D1256030

Library of the
Catholic Foreign Mission Society
of America

35556

The Catholic
Theological Union
LIBRARY
Chicago, Ill.

Donated
To The Library by

MARYKNOLL COMMUNITY, NY

© DEMCO, INC.—Archive Safe

THE CRESCENT AND THE CROSS

The Fall of Byzantium: May, 1453

THE CRESCENT AND THE CROSS

The Fall of Byzantium: May, 1453

DAVID DEREKSEN

G. P. PUTNAM'S SONS
NEW YORK

© *1964 BY DAVID DEREKSEN*

All rights reserved. This book, or parts thereof, must not be reproduced in any form without permission. Published simultaneously in the Dominion of Canada by Longmans Canada Limited, Toronto.

Library of Congress Catalog
Card Number: 64-18017

MANUFACTURED IN THE UNITED STATES OF AMERICA

VAN REES PRESS • NEW YORK

THE CRESCENT AND THE CROSS

The Fall of Byzantium: May, 1453

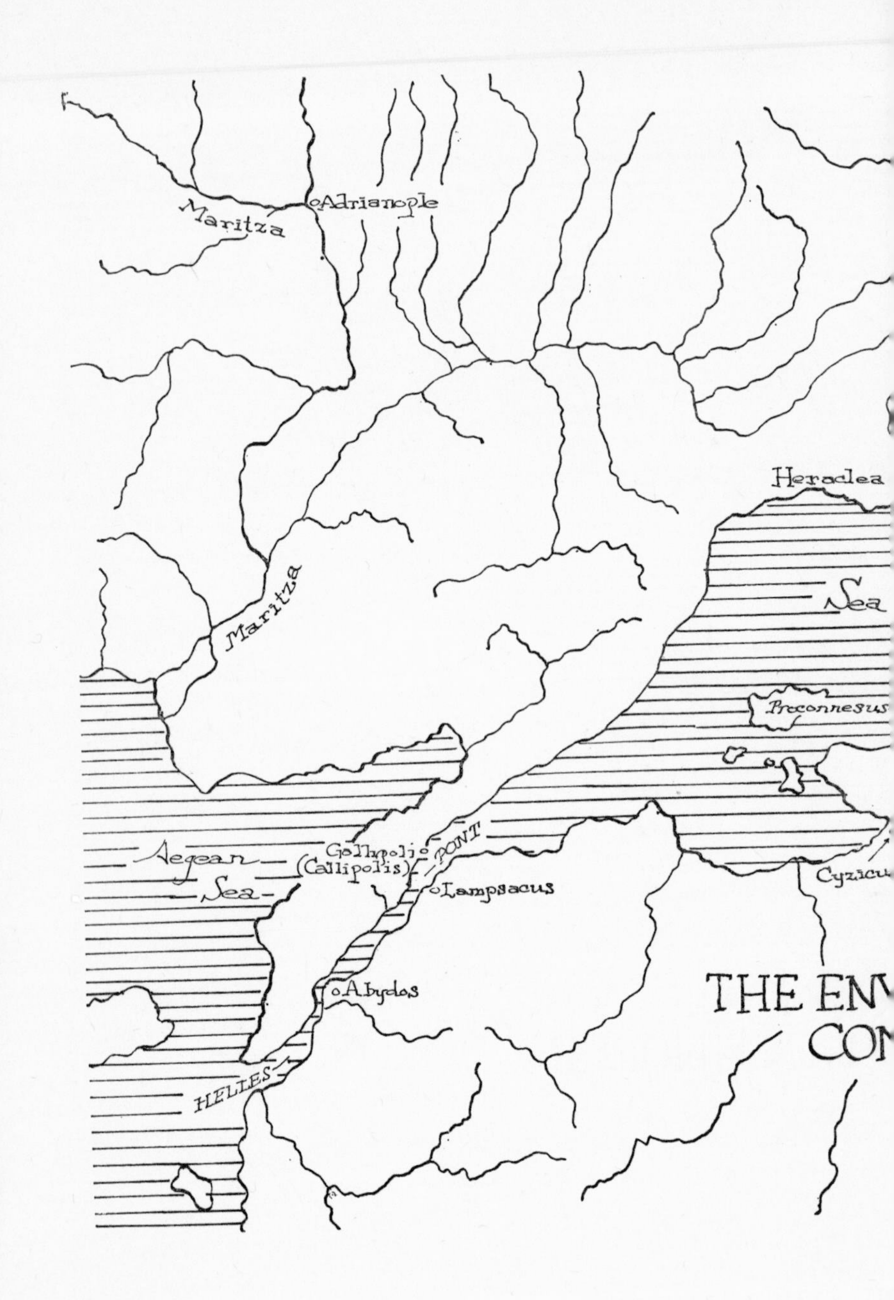
Adrianople
Maritza
Maritza
Heraclea
Sea
Proconnesus
Aegean
Sea
Gallipolis
(Callipolis)
PONT
Lampsacus
Cyzicu
Abydos
HELLES
THE EN
CON

Euxine
(Black Sea)
-PHORUS
THE HOLY MOUTH
The Long Wall
Rumelia Hissar
Anatolia Hissar
Diplokynion
Pera-Galata
CONSTANTINO-PLE
Scutari (Chrysopolis)
Chalcedon
Selymbria
BOS'
Pelekanon
Nicomedia
The Isles of Princes
of Marmora
(Propontis)
Nicaea
Brusa
RONS OF
STANTINOPLE

I

WHEN Constantinople, which is to say Byzantium, was captured by the Turks on May 29, 1453, the laments were loud, long, and many, and some of them were even sincere. "O city, city, head of all cities! O city, city, center of the four quarters of the world! Oh city, city, pride of the Christians and ruin of the Barbarians! O city, city, second paradise planted in the west!" and so on for pages, wailed the Greek historian Ducas. Even in translation, it may be sensed that this threnody is not a masterpiece. It is, indeed, an exact imitation of the lament Nicetas Acominatus wrote in 1204 when the city fell to the Franks, a term by which both Muslims and Greeks referred to those inhabitants of Europe who were not themselves either Greek or Muslim.

At the far end of the Black Sea, a Georgian chronicler professed to believe that the sun had been darkened all that day; and the Holy Roman Emperor, Frederick III, called the event a general disaster for the Christian Faith, though he had done nothing to prevent it, and perhaps had not wanted to (the Byzantines had never recognized his right to be regarded as emperor of anything).

"The Germans," said Aeneas Sylvius Piccolomini, the future Pius II, of this ruler's quarrelsome domains, "are greatly divided and have nothing to unify them." Pope Nicholas V had tried to raise a crusade for the city's defense, with negligible results. "Christendom is a body without a head," added Piccolomini, "a republic without laws or magistrates. The Pope and the Emperor may shine as lofty titles, as splendid images; but they are unable to command, and none are willing to obey; every state has a separate prince, and every prince has a separate interest. What eloquence could unite so many discordant and hostile powers under the same standard? Who would undertake to feed such an enormous multitude? Who would understand their various languages, or direct their stranger and incompatible manners? What mortal could reconcile the English with the French, Genoa with Aragon, the Germans with the natives of Hungary and Bohemia? If a small number enlisted in a holy war, they must be overthrown by the infidels; if many, by their own weight and confusion."

Piccolomini was an astute and experienced diplomat. His summary is accurate. And he himself, though soon to be Pope, while most piously regretting the downfall of the Eastern Church (whose autonomy it had always been the first wish of the Western Church to destroy, and now seemingly the task was done), was more concerned with the loss to learning (manuscripts from the Byzantine libraries had been carted into the streets and sold in job lots at one gold coin the piece—those manuscripts, that is to say, the monks had not already torn up to use as gunpowder wrappers).

Nonetheless, the fall of the city consternated Europe and was disastrous to the prestige even of the Latin Church. In Burgundy, a state then much more powerful than France, the event was mourned at a banquet held at Lille, in Flanders. At the climax of the feast, a gigantic Saracen entered the hall, leading a factitious elephant with a castle on its back. The castle was made to open and there issued from it a matron dressed in mourning, who symbolized Religion. She wrung her hands and deplored both her oppression and the slowness of champions to come to her defense. The Herald of the Golden Fleece advanced, bearing in his hands a live pheasant (an emblem of fidelity). Philip of Bungundy thereupon engaged to crusade against the Turks, his fellow diners following his example, and swore an oath to do so by God, the Virgin Mary, the ladies present, and the pheasant too. Saracen, mourning lady, factitious elephant and castle then left the hall, and the performance concluded with a little music. For the next twelve years the duke held himself in readiness for departure, but died before he could leave. No doubt he meant well—we are told he made some show of piety—but things had a tendency to intervene.

The feast was widely mentioned. What nobody mentioned was that the fall of the city was a political catastrophe of major proportions, about which no one had done anything whatsoever. In particular Venice, the one adjacent power which could have saved the city, had done nothing except to promise a little and then dally, for Venice, which had formerly been under Byzantine protection, was more concerned to see a once powerful trade rival finally crushed than to realize that once the city had fallen, nothing any longer stood between Europe and the steady advance of the Turks. And Genoa, whose citizens had controlled what was left of Byzantine trade for almost two hundred years, was not only at war with Venice more or less continuously but not in the least uneager to see those of its citizens who held the Byzantine suburb of Galata prosper at the expense of the mother city.

True, the Pope had sent a papal legate, a little cash, and three hundred soldiers, but what are three hundred soldiers against a combined besieging horde of almost 200,000; it was very little cash; and as for the papal legate, though he helped to man the defenses, in the end he counted himself fortunate to be able to escape the fallen city in disguise, aboard a skiff, after having been sold as an anonymous slave and then ransomed for considerably less than would have been demanded had the Turks guessed his identity.

The slow decline and quick collapse of the Byzantine Empire is a pivotal event in the history of Europe and the Near East and, as such, an appallingly complete example of those inevitable if variable processes which it is the object of geopolitics to study. The state ages like the body and, like the body, grows corrupt and can no longer fight off invasion. Byzantium was a theocratic state, and though there is nothing wrong with a theocratic state as such, the Eastern Empire was something much worse and rather different—a civil theocracy, in which the Church was allowed to interfere in politics and politicians to make use of the Church, to their mutual frustration and befuddlement. This state not only decayed from within but was collapsed like a hollow shell by two simultaneous outward pressures: the rise of secular nationalistic commercial states in Europe; and the migrations of peoples forced out of Asia and Russia into the Empire.

From the earliest times of which we have record, the process of cultural renewal has always been the same and had the same cause. Migrating peoples, weaker than those who pushed them out of their homeland (ethnic or temporary) but stronger than the peoples upon whom they descended, have destroyed an old and dying culture, and built a new one out of its ruins. In the past, this movement was geographic and lateral. At present, with the rise of Negro and Asiatic peoples and the downfall of the colonial systems, it is vertical, economic, and political. But the process is much the same.

Historians in our day seem to prefer, for almost religious reasons (it is the religion of the impersonal), their history without faces; to reduce it to statistics, movements, significances, and set pieces, and to leave individuals and their emotions out. But it is wrong to leave either out. The laws of historic process, if any, are based upon causes so complex as to defy individual motivation, but as in surfboarding, so in history: the clever and those who by accident have balanced themselves properly and taken their moment well, ride the wave in on the crest and the rest would drown in any case. And so it was with the fall of Byzantium. It drowned most men, but others rode it safely in.

The contemporary demotic Greek poet Cavafy once wrote a poem, now celebrated, called *Waiting for the Barbarians*. The functionaries of Byzantium have gone out in their most splendid panoply to greet the Barbarians. But dusk comes and the Barbarians do not arrive. Disappointed, the crowds go home, and so do the Emperor and the court officials.

Night has come, but the Barbarians have not come.
Some people arrived from the frontier
Who said there aren't any Barbarians any more.
And what shall become of us without Barbarians?
The Barbarians were a kind of solution.

Surely, in the last weeks and days of the Empire, not to mention the last centuries, with the machinery of government rusted; the Empire gone; the land captured up to the walls of the capital; with the same ancient ceremonies taking place the same way to no purpose, through weed-infested streets, in broken buildings; with the trade and business in foreign hands, and so nothing for the citizens to do but idle; with the huge convents and monasteries more than half empty, the houses and suburbs gutted, burned, abandoned, and tumbled down—the people of Constantinople, all of them, from emperor (of whom there were sometimes several simultaneously) to beggar (and there were many beggars), must often have felt like this. And yet the years disappeared, over two centuries vanished, and still the city did not fall. Generation succeeded generation, and nothing happened. Any change would have been a relief, to interrupt the tedium of waiting for the end. Only the literate had at least the diversion of describing what was not happening. Perhaps for this reason, later Byzantine histories are interminable. No one yet wrote a short book in prison, and there is certainly a smack of prison literature about these endless records of minutely remembered particulars.

But they have their value, for it has seldom happened in history that we have precise records for the end of anything. Rome did not so much fall as dwindle away; Romulus Augustulus, the last titular Roman Emperor, died neither an heroic nor a coward's death, but merely retired to a pleasant villa at Baiae. There is no account of what the first Ptolemy said to the last degenerate Pharaoh. Nor, though we have testimony to what Cortés said and did, do we know what those besieged inside Tenochtitlán said and felt about it.

With Byzantium we are better off. There exist two minute

eyewitness accounts of the final siege, and many partial ones. We know what happened to the last minute on this, the world on the last day of a civilization which had by then endured for some 1,123 years.

It is a dramatic story, and perhaps the most dramatic thing about it is that though it was a battle fought between unequal forces, the one fanatic and enormous, the other picayune and tired, it was also in some measure a duel between two men, Mahomet II and Constantine XI, who in courage, determination, ingenuity, and personal resource were more than a match for each other; the one defending, with little or no help from his own subjects, an ancient patrimony, the other willfully decided, for he already had everything else, to take the capital of his foe as well.

Of these two contestants, Turk and Christian, to his own misfortune the weaker—though personally he was both brave and admirable—was Constantine Palaeologus, 81st and last Emperor of the Romans. A more than competent soldier, he had defeated the Turks before and hoped to do so again. At the time of the siege he was probably (for accounts of his birth date vary) a vigorous man of forty-nine. His opponent, Mahomet II, if not the most polished, certainly the most enterprising of the Osmanli dynasty, was equally vigorous, a logistic genius, impetuous, and only twenty-one. Nor did he have much respect for the House of Palaeologus.

To neither of these contestants did it occur that Byzantium the city, which was known as the Jewel of the East, had been for several centuries now fatal to those who held it. Not that there was anything intrinsically mephitic about the place, which was in fact beautiful, but it had been for some time now the point at which two systems of corruption, Occidental and Oriental, met and melded and flourished to the exclusion of common sense.

To the Osmanli Turks, who wished to take it, Byzantium was only an overripe plum. They were realists and wanted power. The Byzantines, who were not realists, wished to keep it because it was theirs, and peered out at the world from the musty interior of their own myth. For it was a myth and no more. What had been a powerful empire had shrunk, by 1453, to the virtually autonomous despotate of the Morea, cut off from the mother city by the Turks who held the intervening parts of Greece, and to Byzantium itself, also cut off by the Turks on all but the sea side.

II

THE city Mahomet so much wanted for his own had been founded, or rather refounded, by the Roman Emperor Constantine in 330 A.D. The site had been inhabited for centuries before that, for it was the natural place to put a town, strategically, politically and economically, since, dominating the only passage between two seas, it was at the most convenient ford between two continents.

The Aegean and the Black, or Euxine, Sea are connected by the serpentine 16 miles of the Hellespont on the south and the more nearly straight 8 miles of the Bosphorus on the north, with the 150 miles of the Sea of Marmora between them, which on the map has the shape of a chewy candy wrapped in wax paper. Both the Hellespont and the Bosphorous are not much wider than half a mile at their narrowest point, the Bosphorus being slightly the narrower, and both have steep banks. They are thus easy to patrol, close off, or defend.

Constantinople stands on the increasingly rocky tip of a small peninsula which juts out into the sea opposite the entrance to the Bosphorus, and which has the shape of a distended uvula. On the north the city is bounded by an estuary, the Golden Horn, which in ancient times had many inlets, now silted up; on the east and roughly the south, by the Sea of Marmora; on the west, its vulnerable side, by roughly four miles of double wall. In ancient times this was not only considered, but proved, to be impregnable.

Even today, cluttered as it is with the worst and most elaborate architecture the nineteenth and early twentieth centuries could devise, and with its classical remains virtually obliterated, the beauty both of the city and of the site are spectacular. The Sea of Marmora is surrounded by low but steep hills with a narrow foreshore, and the cities and villages around the capital are banked against them. The view is magnificent; the climate, despite winds and a sometimes harsh winter, excellent but humid, and so somewhat enervating.

Even in neolithic times, there had been a small, perhaps seasonal, fishing and shell-gathering community on this foreshore, but it was Greeks from Argos and Megara who first settled the area, around 657 B.C., having first for some unknown reason chosen the less favorable Chalcedon, directly opposite, an example of blindness to one's own advantage which became proverbial. The site of modern Constantinople was selected by a Greek pilot named Byza, hence the alternate ancient name of Byzantium. Since the fisheries were profitable in those days, the Greek coinage bore a tunnyfish as its coat of arms as well as an ox, the meaning of the word Bosphorus. As to why the Bosphorus was called the Bosphorus, explanations are conjectural. It may have been because of the legend of Europa and the Bull, because of the legend of the founding of European Thebes, or simply because it was possible to ford oxen there.

It is interesting, by the way, that the star and crescent, universally taken as the symbol of the Osmanli Turks, was also the emblem of the old city, to commemorate a meteor shower or displaced aurora observed in 339 B.C., by whose unexpected light the inhabitants were enabled to observe the armies of Philip of Macedon creeping up for a night attack, and so to greet them without surprise. On the other hand, the star and crescent is an extremely ancient symbol, of Near Eastern origin, connected with the worship of the moon goddess and of the planet Venus, her attendant in the dawn and evening sky, and as such occurs independently among the Turcomans as early as the third century B.C., and probably earlier.

Byzantium prospered, but was never one of the great Greek cities, either as a mother or as a colonial. It remained a free city, however, under the Romans, after the conquest of Greece, until Vespasian stripped it of its privileges in 73 A.D. For the next two hundred years it was alternately sacked or supported by rival and contending Roman emperors, and sank greatly in both wealth and importance as a result. In 323 A.D., Licinius, the rival of Constantine the Great, barricaded himself inside its walls, but was defeated by Constantine. For some time Constantine had been looking for a site for a new capital, one being needed for administrative, political, and therefore military reasons in that part of the Roman world. After some hesitation, the temptation to refound Troy out of patriotic piety being strong, he settled upon Byzantium, and himself marked out the limits of the new city, planning it from the beginning on an extensive scale. He called it New Rome, and set its boundaries as a mile wide at Seraglio Point to four miles on the west, thus enclosing five of its seven hills and all six of its valleys. He divided this area into fourteen administrative regions, set his builders to work, imported colonists from Rome, and decorated the city with whatever in the way of classical and hellenistic Greek art happened to strike his fancy, no matter how bulky, sacred, or immovable it might seem.

On the rising ground which overlooks the Marmora, the site of the by then 900-year-old Greek Acropolis, he had 150 acres cleared, built a protective wall, and erected a palace and pleasure garden on the seaward side of it. On the land side stood the original Hagia Sophia, which was burned down in Justinian's day; the Augusteum or forum; a palace for the Patriarch (for political reasons Constantine encouraged Christianity while he was alive, and went so far as to embrace it on his deathbed); a senate house; the Baths of Zeutippos, a Greek foundation but elaborated and restored by him; the Milion, or column from which all distances in the Eastern Empire were to be measured, the so-called Burnt Column, a monument to himself; and the Hippodrome, which was connected to the imperial palace by an underground passage.

The Hippodrome was more than just a track for horse racing; it was the center of the city. It was where people came to gossip; where they rioted either against the Emperor or for him;

where circuses and shows were held; where new emperors first showed themselves to the people, and where, in bad years or if bad emperors, they faced the people if they dared. At the north end of the Hippodrome was the imperial box, an enormous structure, solid as a fortress. On the spina, or central divider of the track itself, stood an obelisk, a tripod, and a column formed of three intertwined bronze snakes which commemorates (it still stands there) the victory of the Greeks over Xerxes in 479 B.C., and which Constantine the Great had forcibly removed from the Treasury at Delphi where it had stood since being cast.

These buildings were huge, but the suburbs, private palaces, aqueducts, gardens, colonnades (the two main streets were lined with them for miles), the porticoes, warehouses, public markets, and forums were equally extensive. A hundred years after Contantine's death (in 337), the city contained a capitol or school, a circus, 2 theatres (for mime only; the Byzantines had no secular drama), 8 public and 153 private baths, 52 porticoes, 5 granaries, 8 aqueducts or reservoirs, 4 large state halls for meetings of the senate and law courts, 5 imperial palaces, 6 domus divinae for empresses, 3 domus nobilissimae, and 4,388 domus, or houses of the better sort (Rome itself had only 1,780), all these set out along 322 streets (Rome had 424, but few of them so long).

The city was consecrated May 11, 330, as New Rome, but from the beginning was known as Constantinopolis, after its founder.

The New was unlike the Old Rome in one significant respect. Except for a few left over from the Greek period of the city, it contained no temples. Constantinople was to be Christian, and this for the most practical of reasons, for it may be doubted that Constantine had any emphatic convictions of any kind. What he did have was an eye to the future; the Empire, already disintegrating despite the extensive and effective reforms of Hadrian, Maximian, and Diocletian, must be kept together somehow; and Constantine, looking ahead, apparently realized that the Church was the one well-organized social unit capable of maintaining it own power. He himself devoted considerable effort to keeping schismatic prelates in order, and saw to it that his sons were brought up in the Christian faith, though there was little he could do to foresee or to control the efforts of his successor, Julian the Apostate, to re-establish the old order. Julian, however, died young. Constantine was careful to see to it, at least in the east, that Church and State should be welded closely together, with the result that the power of the Church swiftly became intrusive, enormous, and meddlesome. But he was at least half right; though the Latin Church did not succeed in holding the Western Roman Empire together, the Eastern Church maintained the Eastern Roman Empire well, if only because it gave the monarchy something to fight against and so, in times of political and military peace, kept it from falling asleep for longer than a generation at the most.

The Church was an expense, but a worthwhile expense. Though bigoted, its quarrelsome patriarchs were, with only a few exceptions, at least sincere in their beliefs, and though they meddled in the government to an atrocious and dangerous degree, they at least had the justification that the laity, and often the Emperor and his staff, were as fanatic as they were. Also the Emperor was titular head of the Church, and thus in a position to arbitrate. When the Emperor was a theologian, as sometimes happened, the results were pyrrhic. When he was practical and astute, he generally managed to maintain order among those whose chief political function was themselves to maintain it, a duty to which they grew increasingly oblivious as the centuries passed, and with them the Empire too.

Abuses these meddlers may have committed, but they became unjustified abuses only in the later days of the Empire when the social system was already imbalanced and the secular power gone. Ecclesiastic power was not only huge but sometimes absurd, and it had some very odd privileges.

Hermits became so popular, for example, that when Lavra was founded on Mt. Athos by St. Athanasius in 963, he found it necessary to lay it down as a rule that only 5 out of 120 should be allowed to establish individual hermitages. The practice had been established by Pachomius of Egypt, at Dendereh, in the time of Constantine, and grew increasingly popular. Even though the clergy was allowed to marry if it did so before being ordained subdeacon, bishops were not allowed to be married, and if a man was elected bishop and his wife refused to enter a convent, he had to decline. This sometimes led to far from pretty domestic dissension when the wives were of a worldly temperament, and certainly diminished their talent for intrigue, since the advancement of their husbands inevitably meant their own retirement. On the other hand, convents were often far from strict, and constituted a sort of cul-de-sac or *béguinage* for fertile daughters of deposed monarchs, the incurably spinster rich, and for the ambitious, there being few careers open to women in Byzantium above the level of hetirae and below that of empress, though a few landowners became manageresses of their own estates.

Though one might put aside a wife, divorce and remarriage were frowned upon. A second marriage was permitted; a third permitted only under penalty; and a fourth incurred excommunication. Thus Leo VI the Wise (866–912), who was able to beget a male heir only upon his mistress, whom he thereupon made his fourth wife, had considerable difficulty with the clergy in order not to become an excommunicant.

On the whole, hermits had a happier time of it. Some of them, in emulation of St. Simeon Stylites, stood for years on columns about the city. Others, the dendrites, lived in trees, one of them "in an almond tree like a singing bird." Sometimes, for no other reason than an ability to stand on one foot for long periods of time in all weathers, they became esteemed for their political advice, often with disastrous results. In 860, for instance, when a fleet from Russia (the only unified Russia of those days was the Norse colony) arrived to attack the city, an ikon of the Virgin Mary was carried down to the shore instead of an armament. Since a storm blew up and dispersed the boats, this set a delusive precedent. And as the prerogatives of the Eastern Church grew, and resembled less and less those of the Western Church, schism between the two arose, to such effect that in 757 Pope Paul I announced his election to Pippin of France and not, as courtesy would demand, to the Greek Emperor, who was further slighted when in 800 A.D. Charlemagne had himself crowned Holy Roman Emperor at Rome, in despite of the Greek claim to that title.

Much more disastrous than the power of the clergy was that almost Oriental love of intrigue, particularly among the eunuchs, and that shift of palace power to the eunuchs which had already been introduced into the Empire by Diocletian, who, in order to bolster the prestige of the Roman Emperors, much as Louis XIV was to do later among the squalid boredoms of Versailles, had adopted the Oriental custom of setting up a secluded, invisible, and unapproachable authority, barricaded in the palace, out of touch with the people, and so at the whim, ultimately, of palace cliques for its unreal information about what was actually happening in the real world outside. Eunuchs or the eunuchoid always invade social systems toward the period of their decline, and they always get out of hand. The results of this may be prolonged, but are as inevitable as is the process itself. Since, however, the Byzantine mind, with its passion for categories, recognized over thirty different degrees of eunuchs, from the real to the imaginary, these people somtimes stopped twittering and acted with amazing vigor. Narses the Eunuch, for one, was a great soldier in Justinian's day, under Belisarius (*circa* 555).

Constantine the Great divided the Empire among his several sons. The result was inevitable civil war, and then a new line of absolute emperors. The Eastern and Western empires were separated upon the death of Theodosius the Great, in 395, the Eastern going to Arcadius, the Western to Honorius, and went their different ways, the one up, the other down, except when reunited by the conquests of Justinian in the sixth century, a consolidation which scarcely lasted his lifetime.

For the first two hundred years of its renewed existence, Byzantium stood much as Constantine the Great had left it, except that Theodosius I extended its limits to include the landward suburbs and the last two of the seven hills and built a new wall, which Theodosius II (408–450) reconstructed and further strengthened with 192 towers, after the earthquake which occurred during his reign.

The next notable emperor was Justinian, who was co-ruler with his uncle Justin, who died in 527, and then ruled alone until his own death in 565. In addition to his political and legislative accomplishments, he was also a great builder, and so completely transformed the appearance of the city, a good deal of which had been destroyed during the Nika Riots (532), an uprising in which the citizens had demanded an autonomy their subsequent conduct showed them but little qualified to obtain. Justinian's rebuilding created the Byzantine style as we know it, a mixture of Persian, Syriac and Roman structural and decorative techniques. Hagia Sophia, his chief monument, the most famous building in the city, was designed to replace the earlier church built on the same site by Constantine, which had burned down during the riots, and was dedicated December 26, 537.

No matter what the political or economic reverses or successes of the next five hundred years, later emperors went on adding to, embellishing, and repairing the city, until in its heyday, about the year 1000, it was the largest, richest, and most beautiful city in the Western world, with a population of between 500,000 and 1,000,000 people living within 12 to 16 miles of double wall, and in the surrounding small towns and suburbs. Indeed it was the *only* large city in the West (Rome had shrunk) and, if we except China and India and the cities of the New World, of which nobody then knew, the only large city anywhere.

It was a true cosmopolis, for its population was not to be predominently Greek until the last two centuries of its existence. The habit of moving peoples wholesale across the map for political reasons is not a modern one. In the seventh century, Constans II had moved large numbers of Slavs into Asia Minor. In 747 Armenians and Syrians were forcibly settled in Thrace. In the twelfth century large groups of Serbs and Hungarians were removed to Asia Minor; heretical religious communities were arbitrarily scattered and resettled, there being no other way to deal with them, and Anatolia, from being mostly Greek, became 75 percent Armenoid, as it is today. And as not infrequently happens in large commercial and colonial empires with a centralized administration—for instance, England and London —the actual work of the capital, and of administering the Empire from it, was soon done, not by the native Greeks (or English) but by emigrants to the capital and by outlying peoples who were subjected to imperial control without being merged with it—in the case of Byzantium, the inhabitants of Macedonia, who soon founded the most successful of the Byzantine dynasties (867–1057); in the case of England, the Scots after the Act of Union.

Byzantium was fabulously wealthy, chiefly from trade, until the Empire began to lose its African and Asian provinces: Syria to the Arabs in 636; Palestine in 637 or 638; Egypt, the richest of all, in the late 640's; parts of Asia Minor [Anatolia] by 650. Constantinople itself was first besieged by the Arabs in the early 670's, several times, though by 677 they were forced to depart. Their first incursion had been to sieze the unimportant fortress of Bosra, on the far side of the Jordan, in the early 630's.

Despite the lost provinces, this wealth poured in until the end of the twelfth century, for Constantinople was the transshipping center of the Western world's trade with Asia and Russia. It would have remained rich even after that, despite the opening of new trade routes to North Europe up the Danube, to the Far East through the Crusader cities established in Palestine, if it had not allowed its commerce to fall into the hands of the Catalans, Pisans, Venetians and Genoese, after its navy collapsed at the end of the twelfth century. The navy and merchant marine fell into disuse for three reasons: their expense could no longer be afforded; the negligence of the wrong emperors at the wrong time; and the disadvantageous treaties forced upon Byzantium as the only means available to it whereby to pay its allies for their assistance in ruinous but unavoidable wars.

There were other reasons for financial collapse. Both customs (10 to 12½ percent, as opposed to 2½ percent at Rome and

Ostia) and land taxes were pitched much too high. The loss of Asia Minor meant an incalculable loss in produce, tax revenue, and, most important of all, manpower. The noble estates were too large to allow of a free economy, and badly managed besides. Hoarding was a national vice, with more money buried in the garden than was in circulation, or so at times it seemed; the expense of the religious establishment was staggering (Hagia Sophia alone had 365 estates in the city, all exempt from tax, and these were merely its town estates; the four other principal churches were similarly endowed, and the monastic establishment was so large that even in the last days of the city, out of a population of perhaps 60,000, 18,000 were monks, priests, clergy, and nuns); and, during the last century, the nobles and richer traders could not be induced to part with a penny toward the defense of that realm which, after all, if it did nothing else, at least gave them somewhere to conceal their wealth, which was all the smaller since the coinage had been debased repeatedly, but was still huge. For a time, indeed, there was no gold coin in circulation at all (after the death of Andronicus II, 1328). Manuel II (abdicated 1425) endeavored without much success, but with some, to make the coinage once more sound, but by then it was too late. As a medium of exchange, the bezant had been driven out by Venetian and Genoese money.

What with pestilence (the Black Plague first entered Europe through Byzantium in 1337, either from the Near East or from the trading cities of the far shore of the Black Sea, raged the first time for two years, spread to the Morea and from there to Europe, became epidemic, and ravaged Christian and Turk alike in seven acute recurrences in the next 85 years, not to mention the minor ones), sudden natural depopulation as the result of a plummeting birth rate, the sacking of the city by the Crusaders, the several disastrous set fires, and the selling into slavery of whole populations, not to mention the engrossment of trade by the Genoese and Venetians, by 1450 the city was a hollow shell in which perhaps 60,000 people (the highest estimate is 100,000) lived in an area planned, and spaciously planned, to accommodate a million (the contemporary population of Rome was 125,000, with 10,000 Jews who, though not counted as inhabitants, were there to keep the cardinals and the black aristocracy afloat with loans, and so indispensable). The city Mahomet so coveted was neither what it had been, nor what it seemed to be.

The greater part of the residual population was almost completely idle. With no empire left to administer, and with its international trade entirely, and its local trade chiefly, in the hands of foreigners—the Genoese at Galata, the Venetians in their own quarter of the city—there was nothing to do but read, indulge in theological squabbles, go to an animal show at the Hippodrome, if there was one (recently there had not been many), cabal at court if one was noble, or carouse at a tavern if one was not. Like the mob of Rome, they had been provided with a free corn ration to keep them quiet, but with first the loss of Egypt, then Asia Minor, then the Ukraine, and finally of the fields around the city, the payment of this had become irregular. Therefore the mob often went hungry; when it was hungry, it smashed things; and meanwhile it got poorer and poorer and poorer.

The city must have presented such a sight as is to be seen in Spain today, where there are too few children and young people about; there are too many priests and monks very much in evidence; most of the churches are shut up; the monasteries have been partially turned to other purposes; most of the churchgoers are old women; the houses are tumbledown and abandoned, with one or two here and there almost impertinently natty; moss, grass, and weeds grow from cornices, towers, and roofs, and the streets are most usually empty.

The Emperor Constantine, with several palaces to choose from (all in disrepair) but without enough domestics to staff them, alternated between the enoromous complex of the Great Imperial Palace, which was mostly in dusty ruins and used only as a point of departure for the daily ceremonial ride to Hagia Sophia, and Blachernae, on the Golden Horn, some three and a half or four miles away. This had been the personal imperial residence since the twelfth century, though every emperor from 300 to 1100 had added something to the imperial palace complex. Even at Blachernae, large sections of the buildings were roofless, shut off, and abandoned. The church attached to it had been gutted for some time. There had been no money with which to restore it.

All of this was a considerable contrast to the conditions of even a hundred years before. Then the city had been all but self-sufficient, only grain having to be imported. The Marmora and the Bosphorus teemed with fish; and fish, with bread and vegetables, were the staple diet of the plebes. The rich had game, poultry, and pork in addition. The modern culinary term *macédoine* derives from the mixed vegetable salads, doused down with oil and vinegar, of Byzantium. Sallets and other greens formed a larger part of European diet until the end of the Middle Ages than they did until their recent revival. Each monastery had its kitchen garden.

The religious of Byzantium were vegetarians, and the religion compelled even the laity to a diet of interminable fish, as, for that matter did the Latin Rite. Indeed not least among the effects of the Reformation was the ruin of the Hansa cities, whose essential wealth came from their monopoly upon the supply of fish to Europe, for which there was then less demand. The Orthodox Church, however, frowned upon monastic meat consumption entirely, so that one of the stipulations made by the daughters of Constantine VII in 959, when they were compelled to enter a nunnery after his death, was that they would consent to go only if they were granted a special dispensation so that they might continue to eat meat, of which they were inordinately fond.

Byzantine cookery was partially Roman (fish sauces and mixed leched meats), partially Greek (resinous wines, grape leaves, salads, roasts), and partially Armenian cum Anatolian cum Persian (sticky sweets, sesame seed cakes, and mixed meats wrapped in vine leaves and then baked). Bakers were so important that they were exempted from all other civilian and all military duties, and from most taxes. In the later centuries, both Turkish fashions and Turkish modes of cooking became popular, especially almond cookies, shish kebab (also Armenian) and sweet breads. There was, of course, no sugar. Sugar cane is a New World plant. Honey was used instead, and better so. Though infinitely more fattening, it was also a better source of energy and far less deleterious to the teeth.

Foodstuffs were sold in the great covered markets and at hole-in-the-wall shops in the different quarters which dealt in charcuterie. Perfumes, oddly enough, were sold before the ikon set up in front of the imperial palace. For the poor, there were communal bake ovens. The government regulated the sale of everything. There was a law, for example, that retailers had to buy fish from the boats as they docked, rather than buying the catch at sea. This was partially to assure a supply of fresh fish, and partially in order that the tax inspector could see it in order to tax it.

The city maintained ample supplies against possible siege, and there were so many cisterns and wells that over forty of them survive to this day. Some of these were extensive underground reservoirs, others were open lakes. The aqueducts which brought water into the city were not in themselves a necessity but a luxury, the Byzantines being physically fastidious, at least by comparison to their western European contemporaries, and so delighting in daily baths that the baths themselves became institutions rather like modern clubs. In time of siege, it mattered not at all whether the enemy cut the aqueducts or not. Therefore they were never cut.

Under the city lay an elaborate drainage system leading into the sea. It was so much taken for granted as to be forgotten, with the result that it fell into disrepair, the water and the sewage systems sometimes breaking into each other, thus leading to outbreaks of typhoid and dysentery; but it was so well built that it survives to this day.

Nor was hygiene forgotten in other ways. The Church ran large and remarkably clean and airy hospitals, where the diet, though vegetarian, was balanced. At least one woman physician is on record, she a specialist, and in general, though not much is known about the subject, Byzantine medicine was in advance of European practice. Sanitation, hygiene, invalid diet, and the principle of isolation, though not the reasons for it, were well understood. Despite the absence of any anesthetics but muscular pressure, alcohol, narcotics, or a knock on the head, a wide range of successful operations was performed. The only disinfectants known were soap and hot water, but these, in contradistinction to contemporary European practice, were used. So, of course, was a great deal of mumbo jumbo, but there were known specifics, too, and a considerable pharmacopoeia, some of it Greek and Roman, some derived from the Orient.

Both Church and State ran poorhouses, orphanages, and almshouses, and ran them well, though there were always more poor than there were houses, partly because of the onerous taxes, partly because of the condition of the Empire, partly because of the free grain allowance which encouraged the existence of a professional beggar class, partly because poverty is inevitable in any lodestone cosmopolis where a large part of the population would rather starve in the presence of luxuries it can never hope to afford than remain provincial in the country, where it could at least earn enough to eat. Nonetheless, the principles of economic health were badly understood and worse practiced by the government, sometimes because it knew no better, sometimes because it knew but did not care, more often because though it knew, it was impotent to act.

These people were not, of course, at all like a modern industrial proletariat; no such thing existed until the end of the eighteenth century. Constantinople had factories, but these existed either for the manufacture of arms or for the production of luxury goods, and those who worked in them were well paid and skilled artisans, particularly in the silk and embroidery works, not a proletariat. After about 800 A.D. when western Europe became sufficiently civilized again to demand luxury goods, Byzantium made a fortune from the sale of woven stuffs, which had a Chinese flavor, the patterns having reached them, altered by intervening Sassanid motifs, from there.

Though silks were exported chiefly as imperial gifts and under a strict quota system, there was, of course, an illicit market in them, as in other imperial monopolies. Cloths woven with gold and silver thread were the most valued, but almost everything was passed under the counter for profit, except stuffs in imperial purple—a color which, far from being purple, was actually a shade of mute, deeply saturated red.

Gold was only allowed to leave the Empire for official reasons, but the official reasons had been many; and though there were gold, copper, lead, zinc, silver, and iron mines to draw on, with few exceptions these were soon in Turkish hands.

All the same, Constantinople was a commercial city, and no matter what the state of commerce, there was always something for the small trader to do. Business appointments were most often made in church, those contracting them often leaving before the service was over in order to continue to bargain in the porch. The Patriarch once caused embarrassment by leaving Hagia Sophia himself and joining the others in the narthex, with the remark that it was the duty of a shepherd to follow his flock.

To do business in church was, however, no more than the universal custom of the day. Both old St. Peter's and old St. Paul's went so far as to have booths and stands in the side aisles on Sundays, and were favorite places in which to make assignations and appointments, commercial and erotic both.

The amusements of the city were those of any large city anywhere, but had their peculiarities. The chief of these was that there was no theatre either in the classic or in the modern sense. Though everybody knew the Greek classical drama, it never seems to have occurred to anyone to produce it. Morality plays of a religious content, more primitive than those of western Europe, were performed in the churches as an extension of the drama of the mass and as illustrative of homilies and sermons. The only ones of these to survive were more probably written to amuse the court of the Lusignans at Cyprus than actual examples of the sort of thing to be seen at Constantinople. What the Byzantines did excel in, and what they provided an audience for, was topical cabaret of a satiric cast, as trenchant and lubricious as that to be found in Berlin in the 1920's and early

30's, or in Amsterdam today. Ballet was also popular, in particular children's ballet, which tended more toward mime than choreography, though large dance spectacles must have presented an effect half Sportspalast eurythmic exercise, and half Versailles or Renaissance Italy court dances.

The great entertainment of the entire populace was the chariot races at the Hippodrome, which could seat 40,000 people, though they seldom kept their seats. These were discontinued during the twelfth century in favor of horse racing, spectacle dances, raree shows, animal hunts—though nobody has ever been able to train so many diverse animals so well as did the ancient Romans—and pageants. The upper classes played a sort of polo called Tsykanion, which they had gotten from the Turks, who had derived it from the Persians, and this game was popular with spectators and players alike, there being many polo grounds within the city. It was considered fashionable to admire Tsykanion.

The Hippodrome, into which Manuel II had introduced tourneys of a European style, was not fashionable but obligatory, and far from polite. It was dominated by factions and by clubs halfway between sodalities and New York street gangs. These were led by foppish young toughs, or nobles pretending to be foppish young toughs, who took special delight in customs of a Mardi Gras extravagance, in violence, and in rioting. It was always possible to fill the Hippodrome, even though the city was depopulated and weeds sprouted in the bleachers.

Another addiction of the people, particularly during the later centuries and especially among the upper classes, was, rather surprisingly in a theocratic Christian state, spiritualistic séances. There were elaborate handbooks to proper conduct during these, which advised what to do, for example, in the awkward situation caused when the medium raised the wrong god or goddess—or for that matter, relative—by mistake. Dream books were also popular.

The Church frowned upon revue and cabaret, some of which was naked, to the extent of decreeing that any ecclesiastic caught in attendance would be incarcerated in a monastery for three years, after having been deprived of his office. Of course, mem bers of the clergy went anyway. Wit, in that society, was infinitely preferred to wisdom.

In the vast, denuded, twilit buildings of the official part of the city, the outer forms of the Empire were still, insofar as that was possible, kept up. Just as elaborate stage machinery and furniture was admired during the miracle plays, so was the divinity of the Emperor well hedged. Anna Comnena, in her adulatory life of her father Alexius (1081–1118), who ruled at the time of the First Crusade, devotes chapter after chapter to a fatiguing list of the multiple titles and offices of state which her father either invented or reformed, in order merely to codify the names of the administrators of the Empire.

So multiple had empty titles become under Michael VIII Palaeologus (1261–1282), and so great had been the intrigue for them, that he instituted a new title which had no title, deliberately left vague so no one should know the exact amount of prestige and precedence attendant upon it, the only information given out about it being that it was above the rank of Despot, but below that of Basileus (Emperor). This was usually given to favored blood relatives, whose ambitions were thus halted by their incertitude as to exactly how far they had risen to date. And as for some of the titles so vigorously striven for, in many cases no one could remember to what office or function they had originally been attached.

Now that the Empire was gone, these offices were empty, but they were nominally maintained. Even the Porphorygenitus, the marble chamber in which royal children were supposed to be delivered, though it was in a palace no longer used, and though the dynasty had produced no direct heirs since the days of Manuel II's youth, and though Constantine XI had no empress, still had its attendants, and was inspected from time to time—an empty shrine, like the improvised downstairs bedroom off the main hall at Blenheim in which Churchill was born, in which nobody else ever will be born, but which is reverently shown to visitors nevertheless.

The Emperor was the representative of Christ. Emperor worship was incompatible with Christianity, but the compromise was hit upon that though he was not himself a god, he was the earthly delegate *of* God. Therefore the *Adoratio,* or prostration of the subject before him, was compulsory. To show the equality between the two branches of the state, there was even a ceremony in which the Patriarch prostrated himself before the Emperor, and the Emperor before the Patriarch. In ikons, the Basileus was always shown with a halo. The term Basileus implied that the Emperor was by right emperor of the entire world, even if he lost parts of it. In the natural order of divine creation, they were still his whether he held them or not, for when they came to their senses they would return. For this reason he was called Basileus Rhomaion, Emperor of the Romans, to distinguish him from the somewhat inconvenient Holy Roman Emperor of the West, who was regarded as an impostor. Whether the Emperor controlled territory temporally or not made no difference. Spiritually, since he was God's appointed representative on earth, it was his, and as God's chosen instrument he had no equals. Thus the Holy Roman Emperor was always addressed as King of the Germans, no more, and regarded as a vassal—a view he seldom himself shared. In later days this attitude led to some curious anomalies and a great deal of correspondence which could not be received, even though it was read, because improperly addressed; but at least it explains the absolute certainty with which the Emperors were given to act.

This cult was not a political invention. Only once in the history of the West had it been possible successfully to foist upon the people a synthetic religion, on that occasion when the Ptolemies invented the god Serapis, whose worship swept from Egypt to Rome; and even Serapis was a combination of already existing cults into one name and one image. Rather, the Romans took political advantage of a belief already held. The Asiatic mind—and though Greek, Constantinople was under heavy Syriac, Anatolian, Egyptiac, and Persian influence, not to mention the occasional successful philosophical foray of fakirs from India—did not distinguish between the Emperor who is

God personified, and the Emperor who is God's representative on earth. So the rites and rituals of the court were many.

From the foundation of the city by Constantine, the residence of the Emperor was known as the sacred palace. The Emperor was obliged to deliver a sermon to the court and people during Lent, and to officiate at the altar in Hagia Sophia at Christmas. He was hailed as priest king during Church councils, and though this title was a continuation of Julius Caesar's merely practical contrived election as Pontifex (the position granted him certain kinds of legal immunity to prosecution for debt and treason), it derived equally from the traditions of the Near East.

Thus Roman Pope and Eastern Emperor held what was, in its derivation, the same office and title, the Pope feeling it gave him temporal rights, the Emperor, spiritual, though the first was for the first centuries of Christianity merely *primus inter pares* among bishops, and the second merely *primus inter pares* at his own court.

The left side of the imperial throne was dedicated to Christ, and though it was allowed to remain empty during great church feasts, the Emperor slid over onto it, as Christ's representative on earth, when it was a matter of entertaining ambassadors or adjudicating civil disputes. Light, fire, and incense were sometimes carried before him, in both public and private processions, and it was customary to cense him in church. He was hailed, when he appeared in public, as God's direct representative on earth.

However, God in His wisdom might not always provide a good ruler; and in the *Spuria Athanasia* we may read that when God was asked why He allowed such a monster as Phocas (602–610)—after devoting eight years to murder, and then asking his future successor if he thought he could do the task any better, he was dismembered, and the pieces flung into the Propontis by the mob—to become emperor, He answered, "Because I could not find anyone worse." Phocas, it appears, had been one of those trials with which God likes to test the faith and endurance of His followers. And it must be said that the faith survived the test, though it is perhaps a pity so many of the faithful had to die during the course of it. Whoever the incarnation might be, the role itself remained sacred.

To emphasize this, a throne, with the Gospels open upon it, was set up in the council chamber (and sometimes used for augury, though for that purpose the Old Testament is better); and a mosaic of Christ was inlaid immediately above the imperial throne, with the superscription: King in Christ.

Not that the Church was always content to be meddled with, particularly by those Emperors who fancied themselves, and who sometimes were, theologues themselves. When Andronicus II (1282–1328) refused the Patriarch Calecas' advice, Calecas told him: "I am surprised at your commanding me to mind the business of the Church and to allow you to rule the Empire at your will; for it is as if the body were to say to the soul, 'I do not need your companionship and will not bear your judgment and order of my actions; I will go my way, you go yours.' "

However, in general the Emperor and the Patriarch ran the state in tandem, perhaps because the Emperor could, though at some risk, depose the Patriarch, whereas the Patriarch could not in any manner depose the Emperor, though he could excommunicate him. It had been Constantine's astute policy, since he foresaw that the Church would become all-powerful, to make the Emperor an indispensable part of it as its titular head who could, if necessary, assemble his own bishops and so depose Patriarchs and appoint new ones. Though this frequently led to schism, it averted that incessant temporal war between ambitious Pope and refractory nascent national leaders which so disfigured and enfeebled the West until the Reformation and Counter Reformation imposed some semblance of order upon their usually contradictory ambitions. It is only fair to add that in the West the laity was Catholic only upon Sundays, feast days, and personal occasions; whereas the laity in the East was so consumingly interested in the politics of spiritual affairs as to be theologians in everything.

Alexius Comnenus and his Empress often read theological works to each other at breakfast; and Hagia Sophia had a catering service in the side rooms so that the Emperor and Empress in separate rooms (the sexes were rigidly divided at church, the men occupying the floor, the women the galleries) could be served light refreshments during pauses in the endless ceremonies, and also after them, to fortify them for the short but arduous processional return to the palace.

On entering the cathedral, the Emperor always removed his crown. As he left, he always gave the Patriarch a bag of money, and the Patriarch always put his crown back on for him in the narthex. Whether one be an agnostic or a true believer, the symbolism of this ritual is obvious.

Four things kept the throne secure: since the Empire was almost continuously in a state of military emergency, for the more than 1,100 years of its existence, it never occurred to the people to question the existence of a supreme and absolute central authority; since it was the fact of supreme and temporal incarnation that was important, not its specific embodiment, a bad emperor, though he might discredit himself, never discredited the office; though co-emperors might be admitted to the throne, only one of them at a time was ever given absolute authority in the state, the others being honorific; and most important of all, there was no law of primogeniture (even in feudal Europe, this principle achieves the status of immutable right surprisingly late, not until the fifteenth century in fact, though here and there it had been observed in practice earlier). The Emperor was elected, and though he usually appointed his successor, and the appointment was customarily ratified, this need not be, and often was not, always so. The candidate could be chosen from members of the royal house, from those who had married into it, and even usurpers could legitimize themselves by later marriage into it, so the perils of hereditary incompetence were usually avoided. If the chosen emperor was under age or useless, his powers could be transferred to a co-emperor without diminishing the legitimacy of the throne. And even an usurper must have some talent, though not necessarily the right one, otherwise he would not be able successfully to usurp. So, except for a few disastrously long reigns on the part of tolerated muddleheads, on the whole the imperial system worked well.

There was no way to remove an emperor from the throne except by revolution. Mommsen's definition that "the imperial power is an autocracy tempered by the legal right of revolution" exactly covers the status of revolution in Byzantium. It therefore in no way discredited the legal authority of the throne.

There were only two essential qualifications for an emperor: membership in the Orthodox Church (since after all the Emperor was titular head of it), and full possession of bodily and mental powers—an emperor, like a priest, being supposed to be intact (hence the taste for blinding as a means of putting down rival claimants). Even though he might be, and very often was, a schismatic, the clergy never questioned the Emperor's authority as such over the Church, though they might question, and often did violently, specific of his acts. This attitude greatly strengthened the power of both sides.

Unfortunately, in Byzantium everything was done by precedent, and if there was not a precedent, it was not *done*. This attitude, though useful to the parvenu, hampered the initiative of the established, but thus, by accident, assisted that circulation of the classes which is as essential to the longevity of a society as the proper circulation of the blood is to the longevity of the human body.

The Emperor was swaddled, and sometimes smothered, in ceremony from birth, and well wrapped around with ceremonial thereafter. This often went to ludicrous extremes, since though the Byzantines did not lack wit, like most witty people they were almost totally devoid of humor, the one being merely a mental finger game vastly enhanced by the innate dexterity of malice, the other requiring the more arduous if amiable ability to perceive incongruity. For instance, while the visitor was prostrating himself before the Emperor, particularly if he was an ambassador from an inferior state (and all states, in being foreign, were inferior per se: the old Greek attitude of Greeks and Barbarians never died), the throne was cranked up so that when he rose, it should be even higher above him than it had been before. Even if hydraulics were made use of for this purpose (we do not know how it was done) the sound must have been somewhat peculiar, ancient machinery not being notable for the silence of its operation. It was perhaps to conceal the sound that on either side of the throne gold birdcages were placed, containing gold pomegranate trees, on the limbs of which gold birds sat and by clockwork sang. The Emperor himself never spoke directly. The high chancellor spoke in his name. This, too, is an Oriental custom, and was soon adopted by the Osmanli Sultans, for each nation borrowed the habits of the other continually. As is well attested, we all come to resemble that which we fear most.

The love of mechanics of this type is also an Oriental trait. The Jesuits obtained valuable privileges from the Ming emperors by sending them a life-size mechanical lion; and Elizabeth I of England later obtained trading concessions from the Porte by sending out Thomas Dallam with a clock embellished, among other things, with life-size automatons and a mechanical orchestra which played Occidental tunes upon the hour, complete with cymbals, fife, snare drum, traps, and continuo. As for Byzantium itself, one of the chief entertainments of the Hippodrome was a vast water organ, somewhat like that which once ran at the Villa d'Este and was so much admired by Montaigne, though according to an Arab traveler who heard it, the sound was more ponderous and frightening than melodious. This instrument, a favorite classical wonder device, had first been developed by scientists at the Museon in Alexandria, under the Ptolemies. It was in fact a kind of steam calliope upon a monumental scale.

The bureaucracy which ran the Empire was deliberately fragmented, so that no one part of it could present a threat to the power of the Emperor. Its officials were good at extending their functions, as are entrenched officials anywhere, so that the minor office of postmaster became through the centuries first that of Logothete, an office originally pertaining to financial administration, then (more or less) that of Minister of Foreign Affairs, with a staff of translators at his disposal, and finally that of Great Logothete, or High Chancellor, the eventual title of Phrantzes, the historian, confidant of the last Constantine and himself the last head of the bureaucracy.

There were several unusual aspects to the Byzantine government, for though the bureaucracy was expensive, top-heavy, laden with precedent and corrupt, it was also unexpectedly efficient and adaptable, its officials seeming able, unlike most officials, to differentiate between the proper channels through which things should be done and those other channels through which they could. As a result, they maintained both simultaneously, and for so long as there was anything to administer, they managed to administer it well.

The class system was so rigid that at the martyrdom of the 42 saints of Amoria, the victims, who were all officers, insisted upon being presented to their Ethiopian executioner in strict order of rank, and when this was allowed them went to their deaths with complaisance and even, it may be, some sense of self-congratulation: they had maintained the proper forms until the end. Nonetheless, it was possible for those of exceptionable ability to rise through the ranks from peasant to emperor, or what was even more difficult, from peasant to court official, if they sufficiently exerted themselves. This at least eliminated the dullards and encouraged the clever, which is more than any system of equal opportunity can be said to do, and supplied tiring regimes with a constant supply of the energetic and the supple.

Civil servants were educated to an almost Chinese extent, and in an almost Chinese manner, a university having been founded for this purpose by Theodosius II in 425. Here future bureaucrats studied law, literature, history, philosophy, and the polite arts so intensively and with such a disregard for practical affairs that in the fourteenth century Theodore Metochites compained that he found only those parts of Euclid and Nichomachus being taught which had some bearing on philosophy. Education in practical affairs was taught empirically, when the graduates took up their first positions and began to jockey for advancement.

Theology, oddly enough in a theocratic state, was not part of the university curriculum, but was taught only at advanced schools operated by the Church—technical schools, one might say.

On the upper levels, promotion in office was by seniority, on the lower by merit. Thus the administrators, at least those in responsible positions, were much more apt than their coevals in the West to be wordly-wise and knowledgeable men, which may explain the flexibility of the bureaucracy in practice.

In the later centuries, high offices persisted even though their functions were at best as vestigal and as easily inflamed as the vermiform appendix. There was a Grand Drungarius, or High Admiral, long after there had last been a fleet. There was an entire hierarchy of administrators whose daily task was to govern the affairs of provinces which no longer existed. There was a military General Staff, but no army. The official war cry was "The Cross has Conquered" long after it became evident that it had not, and the most popular war songs were all hymns (indeed they always had been, a church choir often accompanying the armies into battle). Somewhat pathetically, military honors became the *dernier cri* of the expiring Empire, and it was occasionally necessary to sack hypothetical towns in order to obtain them, though a brief afternoon excursion into an adjacent suburb would sometimes do. It was perhaps for this reason that one of the later emperors chose to do battle with the distant border towns of Karamania, over two Arab stallions, rather than risk defeat by an engagement with incursive Serbs in nearby Thrace.

Toward the end, the Oriental influence became stronger, fashion always going so (Empire fashions, for instance, swept more of the world than Napoleon was ever able to secure). The Turks and the Byzantines, though political enemies, had intermarried with each other for over a century and the city already had many Oriental customs and some Oriental institutions, including several mosques, outside which dervishes could be observed spinning, even on Christian holidays. And when the Empress Anna married off her daughter to the Sultan Orchan in 1346, one of the stipulations of the marriage treaty had been that the Turks should be allowed to sell their Christian slaves in the markets of Constantinople. This produced at one and the same time an affecting spectacle, a profitable trade, and a curious situation, not unlike that which holds true in Addis Ababa today, where, if something is stolen from you, you do not bother to report it to the police, which takes money, patience and time and is seldom effective even so, you just go down to the Thieves' Market the next morning and buy it back for a fraction of what a bribe to the police would have cost, who would merely have done the same thing and charged you more. In Constantinople, if you had lost a friend, a lover, or a relative to the Turks, and had the money, and should happen to want him or her back, there was an excellent chance you could arrange the transaction at the market, and this was a convenience to both sides.

Another Oriental aspect, and this one neither admirable nor convenient, though it was as old as the Empire, was the palace eunuch, a profession, more strictly a condition, dating back to Diocletian's day, but extinct in the West until revived in the form of the Sistine Chapel Choir and the sixteenth-, seventeenth-, eighteenth- and early nineteen-century castrato opera singer. They lived by extortionate bribery and their intrigues sometimes proved dangerous. They clogged the machinery of government, they were a pain in the neck and an affliction to the ears; to the eyes they were an eyesore, and there is not much good to be said for them; though it must be said that not all of them were eunuchs by their own consent (future political rivals were sometimes nullified in this way, also children of deposed rivals); that many of them turned out to be competent men, both as statesmen and generals, and several, owing to the meticulous scrupulosity of the classification system, even produced children, one testicle being as good for this purpose as two, and under the circumstances an undescended one best of all. In general, however, they produced an atmosphere as clamorous, futile, and clammy as is to be found, in our own day, at any vernissage in the art world, intrigued with just as much malice to as little purpose, and their whole endeavor was much the same, i.e. to dine with the duchess and put the prices up. Their power they owed to much the same cause: they were intermediaries between the claustrated source of supplies and those who wished to procure them; they provided just as much misinformation at just as high a rate; and they fattened accordingly. A few of them even sang well. They were debarred only from high office in the Church, and from the throne (though one emperor is known by this epithet).

In later days they were reduced to a vestigial, tittering remnant of harem attendants in the women's compartments of the palaces, pensioned off and reduced to tea-table chatter, growing older and their ranks no longer replenished, just as, in our day, the leftover attendants of the Imperial Court were maintained in the palace at Peking by the Nationalist Government of China, and perhaps by—for there must be one or two of them left, though they would be eighty or ninety by now—the Communist Government as well.

Of all the problems with which the later emperors, and in particular Constantine XI, had to deal, however, the worst was the unscrupulous, dishonest, and treacherous behavior of the Genoese colony at Galata on the far side of the Golden Horn, facing the city. They had proved just as tenacious as and far worse than the Venetians, who were quartered opposite them in that section of the capital which faced Galata, and just as expensive and unreliable. A few years before, for instance, they had ferried Murad's troops across the Bosphorus at a gold piece a head, so they might attack the capital. At this period in their development the Genoese—unlike the Venetians who, though just as rapacious as traders, took some pride in the embellishment both of their mother city and of themselves, and so soon became collectors, connoisseurs, gourmets, and proprietors of a colonial empire as well—were interested in business and only in business. Despite the sixteenth- seventeenth-century splendors of Genoa, their home city, they never produced and were never interested in producing, as did Venice, a civilization. In the Eastern Empire cities of Byzantium, at Trebizond, and in the Crimea their highest architectural accomplishment was the warehouse, their highest cultural aspiration dishonest bookkeeping, and as a result they left nothing behind them but a ruined economy, the defensive walls of Galata, and the singularly sparse and uninteresting church which they eventually built for themselves out of the stones and architectural elements of the Venetian bailo's house at Constantinople. The Venetians, who had lively minds and an interest in almost everything, and who spent more time resisting the power of the Western Church than in cooperating with it, since 1204 had produced their own unique culture, a blend of Byzantine, Gothic, and early Renaissance elements, and those of them resident in the city at the end, though of as a practical turn of mind as their ancient rivals, were at least willing to help defend it. The Genoese were not.

They had gotten their foothold under the secret clauses of the treaty made at Nymphaeum with Michael Palaeologus in 1261. He, being afraid of them, and with cause, finally settled them at Galata, refusing to have them in the city. They thereupon turned pirate in the Black Sea. Michael had Galata, then unwalled, surrounded. Since the Genoese had been the offenders, this was an affront they did not soon forgive, and after the Venetians burned Galata to ashes during the reign of the elder Andronicus (1282–1328), the Genoese obtained permission to fortify the town with walls and a sea moat. Behind these they soon grew rich, and Byzantium just as soon found itself at the mercy of its own suburb, which declared war on the then emperor, John Cantacuzenos, in 1348, sank his shipping, pillaged everything outside the city walls, and fired stone balls into the city by means of ballistas. Indeed, if Venice had not triumphed over Genoa elsewhere, if not in the Sea of Marmora, the capital would have fallen to Galata rather than to the Turks.

So what with one thing and another, Constantine was less emperor of an empire than of a rotten borough.

The rotten borough however, even though more than half in ruins, was still a city of great beauty. Its chief monument, then as now, was Hagia Sophia, one of the two best preserved European buildings dating from antiquity, the one saved because it was turned into a mosque, the other—the Pantheon—because it was turned into a church. Of the two Hagia Sophia is the more nearly intact, the bronze sheathing of the Pantheon having been stripped off to cast the Baldinchino of St. Peter's. From its rise of ground, Hagia Sophia dominates not only the city but the straits.

"Glory be to God who hath deemed me worthy to complete so great a work," said Justinian on the day of its consecration. "I have outdone thee, O Solomon." This was no more than the truth: he had.

The cathedral was built between 532 and 537, to replace the Constantinian church wrecked during the Nika Riots, when the mob destroyed the better part of the city in order to prove its right to self-government. Dedicated to the Holy Wisdom, it was deliberately planned to outshine the splendor of any other church than standing in Christendom. Its architects, Anthemius of Tralles and Isidore of Miletus, were both Asiatics; the result looks Syriac, if not Asiatic; and the riches of Asia Minor were spent on it. It cost 300,000 gold pounds, the equivalent of 75,000,000 pre-war British pounds sterling or $375 million—enough money to endow the chair of law at the Byzantine University of Constantinople, always an extremely well paid position, for 75,000 years. Since it was built of the best imported marbles, the blue for its mosaics was ground lapis lazuli, even in antique times an expensive material, the gold was more apt to be solid than leaf, and the altar, pulpit and sacristy (as head of the Church, the Emperor was the only lay person allowed in the sacristy) were made of silver, the total cost is by no means surprising. More to the point, the building is an architectural and decorative masterpiece, a thing which so much expense usually rather more often prevents than assures.

It was never impressive from the outside, except by reason of the articulation of its bulk, which was left plain. Externally, it measures 250 feet long, 235 feet wide, the walls being 180 feet high, the central dome being 102 feet in diameter. The core is of brick. Today the building is cluttered with four minarets, five Turkish chapels at the base—one of them, however, an original building converted—and other parasitic structures, in addition to which its original forecourt was demolished during the nineteenth century; but even so, the effect is majestic.

Originally it was approached by the atrium destroyed in 1873, by an exonarthex, and by a narthex from which nine bronze doors open into the building proper, the central one reserved for the Emperor. The interior was a swirl of light and glitter, mostly from the mosaics, which were plain and merely decorative in Justinian's day, most of the ones there now having been added in the tenth and eleventh centuries under the Macedonian emperors.

Hagia Sophia was less an architectural than an engineering feat, and as a successfully solved problem in stress and strain would have been remarkable in any day, and was doubly so in its own. Its only weakness was not in its construction, but in the nature of the bedrock at the eastern end, which was insufficiently balanced to withstand earthquake. The apse and part of the western dome were thrown down in the tremor of 538, but soon restored and did not fall again, but the eastern end of the building had to be reinforced by Andronicus in 1317, and the eastern hemisphere fell in 1345, to be restored by John VI Palaeologus, who was the last to make important repairs until the Turks strengthened the building, and admirably, in the nineteenth century. It became as holy to them as a mosque as it had been to the Christians as a church, and except for whitewashing over the mosaics for hagiographical reasons, they took excellent care of it, removing the forecourt only because it had been fallen down even in Constantine's day, and was, after four hundred years, beyond repair. They did not cover up the angels in the pendentives, first because Islam recognizes the existence of angels, and second because it would have been too much trouble to try to reach them. What they did do was remove the church furniture, install their own, and hang up large calligraphic shields—which, now that the building is a state museum, have been removed.

Because of the double nature of the state, Hagia Sophia in

Byzantine times was more than merely a church. It was the Palladium of the Empire and of the city, to a greater extent than was, say, the Miraculous Ikon of the Virgin attached to a pillar before the forecourt of the official palace; and so of greater importance than any other place in the city, with the possible exception of the now semideserted and disused Hippodrome. The Emperor or his representative went there every morning, for 1,123 years, counting both old and new buildings, and it was where everyone went in time of trouble or of rejoicing. Synods were held there, state trials were held there, court rebellions against authority often happened there. Though in plan it looks a simple enough building, in actuality its walls contain a multitude of easily overlooked maintenance corridors, staircases, storerooms, and cubicles.

Justinian commissioned at least three other of the major churches of Constantinople: SS. Sergius and Bacchus; St. Eirene; and the Church of the Holy Apostles. The last of these fell into ruin and was destroyed, but St. Mark's in Venice is supposedly modeled after it. Of these Hagia Sophia is justly the most famous, but all three of the surviving churches might be described as baroque without the swirl, for though they have not the baroque ellipsis or tension, spiral, or undulant wall, they are flooded with shifting sources of light precisely calculated for the possible architectural drama of dawn, day and night, and they open out by means of arches, arcades, and superimposed galleries into a deep and constantly shifting space. And they are domed. For much earlier than the Western, the Eastern Church was pervaded by a spirit of mysticism of Near Eastern, even ultimately of Indian, origin, and mysticism always expresses itself in terms of light, sometimes of light so intense as to produce the negative; and this light, always in motion, aspires upward, not in the direct Gothic manner but with a spiral or circular roil. The square plan of these churches derived from Syria, the vault and dome construction imposed upon it from Iran, the combination was Byzantine.

Building, in being the most expensive of manias, has always been the hobby of princes, and Constantinople, as a result, was so full of church by Macedonian and Comnenan times that even the devout could find no excuse for the bulding of more. There thus arose the unique practice of doubling, or enlarging existent churches by building an exact replica of them next door, and then either knocking an opening between them or equipping them with a common narthex. Sometimes they were even tripled.

A curious feature of these buldings was that the religious ikons were skied. The reason for this was that in the ninth century the Empress Irene (independently regnant 797–802), a remarkably stubborn woman but also a remarkably clever one, had settled the ruinous iconoclastic controversy—the quarrel as to whether religious images should or should not be used in churches, which led, as theological matters invariably did in Byzantium, to political violence—by decreeing that ikons should be hung in the churches (she was also a sensuous and picture-loving woman, as well as superstitious), but out of reach of the faithful (who were not, and whose superstitions sometimes took a destructive turn). She had thus been able to combine the sweet reason of compromise with the sheer frustration of her opponents in an admirable, if thoroughly feminine, way.

If they repaired nothing else, the Byzantines were always careful to keep both the walls of the city and Hagia Sophia in working order. And by 1450 they were able to restore nothing else; they had neither the manpower nor the means. Curiously enough, one art flourished during the last century of independence; this was fresco painting, which in Theophanes the Greek produced one master before the fall of the Empire, and in Manuel Panselinus of Salonica and Theophanes of Crete, two more a hundred years after it. It owed its rise entirely to the fact that neither the Emperor nor the Church could any longer afford the preferred but much more costly art of mosaic. It is a defensible theory, demonstrable from the evidence available, as Curt Sachs pointed out long ago in his *Commonwealth of the Arts,* that, allowing for the nature of their function, shape and manufacture, in periods of great stress all objects in a culture from cooking pots to linear representation tend to become more vertical than in periods of relative calm. The figures in Byzantine frescoes of the fourteenth, fifteenth and sixteenth centuries become elongated indeed, even allowing for the ebb and surge of traditional iconographical motives and for the natural generational alternation of classical and romantic periods. The calligraphy becomes scribbly and hectic. In this last period, too, no doubt because of the exigencies of life, the portable picture, or ikon, became popular.

But these arts flourished chiefly at Mistra, in the Peloponnesus. The capital was in disuse. Several centuries earlier, an Arab traveler had noted that large parts of it were now sown to crops or used as truck gardens. This was even more true toward the end, though by then the gardens were less extensive and less well kept, the vegetables and sallets of inferior quality. A good many of the public fountains had broken down or otherwise failed, and many of the cisterns above ground were slimy with algae, those below ground forgotten. The inhabitants let down buckets into bores connecting the surface with the Great Cistern, without any longer knowing exactly what it was that they were letting them down into, the only entrance to it being in the cellar of a private merchant. This, too, had been built in Justinian's day.

Albufeda, in the early fourteenth century, remarked on the sown fields within the city, and that most of the houses had been allowed to fall to pieces. Ruy Gonzáles de Clavijo, a Spaniard who visited Constantinople about 1400, confirmed this, but said that the Genoese suburbs of Pera and Galata were flourishing towns. The contrast was marked. Pero Tafur, another Spaniard —though not a Castilian, to judge by his name—who passed through in 1437, added that the capital was semideserted, the people all poor and ill clad, and even those not enough to form a crowd, but that though the palace was tumledown, the Emperor (at that time Constantine XI Dragases was acting as deputy for John VIII, who was away) still kept great pomp, no office or ceremony being abolished, and that he was "like a Bishop without a See."

He was worse off than that. As titular head of the Church, he was still supposed to process to Hagia Sophia every morning and there, in empty rooms, placate a Patriarch who, no matter how pleasant he might be as a person, was, since Union with Rome had once more to be proposed, almost always professionally angry. Nor was this procession impressive, for even in the day of Constantine's father, Manuel II, the imperial household was so poor that the Empress Irene could take only eight attendants on her state visits to the cathedral, where formerly there had been fifty or a hundred. The procession went on anyway, as it always had, with one attendant to hold the parasol (another Oriental mark of rank) over the imperial head as symbol of imperial protection, one to hold the missal, and so forth and so on, even if they had to double up in order to observe all the rites, and even though there were fewer people to watch their progress than there had been formerly, and no one to cheer it. In fact, on some days, there was no audience at all.

And then, though no one had gone so far as yet as to strip the walls of their marbles or, higher up, of the semiprecious stones which were sometimes imbedded in them, Nicephorus Gregoras, describing the coronation of John VI Cantacuzenos in 1347, says that instead of the customary gold and silver vessels, the court was reduced to pewter and clay, and that though the imperial regalia looked splendid, the gold crowns were gilt leather and the jewels, except for the occasional authentic twinkle of beryl or moonstone, were glass. There were still, however, some pearls, both for robes and for the imperial buskins.

The land outside the capital was a desert, the trees dead, the crops burned over and not sown again, the field walls overturned, the byres empty. Part of the porticoes surrounding Hagia Sophia itself had caved in; what buildings in the city stood, stood in a heap of ancient char; and among other souvenirs of the past, columns stood here and there amid the emptiness, from whose summits ascetics had once alternately prayed and bawled advice down to the current emperor.

As for the monastic foundations and the nunneries, since the eleventh century they had been granted out to laymen, who, in the name of protecting and restoring them, had been able to seize as much as nine-tenths of their income and landholdings, so now they were poor, too. And 18,000 monks and nuns could scarcely fill buildings so numerous and so enormous.

Ibn Batuta, the great Arab traveler and geographer, who visited Byzantium just a hundred years before, had been conducted everywhere by a band of trumpets, fifes, and drums, and had been protected by a symbolic umbrella to show his status as a royal guest. But even in his day the bridge connecting the city to Galata had fallen into the water and had not been repaired, so that a ferry was used instead, crossing beside the broken piers by means of a guide rope.

The saddest and most thought-provoking sight, though, was undoubtedly the huge public markets, built to service a city of half a million people, not to mention transient traders, and now scarcely used at all, goods and vegetables of inferior quality and small quantity being displayed among the empty, dusty, broken stalls. Worse even than this were the warehouses which, once crammed with the luxury traffic of three continents, were now vast dim rat-infested warrens. The Genoese stored their goods at Galata, but even there trade was not what it had been.

Oddly enough, cartographical details of the appearance of Byzantium in the fifteenth century are rare. The Florentine engineer Cristòforo Buondelmonti made a map in 1422, but it merely shows the limits of the 14 administrative sections into which the city was divided, with a written description, and is without delineated detail. It is believed that shortly after the final conquest, Mahomet II ordered the Greek geographer Georgios Amyroutzes of Trebizond to draw up a map, but if this was done, it has not been made accessible, though a Dr. Dickson claimed to have seen it in the library of the Seraglio in the nineteenth century. It is said that Bellini took a copy of this back to Venice with him after his visit to Constantinople, though it, too, is missing, and that sixteenth-century maps of the city are based upon it. Since the city has been extensively built and overbuilt during the centuries, and has been continuously and heavily occupied, archaeologists have not been able to do a great deal either, though the ground plan of the imperial palace, and some other details, have been uncovered. Still, the main outlines are clear enough.

Between the land walls of Theodosius and the inner Constantinian wall, which had long been allowed to fall into disrepair, was an area about four miles long and a mile and a quarter wide which was never heavily built up, and was a garden suburb. Beyond the walls of Theodosius were still more suburbs, shading off into farmland. At the northern end, on the Golden Horn, was the complex area of the Imperial Palace of Blachernae and the Palace of the Porphorygenitus (probably wrongly named). There were large gardens here, and, beyond, the small suburb of Cosmidion on the Horn. These areas had not been developed until the twelfth century. The area between the two sets of walls was more heavily built toward the Golden Horn than in the southern sector, and contained, among others, the Churches of St. Mary of the Mongolians, of St. Theodosia, of St. Laurentius, of Isaiah, of St. John in Petra, of St. John in Trullo, of St. Mary Pammakaristos, St. Mary Blachernae, St. Saviour of the Chora, and the Monastery of Manuel. It also contained one of the largest open cisterns in the city (the largest, that of Moklus, was in the southern part of this area). Almost exactly a mile west of this, a winding ceremonial avenue ran for almost five miles, from the Gate of the Polyandrion (or of Charisius, the present Edirne Kapoussi), and the Church of St. George, past the Church of the Holy Apostles, through three forums, including those of Theodosius and Constantine, to the Milion, or milestone, beyond which lay Hagia Sophia. This was the route the imperial suite took each morning when they went to the cathedral. For the greater part of its length, it was lined with colonnades.

Three-quarters of a mile west of this street flowed the River Lycus, a small boggy stream which was always to cause enormous military inconvenience, since its banks made the walls at the point where it entered the city difficult to defend.

The southern or greater part of this sector contained a few monasteries and churches, but was otherwise bucolic.

Though the northern main street was that in general use,

the ceremonial entrance to the city was by the Golden Gate where the walls met the Sea of Marmora, to the southwest. From here an equally ceremonial avenue ran for about four miles, through the forums of Arcadius and of the Bous, to join the cross avenue in a forum whose name is not clearly established.

The commercial part of the city of course faced the Golden Horn, between Blachernae to the northwest and the Acropolis to the southeast. On the Sea of Marmora side, eight artificial harbors had been constructed, by dredging and by the building of moles. These were those of Theodosius and of Eleutherius, which ran together, were extensive, and lay opposite the Forum of the Bous, though about a quarter of a mile from it; the Harbor of the Heptascalus, doubled to that known as Kaisarius; the much larger anchorage of the Contoscolium, with just beyond it, at the next headland, the New Harbor, which had at its entrance those of Sophia and Julian; and last, near the Palace of the Bucoleon, Justinian's favorite residence but not used much during the last nine hundred years, the Harbor of the Bucoleon.

The Acropolis, or haft end of the axhead which Constantinople resembles on the map, had no harbors beyond this point. Here lay the vast and mazelike complex of the royal palaces, which with their gardens, outbuildings, colonnades, terraces, and service areas stretched around the headland for almost two miles, interspersed, particularly northward, with churches and other formal buildings. The palace area was almost a quarter of a mile wide. To the city side of it lay the Hippodrome, the Patriarchal Palace, the ceremonial square of the Forum of the Augustus, the Senate House, the Baths of Zeutippos, the Stoas and other buildings used by the University, indeed the administrative quarters in general, which was perhaps why, after the twelfth century, the royal family preferred to live at Blachernae, at the other end of the city, five miles away.

The areas not occupied by public buildings, fora, or the two main avenues—and not long in ruins—were a maze of crooked, narrow streets. Over them towered the still-functioning but largely unneeded aqueducts, the domes of the principal churches, and those columns first put up to commemorate emperors but later turned to other purposes, chiefly by stylitic ascetics. However, ever since the mob had accidentally scorched the Column of Constantine during the Nika Riots, the remains of this had been known as the Burnt Column. Most of these columns had lost their original statues, and that of Marcian had fallen into such disrepute that instead of having a square around it, it stood in the garden of a house built on its site.

In the Sea of Marmora were various small islands, chiefly those called of the Princes, formerly pleasure resorts but by the fifteenth century held by the Turks, who also occupied the summer towns on the Asiatic shore.

Not even Rome, many of whose ancient buildings were standing relatively complete at this time, presented so dejected a spectacle as Byzantium at the end, for the ceremonial heart of Rome was always more concentrated, and its population, though small in medieval times, was larger. About the only comparison would be to the great Khmer cities in Cambodia, Angkor Vat and Angkor Thom, which covered an even larger area, and curiously enough had fallen on equally bad days at this time, to the same result and for curiously similar reasons (loss of trade and the rise of stronger peoples around them).

But Angkor was to be abandoned and forgotten. Constantinople was not.

Of the truly nightmare conditions of the city in these last years, Bertrandon de la Brocquière is our best witness, for he had a sharp eye and a lively curiosity. He arrived from Scutari, on the Asiatic shore, by the ferry to Pera, whose operators were Greek. Since they took him for a Turk, he was treated with respect until, finding out that he was not, they attempted to extort a higher fee for the passage. La Brocquière had his sword with him, so though there was a dispute, there was no real battle. He deduced from this experience, and from many others, that he would rather trust a Turk than a Greek, an attitude also shared by most of the Greeks he had to deal with.

It is interesting that at the time of his visit there was apparently no direct way of reaching Constantinople from Asia. No doubt this was as the Genoese of Galata, who levied the tolls, wished it.

Pera, he says (the town was Galata, the district Pera, but they overlapped), was a flourishing settlement inhabited by Greeks, Jews and Genoese, governed on the Genoese pattern, with the Duke of Milan as its nominal overlord (because he was, as secretly as he could manage, in league with the Turks, and thus offered superior protection). A great deal of the actual trading was done by Turks, the port was the handsomest he had seen, but on the land side and near the church, poorly defended.

At Pera he was cordially entertained by Sir Benedicto dà Furlino, the Milanese resident ambassador, who explained, no less cordially, that to make mischief for the Venetians, he had helped the Turks to capture the Venetian-held town of Thessalonica. Since the inhabitants of Thessalonica had promptly become Muslims in self-defense, La Brocquière seems to have felt that Furlino had acted in an unchristian manner.

After two days at Pera, La Brocquière passed over to Contantinople, apparently at Blachernae, where he found most of the palaces in ruins, as were the noble houses near the Golden Gate at the other end of the Theodosian Walls, where later the Turks were to build the Prison of the Seven Towers as a polite place of detention for unruly foreign ambassadors.

La Brocquière says that the open spaces were of greater extent than those built upon. He was also impressed by a small interior harbor, capable of holding three or four galleys, to the south of the city, near a hillock composed of the bones of Frankish Christians murdered on their way back from the Crusades. Atrocity stories of this type were popular on both sides, and for the matter of that, always are. Nonetheless, there was a whitened hill of somebody's bones there, for he had seen it.

He was, of course, impressed by Hagia Sophia. He was told that formerly it had been surrounded by cloisters three miles in circumference, of which three still remained. Despite the sale of relics in previous centuries, the church still contained one of the robes of Our Lord, the tip of the lance that pierced His side, the sponge that was offered to Him to drink from, and the reed that had been put in His hand to break. These he did not himself inspect, but he was shown, behind the choir, the gridiron on which St. Lawrence had been barbecued (a Carib word imported into Europe by the Spaniards who, inspired no doubt by St. Lawrence, one of their favorite saints, applied the method to the natives of the West Indies in the sixteenth century), and a large stone the size and shape of a washbowl "on which they said Abraham gave the angels food when they were going to destroy Sodom and Gomorrah." Even though previous examples of them had been removed, these things were now the chief treasures of the city.

Being curious as to that wicked thing, the Eastern Rite, La Brocquière attended church, where a mystery play was being performed before the Emperor John VIII (the year was 1433), his mother, his wife the Empress Maria Comnena of Trebizond, and his brother Demetrius. The subject of the play was the three youths whom Nebuchadnezzar had ordered to be thrown into the fiery furnace, which is, by a coincidence, the subject of the only surviving complete Byzantine morality play, the one written for the entertainment of the Lusignans of Cyprus.

He was curious to catch a closer glimpse of the Empress, who had arrived with only two ladies-in-waiting, three elderly ministers of state, and three eunuchs, so he waited until after the Empress had refreshed herself with a light meal in a side room and had come out into the courtyard to mount her horse.

He found this ceremony worth watching. First a bench was placed beside the horse. The Empress was then assisted to the bench and while she stood on it, one of the old men took the end of the long mantle she wore, circled behind the horse's tail with it, lifting it well over the rump, and held it over his head at arm's length. The Empress Maria, while this was going on, put her foot in the stirrup and vaulted into the saddle, where she sat like a man, her dress having a split skirt. Once she was in her seat, the old man shook the mantle loose in the air, where it billowed and then settled into place over her shoulders. It was then arranged into becoming pleats and folds. Next, one of those long beaked caps peculiar to the Byzantines, but still worn in our day as the badge of Italian student organizations upon carnival occasions—a cap whose eventual public use was as part of the costume of Sganerelle in Commedia del' Arte performances—was placed upon her head. La Brocquière reported it as very becoming, as indeed they are.

"She looked young and fair and handsomer than when in church," he says. "In one word, I should not have had a fault to find with her, had she not been painted, and assuredly she had no need of it." (In La Brocquière's Burgundy the women of that day did not paint, though the men slightly sometimes, if foppishly, did.)

With a lady-in-waiting on each side of her, also mounted, the Empress returned to Blachernae.

In the square before the church, the Despot Demetrius and some of his cronies were riding back and forth, throwing their hats ahead of them, spurring their horses, and trying to shoot the hat with an arrow before it fell. This was a sport they had adopted from the Turks, and Demetrius seemed eager to master it. The game was also practiced in the Hippodrome, where tourneys were held in the presence of the Emperor and Empress.

La Brocquière went on with his sightseeing. At the Church of the Pantocrator he was shown a stone table "of diverse colors" which Nicodemus had had made for his own tomb, and on which he had laid out the body of Our Lord. While he did so, the Virgin Mary wept beside him, and the tears had remained on the table where they fell. "At first I took them for drops of wax." Or, as Hawthorne said much later, on being shown at Winchester that other table at which King Arthur and his Knights once sat, "I would very much like to believe in this table."

The same church also contained the tombs of Constantine the Great and of his mother, St. Helena, raised on eight-foot columns and with pyramidal lids. The body, or more properly the bones, of St. Helena had been taken off to Venice by the Venetians as a consequence of the Fourth Crusade. Constantine they had, some said miraculously, been unable to burgle, though they had apparently tried, for the lid of his sarcophagus was cracked. Both tombs were of red jasper.

La Brocquière seems to have taken the multiplicity of relics calmly. Of the shaft of the column on which Our Saviour was fastened so He might be beaten with rods, he says only, "This shaft . . . is of the same stone as the two others I have seen at Rome and at Jerusalem; but this one exceeds in height the others put together." A plurality of unique objects never seems to have disturbed the faithful of any cult. No doubt there were pilgrims who made it their practice to see all examples of the same thing, though no one speaks of them. If so, some of them made extensive voyages.

What La Brocquière did not care for was the irreverence with which the Constantinopolitan example was treated, it being merely enclosed by planks and placed upright in an offhand manner, near one of the entrances of what was left of the Church of the Holy Apostles. "The Greeks have not the like devotion we have for such relics."

His own devotions were performed according to the Latin Rite at a church which the Genoese maintained at Pera. It had no relics, the Venetians and Genoese believing, like the gypsies, that anything that isn't nailed down is public property, including the nails, and having sent what relics they could snatch to Europe centuries earlier.

Pera particularly, Constantinople to a lesser extent, was in the control of European and Turkish merchants, each with his own bailiffs and independent self-government, and none loyal to the Emperor who, so La Brocquière was told, paid 10,000 ducats annual tribute to the Porte for Constantinople, there being no other empire but "a castle situated three leagues to the North and in Greece a small city called Salubria [Selymbria]."

It is interesting to note that, having heard that La Brocquière was attached to the court of the Duke of Burgundy, the Emperor sent to see if it was true that the duke had captured the

MARYKNOLL

Maid of Orleans, a thing the Greeks found unbelievable. La Brocquière said it was true.

A few days later he went to a royal tournament, the conduct of which appeared to him strange. Forty knights tilted at a fixed plank with long elder wands, the point being to break the wands. As they broke, and they broke easily, a band of Turkish instruments played a jubilee. The tournament was held to celebrate a marriage. The bridegroom then tied two unbroken rods together, while the Empress and Emperor watched from a window (women being semisecluded in Byzantium, one of the features of the local architecture was the presence of a species of bow window or jalousie on the second floor of most large houses, from which they might watch the world go by).

From Constantinople La Brocquière went on to Adrianople and the court of Murad II, which he seems to have enjoyed more, thus passing from a moribund to a nascent empire. For whatever else they were, the Turks were considered chic. Whereas Byzantium, which had persisted in the same habits for centuries, as always happens when power is gone, from being considered splendid because unique quickly came, to the rest of the world, to seem old-fashioned, fusty, shuffling, and quaint—any figure of tragedy seeming a figure of fun, once seen from the back. The Byzantines were fugitives from time, there, much more than from the Turks.

A serious problem during the last century of the Empire, and sufficient indication of the financial distress prevailing, was the outbreak for the first time in 1,100 years of class warfare. True, the mobs had always been unruly, but only as mobs always are, without in any way wishing to break the thin glass of social distinction, no matter how much they might slosh about within it. In the past the mob had rioted for civil privilege, in order to be given something, for the sheer joy of smashing things and distressing their betters, for theological, or for political reasons. But there had been no class hatred, for though the Emperor's income came to 20,000 gold ducats a day from the tax on city trade alone, it had been a trade profitable to all, despite the heavy excise duties. But this prosperity had been dead for over two hundred years. So in the middle of the fourteenth century the lower classes rose up and for the first time slaughtered the nobles and the wealthy not because of anything they had done or not done, not even to rob them, but simply because they were noble and were wealthy. For seven years (1342–1349) the city of Thessalonica became a republic. "Servant dragged his master, and a slave his purchaser, the peasant struck the *strategos* and the laborer the soldier." A sort of sansculottism spread everywhere, and at last it became impossible for those who ran the capital to enforce their mandate by accumulated authority alone, and having little by way of actual forces, ultimately they gave up trying. There came to be certain places where it was no longer safe to go, that was all, as in the New York or Paris or Naples of today.

And yet, even so, every night Hagia Sophia blazed with lamps—there was always money for that—and because of the round-topped windows which parade around the base of its dome, it shone out like a beacon over the Sea of Marmora and toward the Bosphorus as it had always done, even though the city itself was a mere cracked silhouette of disused buildings and of scurrying, furtive shadows.

The torches of the besieging armies came and went. Hagia Sophia was always there, a pharos alike to the faithful, the unfaithful, the heathen, and the proud. It hummed with yellow light, and when each successive dawn came and the lamps burned down and out, there was the city again, still intact, as by a miracle. So though despondent, defeatist, and nervous, the greater part of the dwindled population still felt safe within their walls (though several thousand prudently fled before Constantine could shut the gates), and when in doubt, looked toward their great church and half believed that God would save them as so often before, in their opinion, He had—or rather the Virgin Mary, in her form of Protectress of the Walls, for Mariolatry had entered the Eastern Church earlier than it established itself in the West (about 1000).

It must be confessed that during the last five months of the city's independence (early December 1452 to May 29, 1453), even this pharos was at last in darkness, because the people had rioted in Hagia Sophia and, while rioting, had smashed the lamps, so that only a few burned there now, not enough to light up the procession of windows around the dome, and those at the Emperor's order.

Nonetheless the faith in divine intervention remained strong. Constantine XI and his advisers, however, knew this faith to be an illusion, for walls, no matter how strong, must be defended; there were over 14 miles of them, they were double walls, which means 28 miles, and of defensive forces there were almost none.

There was one more sight in the Empire even more disturbing than an abandoned Hagia Sophia. This was the Holy Mouth, the area where the soon-to-be-closed-off Bosphorus opened into the Black Sea, so called because since neolithic times temples had been built there. It was a clutter of abandoned and half-forgotten ruined monuments to a hundred faiths, cults, gods, and goddesses. There were tumbledown Christian churches, from every epoch of that faith, built among the temples. Soon there would be mosques as well. Nobody ever paused there. Nobody lived there. Temple and church were alike deserted. Winds blew there, fogs came in, birds nested in what had once been eaves. It was the boneyard of faith, waiting for its next addition. But nobody thought of it, or remembered it was there, for only the Genoese traders ever saw it, and they were not a people thoughtful in that way.

Nonetheless, there it was, waiting. It was built on low land. The sea had already washed some of it away, and it was itself a sort of Sargasso Sea, or ships' graveyard, of man's faith.

III

THE anomalous state of which this city had once been the capital had arisen by inevitable happenstance, out of the political and tactical necessities of the later Roman Empire, as a result of the administrative reforms instituted by the Emperor Diocletian.

We are used to dating events by the Christian era, and so forget that the Rome of the third century was not three but some six centuries old, as far as its empery and machinery of state was concerned; a third again older than that, if we consider the social history of its people. It had thus grown stiff in the joints, and its administrative system was bad.

The Emperor was the head of the state, but no established procedure existed for his legal choice. Augustus had deliberately left the matter vague. Because of the difficulty the Julio-Claudian line had had in producing surviving heirs, inheritance was by adoption and election, though one might adopt one's own son if one had one. It was customary to have adoption and election ratified by both the Senate and the Army, but the Senate was a body known more for its contumacy then its conscience, and in imperial times seems to have existed chiefly to block essential legislation, turn coats, and accept bribes. The Army had early seized effective control of the state, since the state could only be maintained by the Army. It elected and deposed emperors at will.

This would not have been so disastrous a situation, had the Army still been made up of Roman citizens from Latium. Instead, by the end of the first century it consisted of provincial mercenaries loyal to the region where they were stationed, where they had married, and where they had kin. Since troops were no longer shifted about to alien territories, the result was a series of semiautonomous armies without loyalty to the capital who frequently raised provincial emperors and precipitated civil war. Thus the Empire grew weak against invasion. It had a population of about 50,000,000 people, or about 20 per square mile. This was too thin a settlement to obstruct the entry of barbarian hordes, who must therefore be destroyed by armies stationed there. When recruited locally, these tended to fight for their province, not for the Empire, and so the provinces began to claim more and more independence.

The chief incursions into the Empire came across the long, exposed, and shifting frontier which stretched from the North Sea coast along the courses of the Rhine and Danube down to the Black Sea, and from Persia. Persia was a civilized, highly centralized state which could be dealt with, if all else failed, by diplomacy and bribe. The barbarian invaders could not be so dealt with. Buffer states tended either to become independent or to collapse.

At the center of the Roman Empire lay Latium and Rome. Latium was semideserted and Rome was a rotten borough where an idle mob lived off grain allotments from Sicily. The older Roman families had died out, and the chief functionaries of the state now came from Gaul, Spain, Africa, Syria, and the Dalmatian coast. Money was so devalued as to have vanished. Even imperial officials were now often paid in kind. Since the only form of investment known to the rich was usury, at rates of from 36 to 75 percent, the finances of the Empire were so feeble as to be nonexistent. Trade was either in Jewish hands or else there was none. The emperors, almost continuously on campaign, avoided the capital as much as possible. It was administratively inconvenient and socially treacherous.

On the Dalmatian coast, between what is now Jugoslavia and Albania but embracing the southern area of the one, the northern area of the other, was the province of Illyria, which was Latin-speaking (the other provinces had already begun to produce what were to be the Romance languages) and whose inhabitants had always made good soldiers. In the third century they began to make good emperors as well. The Illyrian emperors had no sentimental ties with Rome as a city, regarded it as irrelevant to the maintenance of the Empire, and acted accordingly.

In the latter half of the third century, the first Illyrian emperor, Aurelian, had been able to restore the Empire, fling out the barbarians, reduce the independence of the provinces, and strip the Senate of the power to implement its venal whine. He was murdered by his own troops, and succeeded by Tacitus, from whom the Army drained first his fortune and then his blood. Tacitus was succeeded by Diocletian.

It was Diocletian who divided the Empire in two, taking the eastern half for himself (his seat was at Nicomedia, in Asia Minor) and turning the western over to his colleague, Maximian. It was his intention that he and his successors should be *primus inter pares* among four co-emperors, both he and Maximian appointing Caesars to help them rule, who in their turn would become co-emperors and appoint two more Caesars.

Needless to say, human ambition being what it is, this reasonable scheme led to nothing more constructive than twenty years of internecine warfare among the designated heirs. Constantine the Great defeated the last rival heir, Licinius, September 18, 324; founded Constantinople the following November; inaugurated it six years later, on May 11, 330; and made it his capital until his death in 337. From the start, it was designed to be a Christian city.

Nobody knows for certain why Constantine became, though only on his deathbed, a Christian, nor why he had his children reared in that faith. The explanations are probably as multiple as his motives. The two chief of these are, however, eminently practical, and he was after all a practical man.

Both Jews and Christians had been a nuisance to the Empire for centuries. It had been possible to work out an agreement with the Jews, who were useful to the state and found it useful to their own purposes. The Christians were another matter.

They were seldom property owners, contributed nothing to trade, were in those days pacifist, endeavored to undermine the Army, and corrupted civil obedience. They were bigoted, contentious, and well organized. Despite their rapid growth as a sect, they were everywhere a minority except among the ruling class of Alexandria, which controlled Egypt, and in Asia Minor, Thrace, Cyprus and Edessa, where they constituted slightly more than half the population.

But not only were these the most densely populated, they were also, at least in the case of Egypt, the richest provinces of the Empire, and Licinius, Constantine's rival, a redoubtable anti-Christian, had taken refuge in Thrace. It is therefore not difficult to see why Constantine espoused the Christian cause.

He had a second reason. The Church was the only existent organization strong enough to maintain a state, and in its appeal to the emotional and superstitious obedience of his subjects, a far more effective one than his own, which was merely military. He prudently, however, placed the Emperor at the head of it, both spiritually and, when the Emperor was strong enough to control it, temporally, as he himself was.

More than anything else, this policy of his of welding the spiritual and secular arms of the state together led to that eventual religious schism with the West which was to cause so much trouble later. In 554 Justinian the Great granted to the chief bishop of Rome certain civil and administrative powers. During the latter half of the sixth century the two Popes Pelagius were given the right to deal with Lombard invaders independently of Constantinople, and the Exarch, or representative of the Eastern Emperor at Rome, being politically impotent, his position was abolished. The Pope was therefore forced to step into the temporal vacuum so created in order to maintain order, thus laying the foundations both of the Papal States and of papal pretensions to universal dominion over lords temporal. Since these pretensions were usually impossible to enforce, the result was dissension all around. For many centuries the Orthodox Church and Byzantium were coterminous and worked harmoniously together and, as Constantine had foreseen, despite friction, reinforced each other's power. The Orthodox religion became a state religion, and made few efforts to proselytize areas not Byzantine. It claimed equality with the Popes, but not dominance over them. The Western, or Roman Catholic, Church worked harmoniously with no central government—there was none—but only with one European power against the other, in constantly shifting patterns; maintained its own secular states, which were unfortunately usually temporally weak, and claimed universal dominion over all Christians.

Politically the fiction that the Eastern and the Western empires were two halves of one whole was maintained as late as the tenth and eleventh centuries, but it was only a fiction. The two halves of the Empire became independent after the death of Theodosius the Great in 395. The Western Empire fell, if a shadow can be said to fall, during the second and third quarters of the fifth century. Though in the middle of the sixth century Justinian the Great, another Latin-speaking Illyrian, attempted to restore the original Empire, he did so from Constantinople, and his efforts did not long survive him. Even Latin was lost. The Justinian Code was formulated in Latin, but Justinian himself was forced to publish his edicts in Greek in order to have them understood by his subjects. In the West they were promulgated, but scarcely obeyed. And after his death the Byzantine Empire, though proud to regard itself as successor to the Roman, was in no sense regarded by the West as Roman, but as what it was, a powerful independent contemporaneous state which had nothing to do with Rome or with Europe whatsoever, and most certainly had no claims upon either.

In the year 800 Charlemagne had himself crowned Holy Roman Emperor, thus reviving a delusive dream which was to bemuse men's minds for some time, and to survive as a title until Napoleon's day. But it was only a dream. It had no reality in it .

To Europe, Byzantium became a mythical place at the far end of the Mediterranean, trafficking with Asia and itself a semi-Oriental state. It also became a foreign place and therefore fair game, should anyone ever become powerful enough to take it.

Despite constant warfare, incessant invasion from both the newly arisen Arabs bent on conquest and peoples who swept in from European Russia and down through the Balkans, and a protoplasmic shift in the dimension of its territories, Byzantium prospered. Its wealth came from trade, and continued to come from trade even after it lost Egypt and Asia Minor to Muslim hordes. Its people were fed out of the granaries of the Crimea rather than those of Egypt, that was all. For manpower the government depended upon Anatolia, and when Anatolia was lost, upon mercenaries. Territory after territory was lost, but this seems to have made little difference to the inhabitants of Byzantium or its rulers. They went on living in a state of unimaginable empery, though the state had begun to decline during the eleventh century and, like a once healthy man, was to perish not of one fatal, but of a complexity of chronic diseases.

Unfortunately there comes a time when a trading aristocracy adds, like the Medici, a few balls to its escutcheon, forgets the source of its wealth, and begins to disdain trade; the trade is allowed to fall into alien hands; and so the mercenaries can no longer be paid. Byzantium was no exception to this process.

Disaster overwhelmed it in 1204, some two hundred and fifty years before the eventual fall, partially as a result of its own intrigues. The particular name of the disaster was the Fourth Crusade, heavily assisted by the commercial ambitions of Venice, the incompetence of the Byzantine ruling house, and the rapacity of Pope Innocent III.

IV

AS the inheritor of an empire which had once embraced Egypt, the North African coast, all of Anatolia, the Balkans, and Greece, but now consisted only of Greece, a few Balkan holdings, some places along the Black Sea coasts, and a third of Asia Minor, the Byzantine Empire in 1204 was financially poor but materially rich. Unfortunately its rulers had no idea of what had happened in Europe during the past few hundred years or, more properly, of its significance, being much too taken up with defending themselves against the onslaughts of Arab, Muslim, Slavic, and Mongol invaders, and against each other, to pay much attention.

In Europe, the Popes were forced to maintain themselves by playing one secular ruler off against another, in order to preserve their own temporal power. The Crusades derived their impulsion from many causes, but were of great use to the Church. Since nothing left behind by the Crusaders could be sequestered for debt, they were equally useful to the Crusaders, whose religious motives were often sincere but had a tendency to get mixed up with other matters, as most disinterested motives will.

The Muslims, whom the Byzantine Empire could not successfully repel, had long since occupied the Holy Land, Egypt, North Africa, most of Anatolia, and more recently Spain. They were a menace not only to Christendom, but also to many a Christian prince. They were a menace to shipping as well.

Be these motives as they may, the Fourth Crusade was held up at Venice for want of money to pay for its transport to the Holy Land. Not only were modern states then beginning to take their rudimentary shape, but so was commercial society. Apart from the towns of the Hanseatic League, with which she had connections, Venice was both the most ambitious and the richest of the new trading cities, and wished to be more so. Her rivals were Pisa and Genoa. What she wished to do was to engross Byzantine trade by sacking the city. Alone of the governments of Europe she was well informed as to Byzantine affairs, and thought this could be done. She waited only for a pretext.

The pretext was provided by the then rulers of Byzantium, the House of Angelus. It was a short-lived dynasty, lasting not quite twenty years, and considering the abilities of its members, the brevity of their reign is not surprising.

The founder of the house, Isaac II, was a well-known coward, set up on the throne by the mob as a result of an act of terrified courage (instead of waiting to be assassinated, he had, almost accidentally, killed his assassin). His only notable act was to debase that coinage upon whose immutable worth as a trading unit the prosperity of the Empire depended. He was blinded and deposed, but by some oversight not murdered, by his brother. Isaac II may at least be accused of incompetence; his successor, Alexius, leaves one with nothing to say at all. He used money raised to fight the Bulgars to pay for his coronation. He gave his favorites a monopoly on taxgathering, and so ruined the civil service which kept the Empire solvent and afloat. He spent everything in the treasury, and starved the army. Rather than be put to the fatigue of reconditioning the fleet, his admiral sold off the contents of the arsenal to his own profit. The Emperor himself turned pirate and sent six galleys into the Black Sea to raid his own shipping, a transaction from which he made and spent enormous sums.

His oversight was not to murder his brother and his brother's son. The son escaped to Venice and offered the then Doge, Dandolo, a monopoly of the Black Sea trade in exchange for his own and his father's restoration.

Dandolo, who though blind (probably) and almost ninety

(give or take a year or two) was a man of military, financial, and administrative acumen, not to say cupidity, at once offered the Crusaders free passage to the Holy Land if they would take Byzantium on the way.

Pope Innocent III at first objected, and threatened to excommunicate the Crusaders if they did so. Dandolo countered by explaining that the Pope was acting from political rather than from religious motives, and since Innocent III was known never to act from any motive that was not both, the Crusaders agreed to risk excommunication for an indemnity, and to give their transaction some gloss of probity persuaded the Byzantine pretender (also named Alexius) to recognize the supreme authority of the Latin Pope. Innocent III then authorized the Crusaders to plunder those lands which refused them provisions, particularly if they should happen to belong to the Emperor of the East. His sole stipulation was that such plunder must be undertaken with proper fear of God, without injury to any Christian, and with the intent of making restitution afterwards (though to the Latin Church, not to the plundered).

These seemed fair terms, so the Crusaders sailed for Byzantium during April of 1203, a mixed horde of Belgic, Venetian, French, German, and Lombard freebooters, under the imperfect but astute control of the Venetians.

The Byzantine incumbent does not seem to have bothered much about the coming invasion. His only preparation was to ask Innocent III to divert the Crusaders, as they might frustrate his own attempts to liberate the Holy Land (apparently they existed in his mind, if nowhere else). Byzantium was supposed to be, and so far had proved to be, impregnable behind its walls.

He was right about the Crusaders: they were unable to storm the land walls of the city. He was wrong about the Venetians, who approached by sea, each galley equipped with a tower and a retractable bridge. The water was then closer to the seaward walls than it is today, the boats had a shallow draft, and by anchoring at high tide and then letting down their gangways, the Venetians simply walked to the ramparts and, once there, seized them and the city.

Thus began both the long and final ruin of Empire and city, and the rise of that House of Palaeologus which was last to rule it.

Behind its main avenues, Constantinople was a tangle of treacherous alleys. In order to clear their way, the Venetians fired the commercial district, which burned to the foundations from the royal quarter at Blachernae, on the land wall side, as far as the Monastery of Euergetes on the Golden Horn to the east, and toward the center of the city as far as the Deuteron. The incumbent emperor, instead of rallying his troops, fled in a skiff. Alexius IV, the pretender, was allowed in and reinstated, and his father, Isaac II, allowed out to the same purpose, while nine hundred years of Byzantium went up in smoke. It is worth noting that the siege was successful more by reason of bumbling from within than of fumbling from without, and might be said to have constituted an assault by mutual consent. For the land walls were still impregnable, the Crusaders had not been able to storm them, and the city had been taken merely by a mechanical trick. That this was so was greatly to enhance the disastrous self-confidence of later emperors.

Once in, the Crusaders stayed a year and expected to be paid, and daily, for their dalliance. There was no way to pay them. Like the Spanish conquerors of Mexico some three hundred years later, they had never before seen a city so opulent, so well run, or so luxurious, and marveling the while, they set themselves promptly to loot and to destroy it.

There was no one strong enough to interfere. The Crusaders were persuaded to remove themselves to the northern suburb of Galata, and allowed into the city only in small numbers. The looting went on anyway. Some Flemings, to cover themselves against attack by indignant Greeks, fired houses in their rear. A high wind swept the fire through the city for two days, from the Golden Horn to the Propontis, in a swath a mile and a half wide, and so destroyed the richest buildings in the capital. In destroying the wealth those buildings contained, it made it impossible to go on paying the Venetians and the Crusaders the indemnity they demanded. The Crusaders, less accommodating than locusts, who at least leave after they have stripped everything bare, decided to stay on until the following Easter, in hopes of a second crop.

The Byzantine mob, which had earlier tried to get rid of the Latins by destroying a 30-foot-high bronze statue of Minerva under the illusion that it represented the Latin Genius, now rose up, poured into Hagia Sophia, and demanded the deposition of both emperors and the election of a new one. A man called Murtzuphlos was elected, expelled the Crusaders and Venetians from the city, barred the gates, and prepared for a new siege.

This was regarded by the Crusaders as a provocative act. Pausing only to sign a treaty for the partition of the Empire with the Venetians, they besieged the city once more and once more the Venetians took it for them, by the same method as formerly and so rapidly that Murtzuphlos had not time to rally his troops. To create a diversion, a third fire was set, this time beyond Hagia Sophia at the tip of the peninsula. Villehardouin, the chronicler of the Fourth Crusade, says these fires destroyed more houses than were contained in the three largest cities of then France. There was no way to beat them out. Night fell, and nothing could be done but watch the flames until morning.

While the Venetians and Crusaders were cut off from the Acropolis by the fires they had themselves started, Murtzuphlos made his escape (he was finally caught and flung from the top of a column in the Foro Bous or Tauri), and a new emperor was elected in Hagia Sophia. This was Constantine Lascaris, who, finding the city impossible to defend, escaped to Asia as soon as morning came, where either he or his brother Theodore, who was to succeed him within a few months, set up that Empire of Nicaea which was to win Byzantium back.

It cannot be said that either the Franks or the Venetians behaved well. The loot of Constantinople, despite the fires, amounted to over fourteen times the then annual revenue of England. The Crusaders set a prostitute on the altar of Hagia

Sophia, apparently to act out the Book of Revelations but also to show contempt for any faith not exactly like their own; they smashed the chief surviving public examples of Hellenistic, Roman, and Greek art to prove their superiority to an effete culture; they melted down the bronzes to coin money; and the Venetians, more astute and also more civilized, sent back to Venice everything of aesthetic worth they could lay their hands on, including the horses of the Quadriga, now the horses of St. Mark's. Europe had never before seen a sack of such proportions, if only because there was nothing of such proportions in Europe to sack. Rome in the fifth century had been the impoverished underpopulated ghost of a town. Byzantium contained not only the accumulated wealth of nine hundred years, but the chief treasures of the ancient world, aesthetic mostly, which Constantine the Great had been able to remove there.

The city never recovered from this occupation, and no more did the Empire. By the terms of their treaty, the Venetians were to receive three-fourths of the plunder, the Crusaders one-fourth until the expenses of the Crusaders had been paid back to Venice, after which they proposed to go halves—the Genoese, Venice's trade rivals, to be excluded; the Latin Emperor to have one-fourth of the Empire, for it was proposed to set up a Catholic state; and the other three-fourths to be divided equally between Crusaders and Venetians. Since the Venetians knew the strategic and economic geography of the region and the Crusaders did not, this honorable division of other people's property was to be less equal than it looked on paper. Of the capital itself, the Venetians were to have three-eighths and Hagia Sophia; the future Latin Emperor, five-eighths. Baldwin, Count of Flanders, was elected first Latin Emperor, and so founded a dynasty which was to last 57 years.

The sack of the capital of the Christian world, even if only of the Christian world according to the Orthodox Rite, shocked Europe but left the Venetians unruffled. Crete, Rhodes, and all the best trading centers of the Empire fell into their hands.

Dandolo himself was buried in Hagia Sophia, having lived shrewd, blind, and successful into his nineties. He had dismembered an empire and assured the empery of his own state.

The Latin Empire and its associated duchies and kingdoms, all of them in Greece, had no power—the Venetians were careful to see to that—and did not prosper. It is easy enough to turn out incompetent heads of state; it is impossible to control a population which, if not loyal to its rulers, is at least loyal to itself, and knows the country better than you do. Nor was much help to be expected from the West. The Latin Empire might represent Catholic Christendom in an Orthodox Catholic and therefore heathen world, but the Pope was in no position to send aid: and the secular heads of European states saw in the Latin Kingdom nothing but a rival too puny to be placated and not strong enough to be feared.

Economics was then a subject not yet conceived, let alone in its infancy. The only peoples to grasp the economic advantages of holding control of Byzantium were the Venetians, who had its trade once more in their grasp and so had eliminated their middleman in the Black Sea trade and had no desire to erect another, and the Genoese, whose trade wars with Venice were incessant and who wished to dislodge the Venetians. Politics to the embryonic European states of those days, was associated with dynastic land grabbing, not with the accumulation of power by means of trade, and besides, the Osmanli Turks, who were shortly to imperil Europe, had not as yet either appeared or arisen.

So the Latin Kingdom was left pretty much to its own devices, and went rapidly downhill. Of its six rulers, only one was competent and long-lived enough to accomplish anything, and he was most probably poisoned. The Franks themselves were a brutish people, still feudal in a world newly made commercial, stabled their horses in the churches, got drunk, let their offal rot where it fell, tore up the drains, lived on what they could steal, learned nothing, and grew weaker every day. Fighting was all they understood, and even there, the military tactics of the Slavic and Turcoman peoples they had to fight were beyond them. So was administration. So was trade. They were not obeyed by their subjects, and their effective power scarcely embraced the suburbs of the capital. For 57 years they withdrew into an increasingly abandoned and impoverished city, being unable to hold their territorial possessions; and within that city they rattled around like chickpeas, jarred on each other, and accomplished little.

The last Latin Emperor, Baldwin II, ascended the throne as a minor in 1228 and ruled for 33 years. He had few troops, less matériel, and was so poor he had to strip the copper domes off the churches of the city in order to mint base coin.

He had little affection for his capital, and stayed away as much as possible. A great deal of his time was spent in Europe, begging. His followers quarreled among themselves by way of diversion.

The sack of Constantinople meant the downfall of the Empire as a territorial entity. The islands and Greece were broken up into a multitude of minor principalities and duchies, and though these changed hands from time to time, the Empire, even when re-established, was never strong enough to reunite them into a centrally administered whole. However, the Palaeologi when they came to power wisely put members of their own family into control of as many of them as it proved possible to occupy.

For the 57 years of the Latin Empire there were to be three empires going at once; that of Nicaea, which was to triumph over the others; that of Trebizond at the far end of the Black Sea; and the Latin, which looked impressive on maps, but did not exist on the land under them. There was also that nuisance to all three, the Despotate of Epirus, stretching from Albania down into the Morea, which had claims to the imperial throne, but never achieved it.

V

THE Empire of Nicaea, which was to restore the Byzantine state, was a success almost from the beginning, largely because its first three rulers were clever men and its fourth, a child, found his throne usurped by the founder of the House of Palaeologus, in his own way no less able.

Two-thirds of the peninsula of Asia Minor, or Anatolia, had for some centuries now been in the hands of the Seljuq Turks, the best established to date of the Turcoman tribes which had so often invaded Anatolia. The other third was in Byzantine hands, but was given to the Latins when the Empire was divided in 1204. Though it was only 50 miles away across the Sea of Marmora, the Franks could not hold it, so Theodore Lascaris, who had succeeded to the throne, took it for himself.

At first he had difficulty. The Greeks of Nicaea, the strongest city, would have nothing to do with him, fearing Frankish reprisals if they received him. After he had several times saved them from being sacked by bands of marauders sent over from Byzantium, they were induced to accept him as emperor, in the hope that he might do so again.

Now the Empire was gone and its administrative system wrecked, the only force that could unite the invariably contentious Greeks was the Orthodox Church. Fearing the incursions of the Roman Catholic Church into its territories, the Orthodox Church cooperated, particularly on its lower levels, with the Lascarids. The Patriarchs, if sometimes refractory, were not disloyal. The Empire of Trebizond having formed an alliance with the Latin Emperor Henry in 1206, the Orthodox who had taken refuge there flocked to Nicaea, as did a good many fleeing from religious persecution at Byzantium. The city soon became the principal residence of the clergy, and though they had a tendency to interfere in military matters, their adherence had great effect with the people.

Theodore Lascaris attempted to reach an agreement with Pope Innocent III, who had given the Crusaders what amounted to carte blanche to sack the Empire. Since the Greeks refused to allow the two branches of the Christian Church to merge, with Innocent III, of course, as head of both, the answer was not encouraging. Innocent III's reply, addressed merely to the Honorable Theodore, and so denying his claim to the Empire, was thunder, papal style. "The Greeks having rent asunder the garment of Christ, God has doubtless made use of the Latins as an instrument to punish them for their crimes. The judgments of God are always just, and He frequently punishes evil by the agency of wicked men." Innocent was a politician only thinly disguished as a pontiff; his ambition was spiritual domination figured forth in temporal possession, and it was his view that anyone who refused to acknowledge and to contribute toward the absolute supremacy of the Papacy, which is to say himself, be he heathen, Orthodox, Latin, Albigensian, or Frank, was better off dead, and if possible soon, before he slipped from purgatory into most capacious hell. He therefore finished his diatribe by recommending that Theodore became a vassal of the Latin Emperor, and unleashed by means of his legate, Pelagius, so violent a persecution of the Orthodox in Byzantium that the Latin Emperor Henry had to intercede in order to save the lives of his own staff.

Both Eastern and Western branches of the Church were equally bigoted, intolerant and violent, but with one enormous difference. The Orthodox confined their ruinous theological squabbles to members of their own Church and were remarkably tolerant of other creeds, such as the Muslim, and of other churches, including the Catholic until its pretensions made it intolerable. The Catholic Church refused to tolerate the existence of any other church or schism whatsoever upon any terms, except occasionally and impermanently, for reasons of diplomacy which deceived no one. This one difference probably did more to exacerbate each side against the other than did any point of doctrine or of church government. At any rate, Roman intolerance greatly enhanced Theodore Lascaris' following.

He was not a brilliant man, but he was a good one and also a good commander. He ruled and fought for eighteen years, dying in 1222. The next emperor was his son-in-law, John III Vatatzes.

John III Vatatzes had financial and administrative abilities rare in a military commander, and was ably supported by his wife, Irene Lascaris, and vastly assisted by the political circumstances of the world against which he was fighting. The Latins were losing their military strength, which had never been much. There were desertions every day. Moreover, they had to fight on two fronts, the Balkan and the Asiatic. A Mongol invasion which destroyed the power of the Seljuq sultans at his rear but did not reach his own territories, made it possible for John III to fight on but one, and so consolidate his forces.

He defeated the Latin Emperor in battle, captured and had blinded two of the treasonous Lascarids, cleared the Latins out of such towns as they had been able to hold in Asia Minor, and then crossed over into Europe to commence the final reconquest of the Empire.

It was during his reign that the Palaeologi, who had been prominent nobles for centuries and had intermarried with female members of the various royal houses, and so had as good a right to the throne as any, first got that foothold which was later to allow them to vault to power. Their estates, which were enormous, being in Asia, they had remained rich and powerful among many who had become suddenly poor and therefore weak. They swiftly outdistanced rival noble families, and Andronicus Palaeologus contrived to have himself made governor of Thessalonica and other European holdings won back from the Latins. His son, Michael Palaeologus, the future founder of the dynasty, was a young officer in the Emperor

John's favor. He was twenty-seven years old and an ambitious hypocrite, but lacked neither wit nor ability. Since he was also pleasant, agreeable, good-looking, and well liked by the army, the only way to get rid of him was to accuse him of treason.

These intrigues went on at court every day, and John III, who had his own informers, had the good sense to pay them little heed. Since he was endeavoring to conduct a public, not a private war, he deferred the trial until the end of his current campaign. Two witnesses were then examined, one in the pay of one side most probably, and one in the pay of the other almost certainly, as was the way.

The one declared that Michael had made traitorous overtures to him; the other, that though he had listened to the same proposals from the first witness, he had never discussed the matter with Michael. Since there were no other witnesses, it was decided to solve the impasse by a duel. Unfortunately the first witness killed the second. Somewhat in a quandary, with only one witness left and that one far from impartial, the court turned from feud to faith, and declared that Michael should prove or disprove his innocence by holding a red-hot iron globe in his hand. If it burned him, he was guilty. If it did not burn him, that would be sign that heaven had passed a small miracle in order to prove him innocent.

This was known as trial by ordeal, and was popular in the ecclesiastical circles of the day. It not only assured that no sinner should escape, but provided a legal source of entertainment.

Michael replied that, though he was willing to meet his accuser in battle, he could not expect heaven to work a miracle for a mere sinner such as himself and he would need priestly assistance. Therefore, "Holy Father, as you know so well the power of faith and innocence in a holy trial, take the glowing iron from the furnace, and I will receive it at your hands with faith and submission."

Since of all people who do not greatly care for the clergy, the truly devout greatly care for it least, and since both the judges and the Emperor were not devoid of humor, this verbal ruse was taken to prove Michael's innocence. Of course he was not innocent, he was merely biding his time, but John, who was no fool, for that reason favored Michael because he was no fool either, and he was restored to court, married off to John Vatatzes' niece, Theodora, and not trusted; so things stood much as they had before, except that he had a new wife. As Finley says in his *History of Greece,* "We may admire his ability in defending himself without feeling convinced of his innocence," a statement as tolerantly judicious as it is impartially sane; and such seems to have been the feeling at the time.

This comedy over with, John III turned his attention to other matters. His singular distinction is that he was the only emperor after the Macedonians two hundred years before, and the last emperor ever, to put the finances of the Empire not only upon a sound, but upon a prosperous footing.

The emerging nations of Europe might be forgiven for not realizing that a sound state is based upon agriculture and trade, because in their case their states weren't. They were only just emerging from feudalism. The Latin Empire lived on loans, most of them advanced by Venice. The Papal States made do with Peter's Pence, and maintained a considerable colony of Jews at Rome in order to stay afloat. The Arab and Muslim nations were hopelessly ill managed and never realized that the more prosperous the agriculture and trade, the better the taxes; the more onerous the taxes, the harder they would be to collect. As a result, the strictly commercial cities of the Hanseatic League to the north, and Venice, Pisa, and Genoa had grown enormously in power.

The last imperial-minded ruler in these parts to master these matters was probably Mithridates of Pontus, some 1,300 years before, whose wealth was a constant mystery to the ancient world, but most probably came from an astute manipulation of all trade in the Black Sea. Having no ships, John III, whose recreation was in any event farming, turned to agriculture. Rather than pour money uselessly into public projects, he sensibly developed his own lands. The result was an astonishing solvency; and his revenues became so spectacular that the nobles were persuaded to follow his example. One of his cleverer stratagems was to have a diadem made up out of the profits of the egg money, which the Empress Irene then wore in public. Studded with egg-shaped (and sized) jewels, it was portable proof that Cincinnatus knows best, and both the nobility and the country prospered accordingly. The Empire of Nicaea not having been overrun by the Mongol hordes who had recently devastated the rest of Anatolia, there was a ready market and an undisturbed succession of growing seasons, and though the roads were bad, there were enormous profits to be derived from dried fish, dried fruit, dried anything.

He next concerned himself with the civil service, and by making the wearing of the then fashionable Italian silks an offense punishable by removal from office, was able to rusticate most of the court nobility and to replace them with competent commoners, while at the same time reviving the Greek silk industry.

In short he was a clever prince, the only thing to be said against him being that he was compelled further to debase the currency to two parts gold to one alloy, not only to finance the reconquest of the Empire but also because the rich, instead of keeping money in circulation, tended to bury it in crocks, so that new issues were often necessary. A proportion of two to one was not so bad, but set a ruinous precedent for later princes less astute than he.

John III died in 1254 after a reign of 33 years, leaving as his heir Theodore Lascaris II (he took back the name of his mother, the daughter of Theodore I), himself then thirty-three.

Though competent enough virtually to complete the reconquest of the mainland and of Byzantium, Theodore Lascaris II was an epileptic whose only heir was a child. The Palaeologi began to make their preparations. And so did everybody else.

During 1257 and early 1258 Theodore's seizures became worse, and made him so irritable that his sanity began to be doubted. It was the belief of the time that epilepsy was caused by witchcraft. Theodore set himself to find the witch responsible. The courtiers were thus enabled to remove a few rivals from office by means of denunciation, to advance others, and to plot the removal of still more.

Since his heir was now but eight, some of the court, no doubt for a fee, suggested to Theodore that Michael Palaeologus, descended as he was from the eldest daughter of Alexius III Angelus, and married as he was to John III Vatatzes' niece, would make an excellent regent. Others said that, on the contrary, his niece was almost certainly a witch responsible for their master's seizures.

Theodore had the niece, who was considered beautiful, sewn in a sack up to her neck, so her expression might be observed. The sack was stuffed with cats, and the cats jabbed with javelins so as to scratch her to pieces in their rage. She did not confess to being a witch, but she never looked the same again either, and produced no children.

Fearing reprisals, though there is no record that Michael was particularly fond of anyone, Theodore then had him brought to court in chains. As usual, Michael managed to talk his way free, and was thus on the spot when Theodore died during August of 1258.

There were two regents, the Patriarch Arsenios and George Muzulon, a commoner whose elevation had incensed the nobility. It was a simple enough matter to have Muzulon murdered and Michael appointed regent in his stead, but the Patriarch was more difficult to deal with. For one thing, he was away.

Those who had been coerced into appointing Michael coregent had been prudent not to give him access to the treasury. Michael, who controlled the army, was equally prudent to make free of it without their permission, and by the time Arsenios returned had bribed so many that by particular recommendation of the higher clergy and by universal consent of the army and the nobility, he was elevated to the rank of Despot, made tutor to the boy, John IV, and given complete control of everything.

This, he seems to have felt, and under the circumstances he was right, was not enough. He therefore had his friends talk up an elective monarchy, so John IV might be provided with a colleague old enough to make war. His troops supported the suggestion, there were no other troops, so on the 1st of January, 1259, Michael was proclaimed co-emperor, having first signed an agreement with the Patriarch Arsenios to restore full sovereignty to John IV when that minor attained to his majority. The joint coronation was to take place at Nicaea. Thus was founded the House of Palaeologus.

There are two sorts of men who seek supreme power, those who wish to have it and those who wish to do something with it. Michael VIII Palaeologus was of the former, and so there was little chance of John IV attaining to his majority. At Nicaea, when the time came for the coronation, Michael stepped forward and John was nowhere to be found.

The Patriarch Arsenios was a contentious, contumacious, bigoted, self-willed, overemotional, and powerful autocrat, of conservative temperament. He did not like to be opposed in anything, and he most particularly did not like to be tricked. It is also quite probable that he had been looking forward to such power as the regency would give him. He therefore refused to proceed with the ceremony, but was finally talked around by his bishops, who had been suborned. He was not brought around for long, and so Michael's ambitions gave rise to yet another of those schisms which did so much to weaken the social resilience of the Empire, before Byzantium was even restored.

For the moment this did not concern him. He was a self-seeker of no mean ability, and so could never see far. That he wished a reunited empire goes without saying, but his first concern was to consolidate his position. He therefore emptied a solvent treasury in next to no time, in order to hand out donatives to the army, handouts to the mob, enlarged stipends to the senators, a body of men no more useful than those of Rome had been but equally mischievous, and liberal bribes to the nobility; and not only emptied it, but permanently encumbered the state finances with debts. It proved necessary to withdraw the armies from the field in order to support the tax-gatherers and, even so, not even the interest could ever be paid off. In other words, in less than a year he undid the work of two generations, and permanently undermined the prosperity of the state.

But the Empire was in good order politically. The armies were enthusiastic, chiefly because they were paid in land, and so had something of their own to defend; and the farmers, who had been made owners of their fields by John III Vatatzes, had something to fight for now themselves, and did so. Equally, the Empire's rivals and neighbors were in disrepair. The Seljuqs of Asia Minor had been destroyed by the Mongol invasions, and were prevented by dynastic squabbles from restoring themselves. The Latin Empire at Byzantium had dwindled away to nothing, and might better be called the Latin Empire at Byzantium than the Latin Empire of it, for nothing else was left. The Empire of Trebizond was impotent and far away. That left Epirus and Bulgaria. The forces of Epirus were defeated in the field, and Bulgaria was undergoing one of its many interregnums. Europe was otherwise engaged, regarded the Latin Kingdom as the Pope's business, and did nothing to interfere. So there was only Venice to worry about.

Though Michael schemed constantly, his knowledge was almost as deficient as his statesmanship. And though he knew men's price, he does not seem to have known much about their character. Even men who sell themselves always save out something for their own use. And those who make common cause with us all too commonly see that cause as one-sided. Since he behaved so himself, it is curious he did not take greater precautions against such conduct in others.

Of the two maritime empires of the day, Venice and Genoa, Venice was the somewhat less rapacious, knew the weak condition of the Latin Empire, and though given to extort was also willing to coexist to its own advantage, and would very likely have switched sides. Michael did not even ask. Instead he made alliance with the Genoese, granting them commercial privileges amounting to monopoly, and renewing concessions made to them by the Emperor Manuel Comnenus (1143–1180) in exchange for naval and military aid.

It was a shortsighted and disastrous thing to do. Had he been content to wait a year or two, or had he been more astute, it need not have been done at all; it was to ruin the restored Empire; and as a final irony, it turned out not even to have been necessary.

Byzantium was retaken, much as it had been founded, by happenstance. One of Michael's generals, Alexis Strategopoulos, being in the region, turned aside to see the walls of the city. Its Venetian defenders were away in the Black Sea to wipe out Genoese colonies there, and some Greek peasants of the area simply led him into the city and advised that he take it. So he did.

He found it a smoke-stained, semideserted ruin, littered with filth. Rather than defend it, the Latin Emperor Baldwin fled so hurriedly that he left his crown, scepter, and sword behind at Blachernae. Such Franks and Venetians as were present were more determined, and barricaded themselves in the commercial quarter against the return of the Venetian fleet. Strategopoulos had the quarter set on fire, to force them into the sea and onto such ships as were in the harbor. In this he was successful, though it meant still further destruction of the city. The refugees departed in such overladen boats that many of them died of thirst, exposure, hunger, and drowning on their way to Euboea, the selected place of refuge, safely away in the Aegean.

The Latin Empire had lasted 57 years, 3 months, and 11 days. The restored Empire, and with it the newly elevated House of Palaeologus, was to last for 192 years, but only as a clock running down may be said to keep time until it stops, each day a little slower, each day a little less efficiently, until it ends by keeping its own time, which has nothing to do with the rest of the world whatsoever.

VI

THE nine emperors (and one unrelated usurper) who ruled as the House of Palaeologus were men of unequal merit, a thing which need not surprise us, but it is misfortunate that the three really competent members of the dynasty, a father and two of his sons, should come at the end of the reign, and that the first six (and the usurper) should have included a shortsighted schemer, a theological dilettante indifferent to public affairs, an exceptionally long-lived do-nothing, a scheming equanimous interloping statesman afflicted with short sight, and several lecherous nincompoops who insisted that the power be divided in order that they might strut their day.

Titular power, that is. Of real power there really was not any. Moreover, there began to stir in Michael VIII's reign an entirely new power in the Near Eastern world, that of the Osmanli Turks, which the weakness and destruction of the Seljuq dynasty had let in, and the danger of which was not recognized in time, either by Byzantine or Seljuq, Venice or Genoa, Pope or European—a power which, from its first appearance, though nobody realized it at the time, was well organized and bent on world dominance. It was a military power, and military powers must expand continuously and continually, or else be gobbled up themselves. It is the realization of this which gives them their paranoic drive.

But in 1261 the Osmanli Turks were not known.

The restored Empire, most of which was soon to be lost, consisted of one-third of Asia Minor; of Thrace, though Thrace was shakily held; of the territories immediately around the city; of several strips along the Black Sea coast of Europe; and of some, but not most, of the islands of the Greek Archipelago, together with bits and pieces of the Morea, or Peloponnesus. Greece itself was pitted with independent enclaves.

Of the islands of the Archipelago, Corfu was in the hands of the Venetians; Cephalonia, Zante and Ithaca belonged to the Tocchi family; Rhodes had fallen into the hands of the Knights of St. John of Jerusalem; Crete was Venetian; Chios and Samos were owned by a joint stock company entirely in the control of the 14 branches of the Justiniani family of Genoa; Naxos and Santorin belonged to the Crespi; Andros to the Sommaripà; and the others were similarly the fiefs of petty tyrants difficult and usually impossible to dislodge.

All these people had to be treated with. There was danger that Baldwin might make alliance with somebody, anybody, to get back his kingdom. There was danger the Pope might launch another crusade against a church the West felt to be infidel.

Venice might be expected to intrigue to get its privileges back, and still held the chief trading depots of the Tyrrhenian coast, and many of the islands. The Empire of Nicaea, thanks to the fall of the Seljuq Turks, had had to maintain itself on only one front. The restored Empire had to deal not only with Anatolia and with Europe, but with the independent Balkans, the no less independent Frankish enclaves of Greece, and what was left of the Despotate of Epirus as well.

By being so liberal as to empty the treasury, Michael VIII had deprived the restored Empire of its one real asset, ready money. The sources of mercenary manpower dwindled away; the mercenaries could seldom be paid off; and there was no navy—the Angeli had sold it up. Michael had to fall back on bribery and the moneylenders. John III Vatatzes had been a statesman as well as a commander. Michael, though a good enough commander, was no statesman at all but could only deal with one emergency at a time. Peril was nothing new to the Empire. The Empire had always been imperiled. But it had not now the means to maintain itself on so many different fronts at once. Though the Lascarids had wanted Byzantium back, they had been prudent to be in no hurry to take it, wisely setting themselves to consolidate their own position first. Now Michael proposed to restore the machinery and pomp of previous centuries in a world, both external and internal, to which they were no longer either adequate or suitable. In short, he set about the reanimation of an archaic state in a modern world, and so produced a permanently endangered fossil. He claimed the perquisites; but he lacked the power.

His capital had one-tenth of its original population and, worse, was for the first time predominently a Greek rather than a cosmopolitan town.

The ancient Greeks had been adroit at trade and that kept them prosperous. But as the pomp of the Byzantine state increased, as the hierarchy stratified, and as those in positions of power rose higher and higher from any direct contact with the source of it, they let the business of the Empire fall into the hands of foreigners, either out of ignorance of the consequences or because they had no other means of paying for military assistance, since money was short, than to grant commercial futures and monopolies to foreigners. As a result, one day they awoke to discover that power was gone, only the pomp remained, and so found themselves the gorgeous captives of their own delegates. Their impotence only enhanced the fury with which they caballed against each other for a power which no longer existed; it did not unite them in an effort to recapture it. During its last two hundred years, the Empire was not only gobbled up piecemeal by the Osmanli Turks, but became little better than a counter in the endless trade wars between the two chief commercial powers of Europe, Genoa and Venice. The later emperors tried to play these two off against each other, but since the one thing the cities had in common was their determination completely to absorb the trading wealth, Byzantium prospered with neither side.

Michael VIII was compelled to confirm the Genoese in their privileges according to the terms of the treaty, even though no assistance had been needed or given, and so gave away such valuable perquisites as the monopoly on the alum pits of Phocea, which went to Manuel Zaccaria and his descendants, Genoese with no more interest in Byzantium than an ant has in a milch aphid hung up in a dark cellar until it be plump enough to milk.

Such, partly because of their own negligence, partly because of factors which because of past negligence they were unable to control, was the situation of the Palaeologi, who nevertheless, so great was the power of the bureaucratic machinery, which was self-operating if not self-feeding, managed to endure for almost two centuries.

None of this was evident when Michael Palaeologus took over the city and attempted to restore the Empire, for history has seldom been shaped according to pattern, the pattern becomes visible only afterward, like something woven out of the warp and woof of contingency. The demagogue knows what movements to make, but he has not been shown and so cannot see the figure they will form.

Michael, however, thought himself in command of everything. A courier brought him those imperial trophies which Baldwin had abandoned, and after a week of preparations he made his state entry into the former capital through that Golden Gate used only for processional arrivals at the city. He was the last emperor to do so. After his reign it was bricked up and never reopened, until the Osmanli took the city. He entered on foot, to show his humility, on August 15, 1261.

Before him was born one of the innumerable portraits of the Virgin Mary said to have been painted by St. Luke, and he moved in a cloud of clergy. At the Palace of Bucoleon, near Hagia Sophia, he took horse and rode to the cathedral.

Though 57 years is not long for a dynasty, it is more than three-fourths the normal life-span of a man. There had therefore been a two-generation discontinuity in the habit of obedience to the ruling house. This was to cause trouble both with the Byzantine mob and with the new class of small landholder, but in no way subdued the universal pretensions of emperor and administration. Byzantium was so strongly centralized a state that the habit of looking upon the Empire as the city, and the city as the Empire, persisted long after the Empire was gone. Curiously, perhaps because of their ignorance of Byzantine affairs, European nations took somewhat the same view, so that the prestige of the city was stronger in Paris than in its own immediate provinces. Only Venice and Genoa were in a position to know otherwise; only they were in a position to take advantage of the immediate profits to be derived from a galvanized corpse.

Very little of the city remained. It had been devastated by four fires, the last of them still smoldering. The center of the richest part of it was a cinder heap a mile and a half wide. The eastern suburbs and the commercial quarter along the Golden Horn were almost obliterated, except where here and there the now expelled Venetian merchants had fortified a house amid the rubble. The population had dwindled by 90 percent, and what the Franks had left standing they had neglected, broken, or befouled. Churches stood in the desolation like mausoleums in an abandoned cemetery whose tombstones have long since been cast down. Many of them were boarded up. The drainage system had decayed, so that epidemic and plague cut back the inhabitants every five, ten, or fifteen years; while intestinal parasites no doubt did much to rob the remainder of what energy they had not.

The Greeks, who were addicted to the pleasures of street and table, soon put this situation to rights, but were unable to control either plague or politics. It never seems to occur to those who wish to seize power that they might best first make certain that there will be some power left after they have seized it. Without much thought to the consequences, and in order to make himself sole emperor, Michael VIII had the boy John IV Lascaris, who was now ten, blinded. It was the traditional means of removing rivals.

Four methods were available: by gouging out the eyes with an ornamental eye scoop; by burning them away with a hot iron; by tying a cord around the head so tightly the eyes popped out, though it is difficult to see how the victim could survive this; and by searing the optic nerve with a red-hot bowl held over the face. The fourth was considered the most merciful procedure, and by many Michael Palaeologus was applauded for making use of it, out of compassion for the child. The Patriarch Arsenios excommunicated him for having done so at all.

This was dangerous to Michael's prestige, for the nation would not obey an excommunicated emperor. Michael brought charges of treason against Arsenios, but could not prove them. He had Arsenios deposed anyway, and himself absolved with great pomp by a new patriarch of his own selection. But though he could depose Arsenios, he could not depose his authority, and from exile Arsenios gave orders not only that the Emperor was not to be obeyed, but that none of the priests and bishops, nor the new Patriarch who had absolved him, should be obeyed either. The result was a new sect and political faction, the Arsenites, who were to undermine authority for the next fifty-odd years.

It had been predicted that whoever retook Constantinople from the Franks would lose Asia to the Turks; and this soon turned out to be true. Michael busied himself with the reconstruction of his capital, a project admirable in itself but one which drained off those resources which might better have been spent on the defense of the Empire.

There was certainly much to restore. The Franks had stripped the city, and had been reduced to such poverty that they had been forced to sell the Crown of Thorns to the French, not once but twice, once for 7,000 pounds and later for 10,000 marks. Having discovered this source of windfalls, they had disposed of a large part of the True Cross, of the Lance, the Sponge, and other relics.

These things could be replaced, even if they could not be restored; to replace the city and its population proved more expensive. The nobility was coaxed back with promises of place and pension. Michael settled new citizens brought from the Greek islands on terms favorable to themselves. He rebuilt bridges, roads, palaces, and churches, most of the latter no longer needed (the Church of the Apostles, still standing, was boarded up for want of a congregation).

What he could not do anything about was the Genoese, for he had not the arms to break his agreement with them, and they had the force to see that it was enforced in their favor. Nor did he understand that the trade routes of the world had shifted away from Byzantium, chiefly because the Comnenan and Angelan emperors, and of course the Franks, had allowed the navy to fall into such disrepair that piracy had become prevalent, with the result that the merchants of Russia and the East now found it safer to ship goods overland to the Hanseatic cities of the Baltic or up the Danube. The Danube debouches into the Black Sea, and whoever controlled the Black Sea would control this trade. The real purpose of the Genoese was therefore not to batten upon Byzantium's trade, but to cut the city off from the Black Sea, which they meant to control for themselves.

From the suburb of Galata, across the Golden Horn, which they made semiautonomous in theory and completely autonomous in fact, they did not hesitate to attack, bombard, or blockade the capital whenever they wished still one more concession in their favor. The Golden Horn was the commercial harbor of the city. The Genoese saw to it that most shipping docked on their shore of it, not on the Byzantine. In desperation Michael formed an alliance with the Venetians against the Genoese, but the Genoese won the subsequent battle. This made their demands harder to evade than ever; they soon had 87 percent of the customs fees in their own hands, and the revenues of the Emperor shrank accordingly.

Michael's other acts were no more helpful. Being an usurper, and therefore as fearful of his own forces as he was of the enemies around him, he sometimes most unwisely sapped his own strength. Now that the Seljuq sultans of Iconium, who had contained them, had had their power destroyed by Mongol invasion, the Osmanli Turks began to move down from the Bithynian highlands, where they had been settled by the Seljuqs. At the same time, the minor Seljuq princelings also made war upon the half-abandoned Byzantine possessions in Asia Minor. Rather than attempt to contain them, Michael VIII, who was afraid of insurrection, transported the Greek country nobility out of the interior of Asia Minor to the capital, and refused to allow the installation of strong officials there. Since he had no troops to send, within a generation, from being a Greek community the interior of Asia Minor became a predominantly Turkish one.

The price of military aid from the West was the reunion of the Orthodox and Roman Catholic churches. Michael attempted to effect it. His only reward was that he was excommunicated by the Western Church for having failed, and opposed by the Orthodox for having tried. The Arsenites regarded him as excommunicant. By way of retaliation, he did nothing to defend the rich church lands in Asia Minor, which thereby soon fell into the hands of such Turks as wished to take them.

The one solid accomplishment of his reign was that he was able to secure Mistra in the Peloponnesus to the Empire. A century later it was to become the real intellectual and military center of the restored Empire, and even to be able to send a little money to the capital. He was also able, by means of bribery, to take countermeasures against European schemes to restore the Latin Empire.

But on the whole, Byzantium went back to its old and ruinous avocation of ecclesiastical debate. As far as doctrine was concerned, the quarrel between the Orthodox and Catholic churches turned upon whether the Holy Ghost proceeded *from* the Father and the Son (the Latin view), or from the Father *by* the Son (the Greek). As far as the political facts of the day went, the price of military aid from the West was acceptance of the authority of the Pope, and though rulers on both sides were willing to be conciliatory, their separate peoples were not, so nothing could be done.

The Latin delegates sent to Constantinople in Michael's time were so conciliatory as to say that this doctrinal point was an impenetrable mystery, and did it matter? To which the Greek bishops, who preferred their own authority to that of any other man, answered "non possumus." A scholar named Veccus, persuaded by Michael to advocate union, instead gave a speech in which he said, "There are heretics who are so called. There are some who are not heretics and are not so called. There are some who are so called, but are not heretics, and lastly, there are others who are not called but are heretics, and it is in this latter class that the Latins must be placed." For this mixture of Aristotle and acrimony he was imprisoned, but the clergy and people continued to oppose union of the two Churches, and Michael was excommunicated by the Pope, which meant that any Westerner who could was free to take his territories with the blessings of Western Christendom.

The Anjou of Naples, whose heir, Charles of Anjou, had married the Latin Emperor Baldwin's daughter, assisted by the Papacy and Venice, now prepared to march on Constantinople, presumably, among other things, to restore to the Venetians their lost trade monopolies, to the Pope a supremacy he had never had, and to the House of Anjou those rights which it had so recently married.

The expedition was averted by that complicated uprising to Anjou's rear, the Sicilian Vespers, which was sufficiently bloody —which is to say successful—to cripple Neapolitan power for some time to come, thereby also the power of the Pope, who was hopelessly involved; and Venice dared not risk the attempt alone. A good deal of Byzantine money had been well spent on this uprising. "Should I dare to claim that I was God's instrument to bring freedom to the Sicilians, then I would only be stating the truth," said Michael VIII in his memoirs, with some complacency. He was in the curious position of having both ruined and saved the same empire.

God's instrument died in 1282, leaving his son and heir, Andronicus II, to complete the collapse of the restored state. Andronicus combined incompetence with longevity, as people so often do, and so managed to reign for 46 years without ever having seemed to care over what. Ascending the throne at twenty-four, he had no personal vices to speak of, but more than made up for the deficiency by means of his virtues as a theologian. He was a shuffling, vacillating coward, given to bursts of violent sidelong spite, and like many mediocre men was greatly given to continual proofs of his own efficiency, an activity which he confused with competence. He was therefore meddlesome, intrusive, and refused to allow others to transact the business he would not himself attend to, so nothing got done. The less got done, the more people he seemed to require not to do it, and thus he further increased the financial burdens of the Empire by appointing an army of supernumerary thumb twiddlers, each of whom expected a pension upon retirement and a purse to keep his hands busy in the interim. To finance this labyrinthine bureaucracy, in the midst of which he lurked more like a storm-tossed spider than a minotaur (he was so afraid of his brother that he kept him in an iron latticework litter without which he refused to go anywhere), he debased the coinage again. During his reign the imperial income shrank from seven or eight million nomismata of full value to 1,000,000 nomismata of the new coinage, worth half. Out of this diminished sum he paid bribes to any neighboring state strong enough to demand one, and neglected to pay the army. The historian Nicephorus Gregoras said this was as though a man had tried to buy the friendship of wolves by opening veins in various parts of his body and allowing them to drain his blood until they were satisfied.

Territories lost to the Empire were not thereby lost to the Church, which in consequence began to grow stronger than the State, and from being supported by it now became its chief support. Once the two had been coextensive. Now the State paid tribute, the Church reaped it.

For 46 years Andronicus, apart from conducting a civil war with his grandson and heir, which for a while resulted in two contradictory governments, each with a different foreign policy, to very small profit to the state, ignored the world around him; retired the navy and abolished the army in order to pay for his hobby; and devoted himself almost exclusively to theological debate, electing and deposing eight patriarchs, and establishing a sort of Inquisition to sit upon heresy and to punish it by the confiscation of property. Since he was strict, there were a great many heretics, and so a few souls were saved and a great deal of civil property irrevocably lost.

With no one to restrain them, the Venetians and Genoese fought each other in the streets and harbors of Byzantium; the plundering of the small islands in the Propontis could be watched from the upper loggias of the imperial palace; and pirates induced the Emperor to ransom their captives by sailing past his windows with the men and women exposed, like merchandise, in the rigging. The Venetians burned Galata in 1296, blockaded the capital, and amused themselves by shooting arrows through the windows of the palaces from the decks of their ships. There were 21 civil wars in 34 years; a brigade of freebooters, the Catalan Grand Company, descended on the Empire in 1303, and lived off the sack of it and the sale of its citizens into slavery for the next 12 years; and the Osmanli descended out of Bithynia to burn the towns on the Asiatic shore of the Bosphorus, which made a splendid display at night.

Andronicus II went on installing and removing patriarchs as though his life depended upon it, as perhaps it did. From his reign on, the Empire was to be saved, not by its own exertions but by a series of fortuitous external circumstances. It was to be sunk, among other things, by its own atrabilious talent for ecclesiastical intransigence.

VII

PERHAPS religious passions are harder to understand or to sympathize with after the event than are any others. Their real cause evaporates, leaving behind it only the salts of controversy. One wonders what all the fuss was about. Though insight is undoubtedly the highest moral experience of which man is capable, and though any organized church has always been an invaluable social mechanism whereby to maintain civic order, unfortunately the other and darker side of this indispensable adjunct of the state has often been, in all ages after the prophetic, and in all faiths, an entrenched and far from disinterested hierarchy.

People may serve themselves without realizing they are self-seeking. The last person to realize his own nature is the bigot or hypocrite himself, otherwise he would be neither. It is possible to satisfy the lowest motives while espousing the highest causes. Historically considered, Christianity and early Judaism have a worse record for intolerance than has any other of the higher faiths, even including Islam, probably because they are revealed religions, whereas Buddhism, Confucianism, Hinduism, and Shinto are not. Constantine the Great had been compelled to put down schism almost as soon as he had encouraged Christianity. He had been able to do so only by force.

That for 250 years a once powerful people should let everything they had won back go to ruin while they quarreled over whether a crust of bread was or was not leavened, and over the hypothetical procession one from the other of three symbolic cult figures, passes the bounds of comprehension and makes the mind boggle. But the mind boggles unjustly, for the quarrel was phrased so, but its actual object was which of two enormous ecclesiastical establishments should finally subdue the rights, revenues, and temporal and spiritual dominion of the other. In the event, neither did. In the process, an empire fell.

The Byzantines, at first in the abstract, but later on to protect their autonomy, had been indulging themselves in the minute joys of theological dispute for some thousand years, commencing with the Council of Nicaea. Though Constantine had dealt with Arianism, it did not die, and schism produced schism produced schism.

Later emperors were either even less successful, or else theologians themselves. In the beginning these heresies and counterheresies came from Egypt—to be specific, from Alexandria, where they were the chief delight of a polyglot and mongrel population. Eutyches, a monk from Byzantium, had been excommunicated for Monophysitism (the doctrine that the human and divine in Christ constitute a single, composite nature) in 448, producing a squabble which split the Empire, caused riots in Egypt, and in time led to the loss of that province, since the Copts preferred religious debate to defending themselves against the Arabs.

These dissensions, in providing a handy tool with which to beat almost any neighbor, soon became political. Before long, anyone who wished an excuse for revolt, if not against the Empire at least to gain possession of it, was at liberty to lay waste his neighbors' territories in the name of doctrinal purity. The influence of the clergy grew so rapidly that in 518 the Eunuch Amantius, a Monophysite, managed to upset the succession to the throne by means of an appeal to religious intolerance, calling in Justin, the uncle of Justinian the Great.

The split between East and West was of a somewhat different order. At the time when the two halves of the Empire separated, the Pope was merely chief bishop in Rome, and sometimes not even that. The bishops and archbishops each had authority over his own diocese, there was no personal authority higher, and matters of church goverment were settled by councils. But as the Western Empire fell into chaos and the Eastern prospered, the Patriarch of Constantinople became head of the bishops in the East, and as second highest dignitary in the Orthodox Church was, with the assistance of the Emperor, its temporal head, and sometimes to assist him, able to inforce his authority over an increasingly well-organized separate church establishment.

In seventh-century Rome, with all other authority withdrawn, the chief of the bishops of that place was forced to maintain order himself, and there thus grew up both the Papal States and the concept of the Pope as head of the Church. Since he could not depend upon the secular resources of a coterminous and wealthy state, he was forced to make use of diplomacy, bribery, intrigue, and excommunication in order to survive as a secular power. Without a strong government to work with, he was constrained to work against many weak ones. And since his only power derived from the obedience of the faithful, he was not apt to be tolerant of anyone who did not recognize his authority.

Behind this situation lay a constantly shifting pattern of power politics, and the intolerance of the too well indoctrinated laity of both branches of the Church. Over and over again the heads of state *would* have reunited the two Churches, but the temper of their peoples would not permit of it. This was the plight of the later emperors of the House of Palaeologus.

By the eighth and ninth centuries the two Churches had become mutually exclusive. In the absence of an overlord, the Pope regarded himself as head of Christendom and though there were Holy Roman Emperors in the West again, after Charlemagne forced his own coronation in 800 A.D., the Pope recognized them but paid no more attention to them than he had to. In the East there always had been an emperor as head of the Church, and so the territorial and spiritual pretensions were in harmony with each other, more or less, and despite constant bickering between them.

This rival establishment the Papacy wished pulled down.

Nor did the Byzantine Emperor take kindly to an upstart Holy Roman Emperor in the West, a title Byzantium never saw fit to recognize. In part this attitude sprang from nothing but simple pretension, since the Eastern Empire had no holdings in the West. But it also came from the circumstance that the Eastern Emperor, as head of both Church *and* State, and so superior to the Pope, could scarcely be expected to countenance the rivalry of a possibly similar arrangement in the West. Since the Pope could not countenance it either, it was never a real danger.

The schism between the two branches of the Church became formal and final in the mid-eleventh century, when the Pope's name was dropped from the Eastern liturgy. The work of completing the rupture was undertaken by the Patriarch Michael Keroularios. An ambitious man, he had been forcibly tonsured after attempting to take the throne himself, and his behavior as Patriarch was imperial. When the then Pope, Leo IX, excommunicated him, Keroularios retaliated by declaring Leo IX to be anathema.

Whatever the heads of state, the Patriarchs, even occasionally a Pope, tried to do, the breach became impossible to close, for the people would have nothing to do with Union. They had been too well indoctrinated, resisted change, and expressed themselves often and violently. For example, in 1182 the papal legate's head was cut off and tied to a dog's tail. "It is far better," wrote Pope Gregory in 1073, "for a country to remain under the rule of Islam, than to be governed by Christians who refuse to acknowledge the rights of the Catholic Church." The Byzantines did not agree, and among them "Papa" became a popular name for dogs.

As the only hope the Byzantine Empire now had was to exchange union of the two Churches for military aid, the situation was therefore intolerable. The people had been conditioned too well.

Andronicus II did nothing to better matters, and died February 13, 1332, aetatis suae seventy-four, regretting nothing, regretted by no one, and forgiving none. He had been forced to abdicate and take the habit of a monk, as Brother Anthony. Strange to say, despite his passion for the theology, he did not take kindly to the cloister, and had made the last four years of his life a contumacious hell.

His grandson, Andronicus III, who succeeded him, was cruel, indolent, debauched, contradictory, but clearheaded. He did his best to institute reform, but it was too late. By the end of his reign, the Osmanli and Seljuq Turks, who had crossed successfully over into Europe in 1329, 1330, 1331, and 1332, but had not been able to establish permanent settlement, held four of the principal metropolitan sees of the Eastern Church; their pirates were attacking Mediterranean shipping and raiding the coasts of lower Italy; their soldiers were in control of most of Asia; and the final movement against Byzantium had begun.

To the eyes of the Great World, which means in this case the petty but burgeoning states of Europe, Andronicus III was the rich and powerful overlord of a large if badly conducted state inhabited by a numerous, prosperous, if degenerate people. That the Empire was diminished signified little, for it also extended itself from time to time (Andronicus III was able to regain Thessaly and parts of Albania for a while), and during that period all states were in an amoeboid condition of territorial palpitation, sometimes reproducing themselves by dynastic synapsis, at others, when their environment was less acid, extending themselves polyp fashion. Nationalism was scarcely born. France meant the House of Capet, and after 1328, the House of Valois; Naples the House of Anjou; England, the Plantagenets; Byzantium the Palaeologi; the Germanies many small princelings and whoever happened to be Holy Roman Emperor at the time. These states went about picking up or dropping new properties like a mad dog with a new bone, until a bigger dog wrested it away. Few of them could successfully occupy what they claimed to own, and if they could, there was always another claimant.

The Osmanli Turks, if they had been heard of at all, seemed

nothing more than a transient insurgent troop of brigands who had managed, no doubt temporarily, to extract tribute from a few Greek cities in Asia Minor, and who had laid waste, in passing, some of the home provinces.

No other view of them could have been so misleading.

VIII

THE word Turk, or Turcoman, is generic, and describes a race, not a nation or even a language group. It was the name of a nomadic people of mixed stock, moving back and forth across the wastes of Central Asia and up and down the great passageways of the Near East, Russia, and Eastern Europe. They had been either a danger or a nuisance to the more settled nations since long before the days of Herodotus, the first European historian to mention them (as *tourgious,* transcribed by copyists as *amougious*). In late Byzantine times, they were more fancifully thought (by the historian Phrantzes) to be descended from the Comnenan Emperor Isaac, because he had spoken Arabic well (at that time the Turks did not speak it at all). Isaac, so the story went, had married the daughter of a Seljuq princeling, having by her a son, Suleiman, the father of Ertoghril, the leader of the Osmanli tribe.

Other historians descended them from the Trojans, by Hector and Teucer. Paolo Giovio, in the period of the Emperor Charles V, claimed the name to derive from the River Tereck, a tributary of the Volga.

In actuality the Turks, whom the Chinese called the Tuku, as early as they can be traced, inhabited the region dominated by the Altai Mountains, and from there spread over Central Asia. Turkestan still bears their name and supports the remnants of the original racial stock. To the Chinese and Indian border peoples, they were then noted for their beauty, their archery, their export of the gland of the musk deer, from which perfume was derived, their habit of worshiping the constellations Canopus, Orion, and the Great Bear, and for their incestuous marital habits.

Nothing remarkable occurred among them until they embraced Islam, a militant religion as attractive to the Near Eastern, Steppe, and Persian soldier as Zen Buddhism proved to be to the Japanese samurai, and one which produced even more explosive results. The desert religions, Judaism, Islam, Christianity in its primitive state, tend to be centripetal rather than centrifugal. Until the Persians, followers of Zoroaster, who made his religious inventions among mountains, modified it, Islam was a militant, stark, and violently expansive cult. The Turks produced Ghazis, or militant Muslim leaders, as early as the ninth century.

Christianity, by dispensation, might reward the Christian warrior with heaven (or at any rate, with a little less time in Purgatory), for fighting in a good cause. Islam rewarded the warrior with heaven for fighting at all. The two opposed factions thus went differently to their deaths, and the doctrine of fate, unlike the doctrine of original sin, produced impetus rather than hesitation. It was extremely difficult, in Islam, to be damned, and the Arabs, having no material culture of their own worth mentioning (though they had had once, in the extreme south of their peninsula, but that was long past and forgotten), when they wanted anything tended to purloin it, a habit they have never lost.

The explosion of the Arabs and their rapid conquest of Syria, Egypt, North Africa, and ultimately Spain convinced many of the advantages of their faith; and the convert Seljuq Turks were able to establish themselves in Asia Minor and to absorb two-thirds of Byzantine possessions there by the third quarter of the eleventh century, after the rout of the Greeks at the battle of Manzikert, near Lake Van, on th 19th of August, 1071. These they kept until the Mongol invasions of the thirteenth century destroyed their power.

Conversion seems to have had a similarly exhilarating and accelerating effect upon the Osmanli Turks. In the period of Genghis Khan about fifty thousand of them, under Suleiman, son of Kayalp, established themselves in Armenia, near Erzingian, on the Euphrates. Seven years later, the Seljuq dynasty being in turmoil, Suleiman took his troops down the Euphrates, but misjudging the flow of the river, fell with his horse and drowned. His troops and families thereupon dispersed, some toward Asia Minor, some toward Syria, some back to their homeland.

On his death in 1231, Suleiman was the father of four sons. Two of these returned to Khurasan, taking most of the tribe with them. The other two, Dundar and Ertughrul, with 400 families, moved on toward the Occident, fell in with the Seljuq Turks, aided them against invading Mongols, and as a reward, accepting Aladdin, leader of the Seljuqs, as overlord, were given a domain in Karadjahissar, or the Black Mountains, on the frontier of Angora. The domain was occupied by Greeks who also paid tribute to the Seljuqs. They were extirpated, and the Osmanli thereupon took up their first permanent residence, for until now they had been cattle-herding nomads, in that part of Bithynia, near Mount Olympus, known as Phrygia Epictetos.

Ertughrul ruled for fifty years, but has left few records behind him. Of his three sons, the first, Osman, born in 1258, became his heir and first effective head of the tribe upon his father's death in 1288. The name means "leg breaker."

He also is a shadowy figure but to him is ascribed one of those elaborate dreams which successful Oriental monarchies are wont to direct their sycophants to attribute to their predecessors.

In his dream the moon descended, buried itself in his breast, and thereupon, after a considerable upheaval, a tree shot up out of his loins, branched, flourished, and became a green tent covering the world from the Caucasus to the Atlas, from the Taurus to Haemus. From its roots flowed the Tigris, Euphrates, Nile and Danube. Rich cities appeared, glittering with pyramids, minarets, towers, and colonnades, each dome and spire crowned with a crescent. Then a high wind blew up, the leaves turned into swords and swiveled around until they threatened the principal cities of the world, though most of them faced Constantinople. That city began to glitter like an emerald (in some versions a sapphire). Osman then slipped the resultant ring on his finger, and woke up.

This dream, though variously interpreted, meant, of course, but one thing. The Seljuq power was collapsing, for about the same reasons the Byzantine power was: dynastic squabbles, poor administration, ruinous taxation, the presence of stronger neighbors, and fragmentation. The Mongol and Tartar invasions smashed it into a series of fractious autonomous provinces. The Byzantines were not strong enough to take advantage of the fall of Iconium. The Osmanli Turks were. Also, they were totally devoid of religious bigotry during these early centuries of their rise to power, and therefore had one less cause of dissension with their subjects than Byzantium had. In 1289 the Seljuq sultan bestowed the title of Bey upon Osman, and in 1307 the last sultan, Aladdin III, was driven out by the invading Mongols. As the Mongols retired, the Turks advanced, through the new petty Seljuq states of Karamania, Iconium (a smaller, restored Iconium), Lydia, and Aidin. The rulers of these took absolute powers unto themselves, issued their own coinage and, perhaps not without reason, had their names inserted into public prayers. In a short time, Osman controlled almost all of Bithynia, parts of Phrygia, Galatia, and the upper reaches of the River Sangarius, and had established a new capital between Nicaea and Brusa, two Byzantine towns he hoped soon to take for his own.

Everything seemed to assist him. Even his name was to his advantage, for there had been no one of any fame called Othman (or Osman) since the third Caliph in direct descent from the Prophet, the compiler of the Koran and conqueror of Persia. Osman's followers took omen from this, he himself took the title of Padishah or "sovereign of his people," and the dynasty is named after him; for if he was not its founder, he was assuredly the founder of its power.

He did not take kindly to criticism. When his Uncle Deindar, a man of ninety, feeling that perpetual conquest was no suitable recreation for a prince, suggested moderation, Osman's answer was to pick up a bow and arrow and shoot him dead. After that there was no more opposition.

In 1307, a puny defense on the part of several Byzantine governors failing, the Osmanli marched from the uplands down as far as the Sea of Marmora, devastating the countryside as they went, as was their policy. Osman had taken the title of Sultan in 1302, and meant to prove it. He was greatly assisted by the tidal movements of transasiatic migratory peoples, which during his reign became once more a flood. The Byzantines tried to turn the Tartars, also in movement, against the Turks, but without success. The only effect was that the Tartars occupied the Crimea until driven out by the Turks 200 years later, and that 120,000 of them crossed over into Thrace but were beaten back. In 1326, having already captured Ephesus, Osman took Brusa as well, the strongest and richest Greek outpost in Asia Minor and the ancient capital of Bithynia. For a while it became the Osmanli capital.

In 1327 Osman died, leaving behind him a bead rosary, a drum given him by Aladdin III as symbol of his investiture as Bey, a double-edged scimitar somewhat dulled by use, a ceremonial banner, a wooden spoon, a linen turban, an embroidered caftan, some Arabian horses, some oxen, a few sheep, and the nucleus of an empire. Power had been his only luxury. Personal possessions had interested him not at all.

Osman was succeeded, not by his eldest son but by Orchan, his second, the custom of primogeniture not then being established in the East or, for that matter, at that time in the West either. Succession devolved upon the most competent member of the royal house, which is to say, the one strong enough to take it.

Orchan was fortunate in his family. Instead of intriguing against him, Aladdin, the eldest son, knew both his abilities and his place, and therefore remained content to become grand vizier. The term "vizier" means "carrier of the load"; and Aladdin more than carried it. Whether both men were geniuses in separate endeavors, or whether between them they were the equal of one, is at this distance irrelevant. Two men who work closely together are apt to be invincible, and such was the case with Orchan and Aladdin. Together, they invented an administrative system so efficient that, despite modifications which tended more to weaken than to strengthen it, it ran steadily for the next 600 years and would have run even longer, in all likelihood, had not Suleiman the Magnificent, in the sixteenth century, adulterated its guiding principles with certain absolutist and religious notions imported from Persia and Egypt.

Like the Portuguese two hundred years later, the Turks were confronted with the problem that there were not enough of them to administer and to maintain a conquered empire made up of a hundred disparate tribes, races, religions, and political systems. This problem the Portuguese were to be unable to solve, with the result that their empire soon dwindled. The Turks solved it early, in an original, exemplary, and efficient manner. This solution was the work of Aladdin. He addressed himself to three problems: the coinage, the costume, and the army, thus proving himself a master of economics, of psychology, and of politics.

Osman had been granted the right to coin his own money by the last Seljuq sultan, but had never taken much advantage of the privilege. The chief coins in circulation were those of the Seljuq dynasty, now fragmented and in no position to back them up, and the Byzantine bezant, by now not merely devalued but watered. Venetian and Genoese money was driving out the latter, but since the Turks were notoriously poor sailors and the Osmanli had at this time no navy, the profits of maritime trade as a source of wealth had yet to occur to them. Indeed, they were never to take it over, though they held a tighter rein on the Genoese and Venetians, and for that matter the Greeks, than the Byzantines had been able to do.

Money in those days had a much greater physical, a much less symbolic, value than it has today. It was therefore more apt to maintain its viability by reason of its degree of fineness and weight than by the strength of the government behind it. Aladdin understood this, and so induced Orchan to issue money. As the Osmanli empire expanded, both in size and wealth, so did the power of this coinage, to such a point that before many decades had passed, it was the bezant that was weighed against the asper and found wanting, not the asper against the bezant.

As for costume, the minute legislated particulars of this were concentrated upon the head covering or turban, in the East a sign of rank. Princes wore a red felt cap wound around with muslin, the effect being that of a Wisconsin loaf cheese imbedded in an angel food cake; soldiers and functionaries wore white felt of a sugar loaf shape. Later, white was reserved for the Sultan's immediate suite, red for the soldiers. Elaborate dress, until the mid-fifteenth century, though beyond the reach of commoners was not yet so rich as to lead its wearers to corrupt themselves for the price of something to wear; and by making distinctions immediately recognizable, simple, but difficult to obtain, an inexpensive incentive system was soon in operation, to excellent effect insofar as social discipline was concerned.

However, the greatest creation of Aladdin and Orchan was the Janissary system, designed to produce man power for both the standing army and an elite administrative staff.

It was the right of the Padishah to take one out of every five captured prisoners as a slave for his own use or for sale. Aladdin had the idea to take one out of every five children in the captive provinces, as well as from the slaves, whether Christian, Orthodox, or Latin, Muslim, Pagan, Circassian, or non-Muslim Turkish, and to bring them up in the Sultan's own household. The children were carefully selected, separated from their relatives and parents at the age of eight, and brought up as Muslim orphans, their only relative, and therefore their only loyalty, the Padishah. Since they were obliged to remain celibate, at least during the earlier centuries of the system, they owed allegiance, and in time came to feel it, to nobody else. They were given a rigorous education, both physical and mental, and in their teens separated into two groups, the brightest entering the administration, the strongest the army. Even members of the royal family were reared in this manner.

The result was at first 6,000, later about 12,000 picked troops, trained to fight at any moment and loyal to the Sultan and nobody else; and about the same number of administrators trained to similar virtues. All these people lived in the immediate entourage of the Sultan, or Padishah, and traveled with him from one provisional capital to the next. Their loyalty could be depended upon. In the earlier history of the Janissaries, there is record of only one backslider, Scanderbeg, the Albanian insurgent.

The Christian families in occupied territory on whom this unique tax of one child in five was levied on the whole raised no objection. The Turks were both too successful and too few to be religiously intolerant, the Empire was ravaged alike by war and the taxgatherer, and, left to their own choice, the Greeks tended to prefer Turkish to Byzantine rule and to go over to it whenever they could.

Thus strengthened, Orchan cleared the Asiatic shores of the Propontis and took the important town of Nicomedia in 1337, even though he had lost a large Turkish army in Thrace seven years before. Since the days of Diocletian it had been a powerful town. Nicaea, where in the Church of Saint Synod the Nicaean Creed had been promulgated, fell soon after. Saint Synod became a mosque.

So far the Osmanli had taken territory only from the Greeks. They now showed themselves equally willing to accept it from the princelings of the fragmented Seljuq empire, thus absorbing most of Karamania (Phrygia). Orchan then settled down to consolidate what he had so far, a prudent practice his sucessors were also to observe and one which invariably allowed them to retain what they had, on those occasions when they felt themselves prepared to add more.

Islam had its monastic orders, even though Mahomet the Prophet had expressly forbidden them. These Orchan patronized. He was particularly liberal to a gentleman known as Gheilik Baba, or "father of the stags." The dervishes were useful for stirring up the troops, Islam being a militant faith. They were more successful at this than were the Christian priests and monks, for if one can buy the repose of one's soul, why fight?

And besides, Islam was still a young religion, if not in the first, at least still in the second vigor of enthusiasm.

Orchan also protected the sciences—logic, astronomy, astrology, medicine, and theology—founding excellent schools. Most of the earlier Turkish poets lived at Brusa, which under Orchan and successive sultans became, if not the Turkish Athens, at least their Florence and their mausoleum, too; the first six heads of the house of Osman, their brothers, sons, wives, daughters, and twenty-six princes of the blood (some of them murdered to assure a peaceful succession) being buried there, together with their viziers, beylerbeys, and about five hundred of their pashas, sheiks, rhetoricians, poets, physicians, and musicians.

Under Orchan's rule, the Turkish state enjoyed twenty years of peace, more than enough time to organize the state. He spent them planning the invasion of Europe.

Turks, though not necessarily Osmanli Turks, had crossed the Bosphorus at the end of the thirteenth century, settling on the coast of what is now Bulgaria and from there emigrating out to the Crimea, the islands of the Archipelago, which they ransacked, and the coasts of Greece, which they ravaged. The Osmanli Turks as an organized unit made their first European landing in 1321, though it was only a raid on the coasts of Thrace and Macedonia.

In 1321 the Emperor Andronicus Palaeologus the Elder had called in Turkish troops to put down his grandson, Andronicus the Younger. Andronicus the Younger endeavored to form an alliance with Orchan, and Orchan was delighted to oblige. He crossed to Europe in 1338, making direct for Constantinople with a fleet of 36 ships. But the maneuver was premature, and he was beaten back with the loss of his armada and his armaments both, though he had managed to devastate imperial lands for two years.

Having grasped the often overlooked fact that if the enemy cannot pay the army, no army will come, the Osmanli went right on laying agricultural land waste, holding out attractive terms to Greeks anxious to emigrate away from the onerous

Byzantine taxation, and taking and selling slaves. Because of the double nature of their aggression, the price of Byzantine provisions soared, famine descended, and many fled to the Osmanli territories, the Turks at this time practicing as prudent a religious toleration as they did a fiscal. By these means they soon gained control of Nicaea, and threatened the Asiatic suburbs of the capital.

In Byzantium, Turkish fashions became the rage, and polo popular. But there was no way to prevent the Turks from devastating the shores of both continents to the walls of the capital and its suburbs, occupying the islands, and carrying so many men, women, and children off to the slave markets that the decline in population and fighting power became conspicuous in less than a generation.

IX

ANDRONICUS III died on June 15, 1341, leaving John V, a minor of nine, as his heir. This young man, in the periods when he was allowed to occupy his own throne, ruled, or attempted from time to time to rule, for fifty years. He was noted chiefly for his astonishing physical beauty, but was weak only in his circumstances, for he did everything he could, when able, to restore or at any rate to maintain what was left of the Empire. However, there was not much he could do at the age of nine.

It might be said of his father's chief minister, Cantacuzenos, that he delighted in children, particularly should they happen to be on the throne, if for no other reason than that they were small, light in weight, and so the easier to remove from it. The Queen Mother, Anne of Savoy, resisted his efforts. Each side called in the Turks to help them overcome the other, and so precipitated six years of unrest and civil war and seven of usurpation. Cantacuzenos declared himself Emperor as early as October. The campaigns which followed gave the Turkish mercenaries an extensive knowledge of the Empire's European terrain, and invaluable combat experience over it. Both sides paid their mercenaries by allowing them to take slaves, the best slave market being set up at Scutari, across the Propontis from the capital, where it thrived and made everybody rich. Eventually the Turks decided to back Cantacuzenos rather than the Dowager Anne, probably because they felt Cantacuzenos to be the weaker of the two. The latter entered Byzantium where, during May of 1347, a really remarkable coronation ceremony was held at Hagia Sophia, in the presence of three empresses and two emperors. Cantacuzenos was thus enabled to govern a state which his own ambitions had rendered even smaller and weaker than it had been before. There was nothing left now but Thrace, Thessalonica, Byzantium and its surrounding countryside, bits of Thessaly and Epirus, a narrow strip of the European coast of the Black Sea, the Bosphorus, Mistra in the Peloponnesus, a few islands in the Aegean, and two cities in Asia Minor, Philadelphia and Phocaea, completely surrounded and cut off by the Turks. Indeed, the Turks were everywhere.

So bankrupt was the treasury that the jewels of the imperial regalia were paper pearls and paste diamonds, and the ceremonial vessels gilt brass. By 1346, the Genoese leeched a revenue of 200,000 hyperpyra (a coin of uncertain value) a year out of Byzantium, and the capital was reduced to 30,000 a year. Cantacuzenos attempted to attract shipping to the Byzantine side of the Golden Horn by lowering customs fees. The Genoese promptly declared war from their own shore, burned all Greek shipping in the harbor, set fire to the suburbs without the walls, and blockaded the Golden Horn. This, the so-called War of Galata, was halted only by the intervention of the Senate of Genoa, with Byzantium, as usual, the loser.

The Turkish sultan, Orchan, amused himself by sending troops to fight both on the side of his Byzantine allies and against them. In 1354 his forces captured Gallipoli, and made of it their first permanent settlement in Europe. They were considerably assisted by an earthquake which threw down the walls of that and of several other towns. The occupation of Gallipoli put the Turks within 30 miles of the capital. Cantacuzenos offered Orchan a bribe of 40,000 ducats to leave, but was told it was not force of arms but divine will which had brought the Turks so close, and that the Osmanli were sufficiently pious never to fly in the face of divine will. Orchan then sent letters to various Turkish rulers announcing his occupancy of Europe, much as a new landlord would inform tenants of a change of management.

While these matters were going on, the Byzantines, with the

assistance of the retired Empress Anne, devoted themselves to their last schismatic heresy, that of Palamitism.

It was so named after the monk, George Palamas, who supported it, but was also called Hesychasm after those clerics who lived in silence as hermits, and so were known as Hesychasts. It was the last great mystical accomplishment of Orthodox theology, the schismatics being divided between the Palamitists, who claimed that it was possible to re-create within one's self the mystic light of Mt. Tabor by use of breath exercises, and the Barlaamists, who claimed it wasn't.

One of the basic differences between the Latin and Orthodox points of view was that the Greeks, being Greek, despite the influence of the innately puritanical and subconsciously Manichee Egyptians upon their theology, quite lovably enjoyed the sensational world so much that they felt that at least part of it must be divine, and therefore immanent; and that the Latins, at bottom ineradicably Manichee, though refusing to admit it, felt that since the phenomenal is finite and God infinite, then God is transcendent, and the world to be despised as dross, evil, and uninhabited by Him. Much more than any quarrel over leavened and unleavened bread, these two diametrically opposed attitudes toward existence stood between any union of the two Churches.

The Hesychasts, by some obscure but fascinating connection, had fallen upon vestiges of yoga practice. By sitting with their bodies bent, their chins resting on their breasts, and with their eyes directed to their navels, by repeating a prayer and then holding their breath, they so managed to redistribute physiological tensions as to experience the numen in the fascinosum form, which in their case was called the uncreated light which had appeared to the Disciples of Jesus on Mt. Tabor. The Latins and what might be called the reactionary, conservative, puritanic wing of the Orthodox Church preferred the tremendum. The matter soon became political, and led to riot, pogrom, and civil disobedience, as well as to the production of some profoundly moving mystical literature.

Literature, however, was no help against the Turks. By making one more disastrous alliance with the Genoese, John V, the rightful ruler, succeeded in getting Cantacuzenos to abdicate. He retired to Mt. Athos and spent the next twenty-five years applying liberal coats of whitewash to a well-composed, smooth, but somewhat untruthful history of his own times. The period of his abdication was also the period that the Turks occupied Gallipoli, and on the 6th of August, 1356, the Venetian bailo informed Doge Andrea Dandolo that the Byzantines were ready to submit to any power, Venice, Serbia, or the King of Hungary, in exchange for protection; on the 4th of April, 1356, Marino Faliero had advised the Republic of Venice to annex the Empire, as otherwise the Turks would take it.

The Turks, however, were never in a hurry, but proceeded according to a fixed policy of never attacking until they were sure of what they already had, and of not fighting at all otherwise than out of an impregnable position. In 1362–1365, Sultan Murad I was so successful against the Empire that he was able to establish a permanent European Osmanli capital at Adrianople, the essential preliminary to control of the Balkans.

This city, less than 150 miles inland from Byzantium, at the confluence of four navigable rivers, had been founded in Roman times by the Emperor Hadrian as an ideal place from which to put down uprisings and control migrating tribes in the same area. It was an equally ideal headquarters from which to make descents upon Byzantium and the Euxine shore, and prospered accordingly, becoming celebrated for its rose water, essence of roses, soap, sirops, sherbet, and poets; also for its seraglio, palaces, arsenals, mosque, military barracks, cannon foundry, and strongly fortified, not to say beetling, position.

From Adrianople to Byzantium was three days' quick, five days' slow march, across pleasant if then often ravaged countryside. It was a journey frequently taken.

During their previous depredations the Osmanli had been greatly assisted by the disunity of Asia Minor, and were to be no less so by that of the mainland.

Nobody realized at the time that the Osmanli were bent not merely on crushing the Byzantines and taking Constantinople, but also upon spreading northward toward Europe. And in Europe nobody cared, for the only country directly threatened by the Turks, if we except the depots of trading cities of Venice and Genoa, was Hungary.

Between Hungary and Greece lay the Balkans, a source of trouble throughout the greater part of European history. Migratory peoples had always attacked through them. Their population was either Slavic or, in the case of Bulgaria, Tartar converted to Christianity. Byzantium lost them as provinces during the seventh century when the resurgent Serbs reached Illyria and set up the states of Serbia, Bosnia, Albania, Bulgaria (which was several times to change hands), and Wallachia (one of the provinces of present-day Rumania). The Serb state was refounded in 1085, grew strong enough to attack Byzantium in the fourteenth century, and then declined. Bosnia became independent in 1376. The Bulgarians were always redoubtable, whether Serb or Tartar. The Wallachians, in alliance with the Hungarians, or feudatory to them, fought off the Turks until the end of the fifteenth century. The Osmanli thought it wise to crush these peoples as much as possible before turning on Byzantium.

There being no other way to hold the Osmanli back, the emperor John V once more undertook the shambling, dishonest policy of attempting to unite the two Churches in exchange for military aid. This diplomatic dead mouse was always the last thing the Byzantines brandished when cast upon their own resources only to find they had not any. To this purpose he went to Rome in 1369, joined the Latin Communion, and acquiesced to the *filioque* clause as sign that he accepted the Latin Rite. His sincerity was not in doubt, but it was noticed that there was not so much as one Orthodox clergyman in his suite. Therefore his was regarded, on both sides, as no more than a personal conversion, and so he not only had his trip for nothing but on the way home was arrested at Venice for debt and had to be ransomed.

Murad I's riposte to this maneuver was to revise and reinforce the Janissary corps, to such a degree that he is usually credited, together with his vizier, Halil Pasha, with having created it.

Originally a body of 6,000, the Janissary corps grew every year, being fixed by Murad I at 10,000 men, by Mahomet II at 12,000, by Suleiman the Magnificent at 20,000, and by Mahomet IV (mid-seventeenth century) at 40,000. It is estimated that in the course of 300 years, over 5,000,000 Christian children became Janissaries.

It is perhaps worth mentioning that the only personal possession of the Janissary being the pot in which his food was placed, this became the emblem of his office. The officers had culinary titles, the commander in chief being named the Tchorbadgi Bachi, or First Soup Maker; his immediate subordinate the First Cook; his next, the Water Carrier. The cap badge of the troops was a wooden spoon. All of which must have given an impression of Escoffier on the march, the exact opposite of that epigram from the Palatine, Greek (or Byzantine) Anthology, to the effect that it is not necessary to send troops against the enemy, it is necessary only to send them one's cook.

The Janissaries were used as picked shock troops, reinforced by foot soldiers organized as a territorial militia. The azabs, or free corps, were irregulars. There was a paid cavalry, divided into sipahis, or knights, silidars, or vassal horsemen, ulufedjis, or mercenary cavalry, and a group known as "strangers" which included such troops as Christian allies found themselves constrained to send.

There was little or nothing Europe could or would do against so formidable a force. In 1364, Pope Urban V instigated a crusade against the Turks. The Hungarians, the only Western power actively threatened by them, together with Serbia, Bosnia, and Wallachia, sent 20,000 Christians down the Maritza (Hebrus) toward Adrianople, but the only outcome of this was a resounding victory for the Turks, who had so little regard for the rules of proper warfare as to attack at night. A Serbian army of 50,000 was no more successful two years later. And in 1373 the Byzantine Emperor was compelled to recognize the Osmanli Sultan as his overlord and suzerain in order to keep his throne. Byzantium was further weakened by plague, which had been cutting down the population in sucessive epidemics since 1346.

In 1373 the Osmanli made common cause with the Tartars north of the Danube in order to attack Hungary. In 1381 they resumed war against the Serbs. In 1389 they crushed the power of the Serbians at the first battle of Kossovo (the field of crows). The Sultan was stabbed by an assassin during the battle, but his successor, Bayazid I, was equally competent. Indeed, it was the bad luck of Byzantium (and of Europe) that against all normal dynastic precedent, the first nine successive rulers of the House of Osman were astute and accomplished men. Though Byzantium intrigued to raise up pretenders and so to insert a conveniently weak link in the succession, such efforts were merely expensive failures.

Bayazid's first act on becoming Sultan was to have his brother murdered. "Sedition," says the Koran, "is worse than murder." Bayazid was nothing if not devout, and committed the lesser in order to avert the greater crime.

Seeing that an attempt to take Constantinople was inevitable, John V began to strengthen the walls, repairing the Golden Gate, or state entry to the city, now never used, and timidly disguising the new defenses by means of a triumphal arch built of blocks taken from the ruinated Church of the Holy Apostles and other abandoned religious structures, of which there were many, for the more faithful the faithful become, the fewer there seem to be of them, and there were now more churches in Constantinople than there were congregations to fill them.

Bayazid gave orders either that the defenses be torn down or that John V see his heir Andronicus IV blinded. John V had the defenses torn down.

The Osmanli were assisted by two more attempts to take the Byzantine throne from its rightful owner, one by Andronicus IV, the other by his son. John V appealed to the Sultan who, nothing loath, backed legitimate and rebel by turns, to his own profit and the further weakening of the capital. John V was restored, the eldest surviving legitimate heir, his son Manuel II, being kept as hostage in the Turkish camp, and compelled, as vassal, to assist at the reduction of Philadelphia, the last Byzantine enclave in Asia Minor.

By the time of John V's death in 1391, after a reign of slightly over fifty years, the Empire had so far decayed that the court nobility was selling the paving under its feet to pay for its ostentations. If you wished to see the glories of the capital you went to Venice, which had bought them. Even the relics of the saints, no longer in inexhaustible supply, had been sold up; those of the Three Wise Men, for instance, never popular as patrons of anything, having gone as early as the eleventh century. They are now in Cologne.

After 130 years of what can only be called planned incompetence, and of civil war among heirs contentious for the honor of ruling nothing (which they coveted presumably because there was nothing else for them to take), it is a relief and a pleasure to come to the last three ruling members of the House of Palaeologus, the Emperor Manuel II and those two of his sons who succeeded him.

X

UNLIKE his relatives, Manuel was an admirable man, courageous, talented, conciliatory, and when he had the means at his disposal, firm. "If anyone did not know that he was an emperor, they would certainly have deduced it from his appearance," said Bayazid. During their last years the Palaeologi acquired a sad dignity they had not had before. It was a Man of Sorrows sort of dignity, but none the less impressive for that.

Manuel was a better diplomat and adminstrator than he was a soldier, which was just as well, for there was no longer much territory to fight on or about. These talents were what the situation called for. "Close the gates of the city and rule within it, for I own everything outside the walls," the Sultan advised him. He took the advice, and since only a diplomat could have controlled that unlucky and contentious city, it is fortunate that he was so good a one. He ruled from 1391 to 1425.

The first ten years of his reign were not agreeable. At the time of his father's death he had been at Brusa with the Turkish armies, detained more or less politely as a hostage against Byzantium's good behavior. The news having been brought to him secretly, he escaped and reached Constantinople before Bayazid was aware of what had happened. Bayazid contented himself for the time being with the demands that there should be a cadi resident at Constantinople to supervise Osmanli interests, and that Manuel should declare himself the Sultan's vassal and pay tribute. A year later he attacked and pillaged the Adriatic coast, made a tentative sortie against Byzantium, and retiring, built that redoubt on the Bosphorus known as Anatolia Hissar. As a result of these maneuvers, Manuel was forced to accept his nephew, John VII, as co-emperor, an act whereby Bayazid, who had backed the nephew, received Byzantine small holdings on the Propontis.

Bayazid was decisive, thorough, and immovable. He would probably have succeeded in taking Byzantium, had he not met with an irresistible force. Unaware of its proximity, he put down and totally defeated 60,000 Christians marching down from Hungary at the battle of Nicopolis in 1396. To do so cost him 60,000 of his own men, but since he had 200,000, though enraged by the loss he was not much diminished by it. He spent the day after the battle in having 10,000 captives slaughtered before him, from early morning until four in the afternoon, at which time he graciously consented to spare the remainder in exchange for 200,000 ducats. Manuel and his brother, the Despot Theodore of Mistra, having connived at the invasion, Bayazid invaded the Morea, took Athens, captured 30,000 prisoners to sell as slaves, and settled a transported Turcoman population in the region.

The battle of Nicopolis, even though the Hungarians had been routed chiefly because their French allies had refused to cooperate with the other troops, and so caused a counterwhorl in battle when they should have provided a countercurrent, was rightly regarded as an international disaster. Sigismund of Hungary escaped by sea through the Dardanelles, for the Osmanli now controlled all overland routes. Bayazid had Christian captives lined up on both shores of that narrow passage, to clank their slave chains, moan, and wail, the so to humiliate their defeated Saviour. If they did not moan and wail, they were beaten.

In 1397 the Osmanli invested Constantinople, and there was no one who did not expect it to fall.

Byzantine prestige reached its nadir. Three years before, the Grand Duke Basil I of Moscow had refused to allow the Byzantine Emperor's name to be mentioned in prayers any more. "We have a Church but no Emperor," he said.

The answer to this impertinence had not been long on the way. "It is not a good thing, my son," wrote the Patriarch Anthony to the Grand Duke, "for you to say, 'We have a Church, but no Emperor.' It is not possible for Christians to have a Church without an Emperor, for the Imperial sovereignty and the Church form a single entity and they cannot be separated from each other. . . . Hear what the prince of the Apostles, Peter, says in his first epistle: 'Fear God, honor the Emperor.' He did not say, 'the emperors,' for he was not referring to the so-called 'emperors' of various different countries, but he said, 'the Emperor' in order to emphasize that there was only one Emperor in the world . . . if other Christian rulers have appropriated to themselves the name of Emperor, this has been done against nature and law by tyranny and force. Which of the fathers, which Councils, which canonical rulings speak of these 'Emperors'? They one and all proclaim a single Emperor whose laws, ordinances and decrees hold throughout the world, who alone, with none other, is revered by all Christians. . . . And if by God's decree the infidel has encircled the realm of the Emperor, he still receives today from the Church the same consecration, the same honor, and the same prayers, and is anointed with the same holy oil and is consecrated Emperor and Autocrator of the Romans, that is, of all Christians."

This was ever the Byzantine view, in good times or bad, whether there was an empire or not. Nonetheless, once the Osmanli were blockading the capital, the only Emperor was to be found begging the Russian princelings for help for their religious brethren who "were besieged by the Turk and languishing in need and misery." And in 1397, the year after the battle of Nicopolis, the co-emperor John VII was trying (without success) to sell his claims to the Byzantine throne to Charles VI of France in return for a castle there and an annual income of 25,000 florins.

The Osmanli blockade of the capital was so effective that a measure of wheat soon sold for 20 bezants, and many of the citizens deserted to the Turks rather than starve. Charles VI had preferred to support Manuel rather than buy out John VII;

and Venice and Genoa had been so alarmed by the defeat at Nicopolis that they cooperated in the city's defense. This time Byzantium was saved by the arrival of a Frenchman, Jean de Boucicault, in command of 8 Genoese, 8 Venetian, 2 Rhodian, and one Mytilenean galleys, 600 men-at-arms, 600 infantry, 1,000 archers, but no horses. These reinforcements made it possible to forage the formerly Byzantine shores of the Marmora for supplies and, since the Turks had no navy at this time, to drive off the besiegers, who had no hope of taking the city once it was supplied by sea, and so no choice but to lift the siege. Besides, the Osmanli were prudent never to fight on more than one front at a time if they could help it, and their attention had been diverted by unrest elsewhere.

Since his ambassadors had been able to secure only this small force for the defense of the city, Manuel decided to see if he could not do better by visiting the courts of Europe himself. Leaving his nephew, the Osmanli-backed John VII, as regent of the city, but prudently depositing his own wife and children with his brother in the Morea, Manuel, accompanied by Boucicault, set out for Europe late in 1399. His manner was imposing, his appearance dignified, his retinue an entertaining novelty, but he had little to argue with. His reception, however, was invariably honorable, if only because he was head of the oldest surviving state in Christendom.

He landed at Venice and from there went to Padua, Pavia, Milan, and Paris. Though the Duke of Milan was secretly in alliance with the Turks, it was a very secret alliance, therefore no attempt was made to detain the Emperor. In Paris, Manuel was lodged in the Louvre and allowed to appear in public dressed in white silk and riding a white horse, a privilege greater than one might believe, for to the French, white was the color of absolute sovereignty, which they claimed for themselves. The German Holy Roman Emperor, who had been a recent visitor, had been compelled to ride a *black* gelding, the petty discourtesies of Franco-German relations having ancient roots.

"The Emperor," wrote the anonymous Religious of St. Denis,

"was a man of middle stature, but his broad chest, his muscular members, his features full of nobility, his long beard and white hair, drew on him the eyes of all the people," and made everybody say "that he is worthy indeed to wear the Imperial Crown." His personal costume was found outlandish and piquant. His cause was found outlandish but unappealing. So though he stayed off and on for almost two years, apart from the amusements of an interesting state visit nothing was forthcoming from France, if only because Charles VI was intermittently insane and the real rulers of the kingdom, the Dukes of Orleans and Burgundy, were not.

In England the reception was as splendid and the outcome just as disappointing. Henry IV, himself an usurper, could and would not help. "I thought in my heart," wrote the equally anonymous English cleric who composed the *Chronicle of Usk*, "how cruel it was that this great Christian prince from the distant east has been compelled by the threats of the infidel to visit the far-off isles of the west to supplicate for help against them. My God! Where art thou, ancient glory of Rome? Today the splendour of thy Empire is laid low and it can indeed be said of thee in the words of Jeremias, 'She that was a princess among the heathen and a queen among the nations, is now enslaved.' Who would have believed that thou wouldst sink into such utter misery, that after having once governed the whole world from thy throne of eminence, thou art now quite powerless to help the Christian faith." In other words, in this new day of national states crusades against the infidel had lost their appeal. Manuel started back to Constantinople, arriving there after an absence of two and a half years. He had not bothered to visit Rome, chiefly because there was an outbreak of plague there, but since these were the years of the Babylonian Schism (1378–1406), with two, and once as many as four, Popes reigning simultaneously, he thereby offended no more than half of Christendom.

Deprived of proper aid, the Empire now depended upon coincidence and hairbreadth escapes for its vestigial survival. The next thing that saved it was less a coincidence than a collision.

That marauding freebooter known to the west as Tamerlane, tired of holding merely the Gorgeous East in fee, chose this moment to invade Asia Minor.

Tamur Lenk, or Timur the Lame, and so Tamerlane, had been born in 1335, in Transoxiana. He did not became a successful freebooter until the 1360's, but then modeled his conduct on that of the popular Arab, Turcoman, Mongol and Tartar hero, Alexander the Great. After fifteen years of preparation, he felt himself ready to conquer the known world, and his progress was rapid. Either he could not restrain his troops, or else he was a believer in what until only yesterday was known as total war. The result was a locust army. His soldiers ate everything. They destroyed everything. They killed everything. They slaughtered 70,000 people in Ispahan in one day, apparently for the fun of it; and in Khorasan buried 2,000 men alive as the foundation of a tower. Of course it had long been traditional to bury someone in the foundation of an important building in order that his ghost might protect it, but a platoon of ghosts was perhaps too many. One hundred thousand people lost their lives on the Ganges. However, the problems involved in the murder of such large numbers of people, particularly in warm weather, as has been rediscovered recently, are hygienic and insuperable, so usually Tamerlane's armies moved on as soon as possible, and though unbelievers themselves, left the dead to a Parsee burial.

Tamerlane was not merely a destroyer. The Mongols of whom he was leader were Shiite Moslems. This doctrine, the Persian variation upon the more puritanic Arabic Mohammedan Sunnite belief, produced a sensuous, vigorous sect which would have been, and often was, considered a heresy, had the Persians not adamantly refused to give it up. They had an ancient, rich, and exuberant culture which produced schools of mysticism, poetry, and of the fine arts which are among the unique splendors of human accomplishment.

Shiism is not a religion for confirmed grovelers, and Tamerlane was no groveler. Along with their lands, he also took over many of the avocations of the Persians. He was a builder; he was a patron of the arts; and since Shiites are not as fatalistic as the strictly orthodox Sunnites, he was also a legislator and civil administrator of ability. Incidentally, he was also the first man in modern times to introduce the wearing of uniforms into an army.

This ruthless but majestic phenomenon invaded Osmanli territory on the 22nd of August, 1400, at the age of sixty-five, the pretext being (Bayazid had been eager to supply it) the dismissal of Mongol ambassadors in the most insulting terms the Osmanli could devise.

After several forays, which included the wholesale massacre of the inhabitants of Damascus and the destruction of the city, the armies of Tamerlane and Bayazid met near Angora, in the interior of Asia Minor, on July 28, 1402. The Turks were defeated, and Bayazid and his son Musa taken prisoner. Bayazid died in captivity, March 9, 1403, while being carted around the interior of Asia as both a raree show and a possibly profitable captive. Tamerlane, whose primary interests were Oriental, marched off to conquer China and died on the road in 1405. His empire did not survive him. Nor, at the time, did anyone believe that the Osmanli empire would survive him either. Bayazid's death was followed by almost twelve years of civil war among his heirs.

Of these, not counting impostors and pretenders, there were four: Suleiman, the eldest, Mahomet, Musa, and Mustapha. Mustapha went into hiding for several years; Musa escaped from Tamerlane and barricaded himself into Karamania; Mahomet fought off the Tartars from Amasia; and Suleiman retreated into Europe. Tamerlane intrigued with the three available, dividing them the one against the others, and thinking this enough to assure their ruin, departed for China. The recently conquered states of Bulgaria, Serbia, Wallachia, and the Morea resumed their independence; the leftover remnants of the Seljuq dynasty attempted to reassert themselves, and in Constantinople everyone began to plot at once. Following Tamerlane's example, Manuel Palaeologus made contradictory alliances with the three visible brothers, and thus obtained from

Suleiman the restoration of Thessalonica, a few villages on the Strymon, and a few more on the Black Sea coast. Unimportant in themselves, these reconquests by treaty gave Byzantium assurance. The Despotate of Mistra flourished, though with the Osmanli gone, the remaining Latin lords of the Morea and the resurgent Serbians were soon at each other's possessions again, as usual.

Musa was driven out and defeated by Mahomet, and took refuge with the Emir of Kermian. His flight reduced the contenders to two, each of whom took the name of Sultan, Suleiman in Europe, Mahomet in Asia. Mahomet made alliance with the Turcoman princes, had Musa turned over to him, and sent him to Europe to attack Suleiman, who was at Adrianople indulging himself in sensual and sensuous excess. These minor peccadilloes could have been forgiven him, but as he was also both effeminate and timid, he was abandoned by his own troops. Indignant when a Janissary interrupted him to tell him that Musa was besieging the city, he had had the man's beard shaved off by way of punishment. At this sign not so much of disrespect as of tyrannous indifference, his troops deserted, and he was forced to flee, being killed on the road to Constantinople by some peasants who, seeing who he was, found both the occasion and the license it suggested irresistible.

Musa, who succeeded him at Adrianople, was energetic, enterprising, and courageous, but unfortunately also spontaneously and erratically cruel. His troops deserted him in the midst of battle, and his body was found mutilated in a marsh.

Thus, in 1413, Mahomet I found himself, so far as he knew, sole ruler of an empire whose reputation for invincibility had been destroyed, its possessions partially dispersed, and its resources diminished by more than a decade of anarchic civil war. The Greek Emperor and the Princes of Wallachia, Serbia, Bulgaria, Epirus, and Achaia sent ambassadors to congratulate him upon his accession to a power so limited, if once more unique.

"Go tell your masters that I send peace to all, and that I accept it from all; and may God punish the violators of it," he told them, since it was to take him eight years to restore his possessions to their former condition; and in the meantime he acted with prudence, strength, and decorum. Though not given to the eating of humble pie, he was quite willing to serve it up, so for the time being he temporized. He gave back to the Emperor a few towns recently taken from him, renewed the trading rights his brother had granted to the Venetians, and released the Princes of Wallachia and Serbia from the payment of tribute. He had reason to be mild; he had an uprising in Asia to deal with. Djouneid, the vizier of his late brother, was trying to carve himself a principality out of Ephesus, Smyrna, and Pergamus. The Prince of Karamania had laid siege to Brusa. Mahomet reduced them both, but by way of reward for initiative, made Djouneid governor of Nicopolis.

The Duke of Naxos, a Venetian, had for some time now been preying upon Turkish shipping in his capacity as Lord of the Cyclades. Mahomet attacked him. Since war must not be allowed to interfere with trade, a Venetian squadron appeared under the walls of Gallipoli on May 29, 1416. It flew a white flag, for it had come to parley, not to fight. Unable to believe that so large a fleet could have come for so peaceable a purpose, the Turks fired upon it, and lost 27 vessels in consequence. Perhaps because of this unfortunate misunderstanding, a treaty with Venice was signed on the 9th of July and was ratified in 1417, at which time a Turkish ambassador appeared for the first occasion in western Europe. It was from this period that Turkish fashions, already the rage in Constantinople, began to be fashionable in the West; since Venice was already Byzantine in both its fitments and its pomps, it is only natural that it should follow fancy, too.

Mahomet next demanded tribute from Wallachia and invaded Bosnia and Croatia, where he was defeated by Hungarian troops, the only ones which ever seem to have been a match for him, perhaps because Hungary was the only country in Europe, apart from Byzantium, directly threatened by the Turks, and so able to hone its weapons on a present danger.

Manuel had taken advantage of the interregnum caused by Tamerlane and the Osmanli civil wars to dethrone his nephew, the co-emperor John VII; banish him; suppress the tribunal of the cadi established by Bayazid at the capital; close the mosques; and revoke such trading privileges as he had been forced to grant to the Turks. He also strengthened what holdings were left to him, particularly in the Peloponnesus. Thessalonica he had handed over to his second son, Andronicus, who on his father's death sold it to the Venetians for 50,000 sequins, probably because he realized that the Turks would take it whether he sold it or not; which, in 1430, they did.

In the Peloponnesus Manuel did better. The Despotate of the Morea, with its capital at Mistra, was now the only considerable possession the Empire had left. During the fourteenth and fifteenth centuries it enjoyed a cultural renaissance, and, more usefully, Manuel so reformed its finances that it was able to remit a fixed annual sum to the capital.

Venice, having defeated the Turkish fleet, left Byzantium to its own devices. Mahomet began the construction of another, but died unexpectedly at Gallipoli in 1421, leaving as his heir his son Murad II. Instead of renewing with Murad the alliance made with Mahomet as Manuel wished, the Byzantine Senate coerced the Emperor into threatening war unless Murad sent his two sons to be educated at Byzantium, and into releasing a pretender to the Osmanli throne, to create what havoc he could.

Clausewitz's dictum that war is a natural extension of diplomacy had yet to be formulated; but that diplomacy cannot succeed unless accompanied by the imminence of successful violence is a corollary the Byzantines never seem to have been able to grasp. The Turks put down this paid insurrection without any difficulty, and Murad II, an amiable man until roused, returned the Byzantine ambassadors sent to him with the message that he would himself follow shortly. He was as good as his word, arrived with 20,000 troops, burned the villages and fields around Byzantium, destroyed the vines and olive trees, massacred the inhabitants, and had a trench dug before the land walls of the city. He held out promise of a general pillage, and after consulting the astrologers, attacked on Monday, August 24, 1422.

For once, most of the citizens of the city consented to man their own defenses, and the fighting went on until sunset, at which time the Turks burned their siege machines and retired, no one to this day quite knows why. The Greeks attributed their deliverance to the intervention of the Virgin Mary; and even the Turks, so it was said, agreed that at the height of the fighting the Virgin had appeared clad in a violet mantle of dazzling brightness, and that this had caused them to fall back. Very likely she did so appear. One of the churches contained an ikon answering to this description, which was sometimes toted around the ramparts.

Another explanation, in its way no less miraculous considering the state of Byzantine finances, was that the Sultan had learned of another revolt in Asia, also subsidized by the Greeks. Murad II, thus interrupted, made no further attempt to take Constantinople, but instead dealt with the rebellious princelings of Anatolia, which took him about six years. He signed a temporary agreement with the Greeks, leaving them Thessalonica, a few small cities in Thrace, a few forts on the Strymon, Mt. Athos, for which he had no use, and the Morea, in exchange for an annual tribute of 30,000 aspers. By the terms of this agreement, Constantinopolitan shipping was from now on barred from the Black Sea, whether at the request of the Genoese or not, is not known.

Manuel once more turned to Rome, but nothing came of his efforts. According to the historian Phrantzes, he told his heir, John VIII, that the last defense against the Turks was their fear of a crusade, but that though John might propose Union, he must never allow it to occur, as the result would be civil war. Both John and his brother, Constantine, the last Emperor, were to discover this was sound advice. Manuel added that at this stage. "The Empire did not need an Emperor, it needed a bailiff." This, too, was an accurate remark.

Before his death on July 21, 1425 (the year 6933, according

to the Empire, which reckoned time from the problematical Biblical creation of the world), Manuel, who was seventy-eight, became a monk. This was the custom of the Emperors.

Manuel, who had ruled for 34 years, left six sons, of whom Andronicus II, Prince of Thessalonica, died shortly afterwards, of leprosy; Theodore was too puerile to bother about; Demetrius intrigued constantly to get the throne; Thomas became Despot of Mistra; and Constantine, together with John VIII the only good of a conniving batch, became last Emperor. Fortunately Constantine and John VIII were able to work together harmoniously.

John VIII made an excellent bailiff, but his reign was constantly disturbed by his brother Demetrius, who commenced loyal by rounding up some fugitive Turkish troops and marching on the capital with the aim of making himself emperor.

For once, against all precedent, the Byzantines preferred merit to mediocrity, and would not have him. After plundering the suburbs, Demetrius saw his army melt into the darkness. John made him Despot of Mesembria—a far from extensive fief exactly the dimensions of his merits,—to keep an eye on him, Mesembria being near the capital. Needless to say, Demetrius had revolted in the name of religion. He was his own schism.

John's next care was to remarry. When young, he had taken to wife Anne, daughter of the Grand Duke of Moscow, but she had died of plague in 1417. His second wife had been Sophia, daughter of John II of Montferrat, a distant cousin (a branch of the Palaeologi established itself as rulers of Montferrat in 1305, but became extinct in 1533). Sophia was ugly, sensible of the fact, did not care for the distaste with which John regarded her, liked his mistresses even less, and so ran back to Montferrat. Since he had no legitimate issue, John wished to divorce her, and said he would abdicate in favor of Constantine unless allowed to do so. Constantine being the more vigorous of the two princes, the clergy agreed to the divorce. John then married a princess of Trebizond, for he felt it to be not only the first, but perhaps the only duty of an empress, apart from childbearing, to be beautiful. This Maria of Trebizond assuredly was, but she produced no children. While the negotiations for this marriage were going on (they took two years), Murad II again overran the Morea, and again had to be bought off.

It was not hard to buy him off. The poverty of the rich is never penniless, and though Byzantium had long been stripped of nine-tenths of its empire and its trade was in foreign hands, by the European standards of the day it still commanded considerable wealth. The splendors of the last century of the Empire may have been paste and plaster, but they were splendors all the same. The irreality of the life lived at Constantinople, as well as the presumption of it, was another matter.

To buy off enemies was state policy and sound economics. In the twelfth century, when the Empire was still rich, Manuel Comnenus wrote to Henry II of England that when on the march the Byzantine army and its mercenaries extended over a distance of ten miles. And if armies are expensive to maintain, mercenaries are even more so. Therefore it was cheaper to pay an army to go away, or to subsidize it to fight someone else, than it was to send troops against it. Also, if you paid a bribe you were almost always certain of the outcome, whereas if it came to a battle you weren't. As for the invading army, it too found it more profitable to take the bribe than to fight, so the system worked well.

Once more the question of Union as a solution came up, and John set out for Europe to attend the Synod of Ferrara and Florence (1438–1439). The Byzantines may have lost everything, but they had not surrendered their pretensions, so it was only natural he should plan to depart with a retinue of 700, more men than the rest of those attending the Synod, combined.

Murad II, who had signed a treaty not to molest Byzantium just yet, and who was an honorable man and besides had other matters on his mind, was so alarmed that John VIII might succeed in his plea for assistance that he offered to pay him a yearly pension not to go.

The Synod had been difficult to arrange, chiefly because of

the dissensions attendant upon deciding where to hold it, but also because the bishops of the Catholic Church were fighting among themselves. A council had opened at Basel, in March of 1431. Basel was too hard for John to reach, and therefore the Pope ordered it to transfer itself to Bologna, for the greater convenience of the Greek Emperor. The Babylonian Schism was scarcely healed, Pope Eugenius' authority was not secure, the prelates at Basel were under the influence of John Hüss, who was Protestant, so the answer came back that "the peace of Germany is not to be sacrificed for the old song which has rung in the ears of Europe for three centuries and ended in nothing, the reconciliation of the Greek and Latin Churches." By way of answer to that, Eugenius denounced the Council as the "Synagogue of Satan," refused to crown Sigismund as Holy Roman Emperor, was forced to do so anyway, and with only four cardinals to support his authority and no troops, fled Rome in disguise, lest he be cut down or deposed.

After several years' delay, the Emperor John suggested that the Council meet at Constantinople. Rejecting this compromise, the Council offered to pay his expenses to Basel. The Byzantines, who were not altogether sure where Basel was and much too proud to ask, said no. Representatives of Pope Eugenius and of Basel arrived in Byzantium, but the quarrel between Pope and Council was now so advanced that the Council declared the Pope full of perjury and said he was a schismatic, and the Pope said the Council was not only schismatic but "an assembly of devils." These mutual courtesies were the first stirrings of the Reformation. Fortunately, Eugenius' ambassadors had had the sense to arrive in Constantinople with 3,000 archers, so it was decided, after all, to hold further sessions of the Council in Italy, at Ferrara. Nonetheless the Council at Basel went on sitting where it was. John VIII departed for Ferrara during November of 1447, leaving his brother Constantine, the only man who could keep his other brothers in order, not to say his subjects, at Constantinople as regent.

Rather than land at Taranto or Bari and so risk a long journey overland, John and his party went direct to Venice, where they arrived after a voyage so stormy it lasted 77 days. He had with him, mostly against their will, the Patriarch Joseph, twenty bishops of the Eastern Church, representatives of the lesser Patriarchs of Alexandria, Antioch and Jerusalem (their sees all in either Arab or Turkish hands), the Primate of Russia, and the five chief dignitaries of Hagia Sophia, together with sufficient church furniture to perform the Eastern Rite, which is to say a great deal; a band of singers; an orchestra, and, using the last gold he possessed, a gold-encrusted bed and a gold-encrusted chariot, to make a splendid impression even though everybody knew the imperial treasury was empty and the trip paid for—the journey by Avignon, the expenses of Italian residence by the Roman Pope.

No matter how far it had fallen, as the oldest surviving state in Europe the prestige of the Byzantine Empire was still enormous. In addition, no matter how much they might fight among themselves, the Palaeologi had impressive manners and had never lost the ability to intimidate. John VIII was a man of imposing and incredible appearance, suave, patrician, beak-nosed, dignified, and commanding. There is an excellent contemporaneous bust of him in the Vatican, and his portrait in the Gozzoli frescoes in the Medici private chapel makes the Medici, though fine men enough, look squalid by comparison. His manner was firm, distant, but cordial. His impact upon Europe was personally a triumph. Having no power he ruled by will, and his will was adequate to the task. It was merely that, like his father before him, he had arrived too late.

His reception was as gorgeous as the Venetians could make it, and he had the pleasure of seeing for the first time those works of art which had decorated Constantinople before the sack of 1204.

"You could as easily number the leaves on the trees or the sands of the sea as the gondolas and galleys of the Venetians," said Syropoulos, an attendant on the Patriarch. The historian Phrantzes, by this time the inseparable adviser of the Palaeologi, was no less enthusiastic. "Venice the marvelous," he writes, "the most marvelous; Venice the wise, the most wise; the city predicted in the psalm, 'God has founded her upon the waters.' "

The visitors were then shown the treasures of St. Mark's, where, as Syropoulos said, the thought arose that "these were once our own. They are the plunder of Hagia Sophia and our holy monasteries."

The state visit to Venice lasted fifteen days. John and his retinue then went on to Ferrara, though Murad II had pointed out that under the circumstances a Turkish friendship would be of greater value than a papal one, to tangle with the intricacies of Roman protocol, which were absurd and held the proceedings up interminably.

Unlike the King of France during the earlier visit of Manuel, the Pope would not so far admit John's absolute temporal sovereignty as to allow him to enter Ferrara dressed in white and riding a white horse. After considerable negotiation, a compromise was worked out: John entered the city dressed in white, riding a *black* horse, but a *white* horse with white and gold imperial saddlecloths was led before him.

The next disagreement was about the seating of the Synod, neither side wishing to allow the other precedence. After several weeks of atrabilious consultation, it was agreed that the church should be divided in two by an aisle, and that the chair of St. Peter should be at the head of one phalanx and the throne of the Greek Emperor at the head of the other, not on a line with the chair of the Pope, but opposite an empty throne representing the nonexistent but presumably equal Roman Emperor. The Holy Roman Emperor, Sigismund, who, hated by both Pope and Greek Emperor though for different reasons as an interloper, might have made this game of going to Jerusalem even more complex, fortunately did not deign to attend, but encouraged the Council of Basel instead.

Almost nobody attended, for though one purpose of the Synod was to demonstrate that Eugenius IV represented a united Christendom, it soon became self-evident that he did not. He had four cardinals, 25 bishops, and the Duke of Burgundy to attend him, and that was all. Everyone else was at Basel. He had threatened them with excommunication if they did not come, and had given them four months to do so. Their answer had been formally to depose him. Since he had been elected by only fourteen cardinals to begin with, ten of whom were dead or had defected, his position was far from secure.

Nor was the Emperor John in much better case, for he had with him his brother Demetrius, who apart from hating the Emperor and everyone else too, was a religious bigot, and so cried down any proposal John tried to talk up; and the theologian George Scholarios, equally bigoted, who though he reluctantly agreed to the Act of Union, did so only to denounce his emperor the more roundly for having brought it about—and who, as the monk Gennadios, was to be a potent source of sedition from now until the fall of the city and after. In addition, three of John's coerced bishops fled to Venice, and had ignominiously to be brought back, plague broke out in Ferrara and the Synod had to be removed to Florence.

At Ferrara the bishop of that place had refused to allow the Greeks to celebrate mass according to their own rite, explaining, in his diplomatic manner, that he did not want his churches polluted. At Florence things went somewhat better, though of 62 bishops who finally consented to appear, 50 were Italians and unwilling to come, and the Burgundians, ignoring the Emperor, agreed to salute the Pope only. Despite these continual affronts, it never seems to have occurred either to Pope or Emperor that they were going against the wishes of the populations of Europe and the Empire. After 26 fruitless sessions, Pope and Emperor agreed to suppress all public discussion, and John VIII imposed silence on the anti-Unionists. The stumbling block was whether or not such a thing as the absolute authority of the Pope could or should be said to exist. Cardinal Bessarion found a formula sufficiently vague to satisfy both parties, one which recognized the supremacy of the Pope *except* over the rights of the Eastern Church. Demetrius, Gemisthos Plethon, and George Scholarios promptly removed themselves to Venice, Scholarios agreeing to the terms the better to denounce them later. During July of 1439 the Union was proclaimed in the Cathedral of Florence, under Brunelleschi's new dome, then three years old.

In Venice, Demetrius refused to sign the Act of Union; the influential bishop Mark of Ephesus (his see also in Turkish hands) refused to attend the proclamation; and the Bishop of Heraclea, required to recite the Creed in St. Mark's, did so with pleasure, omitting the *filioque* clause and declaring, on his return to Constantinople, that he would rather have his right hand cut off than have it sign the Act of Union. Four copies of the proclamation for use in Greece omitted to mention papal supremacy, and the Greeks refused to recognize any others, signed or not. The Patriarch had died in Florence and the Greeks held that his death invalidated the proceedings.

The Pope undertook to pay for 300 fighting men to be enrolled in the imperial service, sent two well-armed galleys, and promised to dispatch 20 ships of war within six months. They did not arrive. He also tried to foment a new crusade against the Turks, without success except among the Hungarians, who were eager to defend themselves.

At Constantinople, the mob felt this to be insufficient aid and refused to accept the Union. Mark of Ephesus denounced the Latin Church. The new Patriarch, a Unionist, was openly booed in Hagia Sophia. The lesser Patriarchs of Alexandria, Antioch, and Jerusalem threatened the Emperor with excommunication, and those of Syria and Egypt said they would not recognize the validity of any priests ordained by a Unionist Patriarch at Byzantium. Demetrius endeavored once more to have John VIII deposed, this time in the name of the True Faith.

The Crusade mounted among the Poles and Hungarians came to an abrupt halt when its troops were wiped out by the Turks at the decisive battle of Varna, in 1444, a defeat for Christian, and victory for Osmanli, arms so signal as to startle Europe, but not to persuade it to intervene. If anyone was to fall, it was Constantinople that must fall first. That, Europe seemed to feel, would be the ultimate proof that something was wrong.

John VIII lived for eight more years, during which the Greek clergy clearly seemed to prefer Turkish domination to those compromises needed to secure papal aid. As early as 1436, a notice shows them in Turkish dress, speaking the language of their conquerors, and confirmed in their archbishoprics by the Sultan.

John VIII died in October, 1448, leaving no issue. Of his brothers, Theodore predeceased him, Constantine and Thomas were in the Morea, and Demetrius was just outside the capital. Demetrius rushed his brother's body underground and proclaimed himself Emperor on the flimsy ground that he had been born after his father's accession, whereas Constantine had been born before it and so not in the Porphorygenitus, the red to purple marble chamber of the palace in which imperial accouchements were supposed to take place if the child were to be legitimately declared heir. Since Constantine, the eldest surviving son, is considered to have been born in 1404, the earliest alternate date ever cited is 1396, and his father Manuel ascended the throne in 1391, the only sense to be made of this claim is that Demetrius was, as ever, a wily, dishonest, ambitious, and uncertain prince.

Once more the hierarchy and people of Constantinople would have none of him. The Empress Mother, the Senate, the soldiers, the clergy, and even the Genoese refused to countenance his accession, and as Thomas arrived unexpectedly with a small army and agreed with them, Demetrius was told to go away and Constantine elected in his stead. As Finlay, the nineteenth-century historian of Greece, says, "The absence of truth, honour, and patriotism among the Greek aristocracy during the last century of the Eastern Empire is almost without parallel in history; but Demetrius was too well known and too generally despised to find a large party even in that worthless aristocracy disposed to espouse his cause."

XI

TO this long sad history of revenge, rebellion, and impotence, Constantine XI provides a bracing and conclusive contrast. "If men do not make history they tend increasingly to become the utensils of history makers," wrote C. Wright Morris, the American sociologist, in his most minatory manner. Constantine did not propose to end his life as a utensil, nor did he. But it is some indication of into what a dependent state the Empire had fallen, that it was thought necessary to dispatch Phrantzes as ambassador to Murad II at Adrianople to ask his consent to the legitimate succession's taking place. This was given. To Murad's mind, Byzantium had for some time now been a tribute-paying fief like any other, and that such consent should be asked was as courteous and customary as that it should be granted. The Byzantines looked at the matter differently, for they had long made it their practice, when facts did not square with their own view of them, to ignore the facts and admire instead the view. This attitude, or political squint, it had long been the attempt of Constantine to correct.

We do not know much about what he was like. We only know what he did. No portrait of him survives. The only likeness we have of him is heraldic, upon the great seal of state, of which several wax impressions survive. This large, spidery, and elegant disk shows us a lively gentleman of mature age, thin, wiry and extremely, even cheerfully, energetic, engaged in reining in a Persian-looking horse. The impression of thoroughly competent vigor is immediate and convincing. He was the warrior of his generation of the family, and looks it.

Constantine XI Dragases (so called because his mother Irene was a member of the Serbian house of that name), the 81st (the numbering varies according to how many usurpations and pretenders are included in the final count) and last Byzantine Emperor, had spent his youth fighting the Turks by preference to joining the fratricidal warfare by means of which his brothers passed their time. Since 1444 he had been co- and dominant ruler of the Morea, which he shared with Demetrius and Thomas, who, if not quite so bad as Demetrius, had few if any good qualities.

Sometimes his forays against the Turks were successful, ultimately they failed. He was forced to become Murad's vassal and treated to the spectacle of 60,000 men and women enslaved by way of rebuke to his intransigence. This disaster was entirely his fault, said the Greeks. Since he had lost, he had obviously been born under an unlucky star and should not try to win again. He did try to win again, and so got back a few territories in Thrace.

Being in the Morea at the time of his elder brother's death, he had himself crowned at Mistra, January 6, 1449, entering Constantinople only on the 12th of the following March. Among those present at his coronation were Gemisthos Plethon and George Scholarios, both of whom opposed his policies, and Phrantzes (more properly Sphrantzes, but always so called), his chief adviser, historian, and friend.

Far to the south of the Peloponnesus and heavily defended as well as eminently defensible, Mistra was the capital of a small, brilliant, virtually independent state, being an appanage rather than an appendage of the Empire. It was a handsome stone and pink brick city built up the side of a barren hill. The inhabitants of Mistra, significantly enough, called themselves Hellenoi, not Romaioi.

The first troubles of Constantine's reign were provoked and provided by Demetrius, who called in the Turks against his brother Thomas and made an independent treaty with the trading republic of Ragusa, thus alienating the Venetians (once Thomas had told them what had been done). George Scholarios, though a self-seeking bigot himself, thought Demetrius had gone too far. "You do not fight only for your rights," he told him, "but for the rest of the Greeks who will die in the midst of our disorders. . . . Take the best resolutions in the interest of what remains of our unfortunate race, exposed and apt to blow away at the least wind, or to be eaten up by our enemies."

The advice was wasted.

Like his brother before him, Constantine had had two childless marriages and needed an heir, for nobody wanted Demetrius as emperor should Constantine predecease him. Before his accession, between 1444 and 1449, he had tried to negotiate several marriages, considering in turn the sister of the Prince of Taranto, the daughter of the Doge of Venice (turned down as too plebeian, a slight not soon forgiven), and the daughter of Lucas Notaras, a thoroughly unprincipled man, though he spoke often of principle, but also the chief noble of Byzantium. He now set himself to find someone suitable, sending Phrantzes out to search.

Since Phrantzes now takes a prominent part in affairs, it would be well to say more of him. Surrounded by a court at which any stray information was valued less for its intrinsic merit than for the malice with which it might, and invariably was, repeated, Constantine trusted no one else.

Seven years younger than his master and related to the royal house, Phrantzes had been a loyal councilor and official under both Manuel and John VIII. He had become Governor of Patras, then of the Morea, Protovestiary of the Household, and, eventually, Grand Logothete, or chief minister. Except when away on an embassy, he was Constantine's constant companion, adviser and, as it turned out, biographer as well.

As an historian, Phrantzes is criticized for undue animosity toward the Turk. On the contrary, since his daughter was kidnapped into the seraglio, his son allowed himself to be killed rather than submit to the Sultan's predilections, and he himself had been sold as a slave to the master of Mahomet II's household cavalry, he is more to be congratulated upon his restraint than condemned for his occasional bitterness. After the fall of the city and his eventual escape from it, he retired first to the Morea and then to a monastery at Corfu, where his history of the last days of Byzantium was written.

In 1449 the Empire had not fallen, and it was a matter of some importance to equip the 81st Emperor of the Romans with a consort. Phrantzes was dispatched to the Black Sea, to make choice between a princess of the Georgian House and one of the Empire of Trebizond. This embassy was the last great maritime parade of Byzantine power and pomp, and lasted more than two years. It did not go well. In Constantinople, Constantine's policy was to give no offense to the Turks while trying to organize defenses against them.

In Georgia, Phrantzes asked the King of Iberia how much dowry the Emperor might expect to receive. He was told the King took money, he did not give it. Daughters were valuable and barterable articles in Georgia. Phrantzes, being a diplomat, "allowed himself not to suppress his surprise."

"Well, what will you?" asked the King, displaying his knowledge of the world. "Every country has its own customs and manners. Look, for instance, at Britain. There *it is usual* for a woman to have several husbands at the same time."

Phrantzes set sail for Trebizond and better terms. But when he arrived there, he received the shocking news that the Turkish Sultan, Murad II, was dead. The news was shocking because in his later years Murad II had been indolent enough to leave Byzantium alone, and the same amiable policy could not be expected of his successor, a young and ambitious prince with nothing peaceable about him whatsoever, who moreover had behind him the most powerful fighting force and the most efficient bureaucracy then known.

The marriage negotiations had to be abandoned. Phrantzes returned to Constantinople as fast as the management of a ponderous embassy would allow.

XII

BOTH Murad II, and Mahomet II after him, were diverted from the taking of Constantinople by trouble with Albania, Serbia, and Wallachia, all three of which were continuously difficult to subdue.

In the good deal more than 2,000 years of its history, Albania has been an anomaly, a grievance, and a thorn in the foot to everyone who has come into contact with it, its own rulers not excepted. In Murad II's day, it was divided into two spheres of influence: its southern part, together with Aetolia and Acarnania, belonged to the heirs of a Florentine freebooter called Carlo Tocci, though they could not control it; the northern part was held by John Castriot, a native princeling. The Tocci lands were delivered to the Turks by the inhabitants who, tired of being fought over, exchanged a nominal for the real freedom of having their laws and religious practices respected. When John Castriot died, his domain was divided among his four sons, who became vassals of the Sultan.

At the other side of this pitted uvula of Europe, Wallachia became a tribute-paying state, while in the roof, so to speak, Serbia, then a much more extensive holding than it is today, was forced to contribute troops to the Osmanli armies, and George Branković, its ruler, to donate his daughter Maria to the seraglio. With the aid of these troops, Murad was able to return from Transylvania with 70,000 slaves; with the aid of the daughter, he was able (according to Greek legend, but it seems a legend and no more) to produce Mahomet II, the future conqueror of Constantinople.

Transylvania was ruled by John Corvinus Hunyadi, a Roumanian who was, with Scanderbeg, the relapsed Janissary and leader of the Albanians, one of the two most redoubtable fighters of the day. Through defeats, victories, and countermarches, he was to harry the Turks and sometimes to win out over them for the next twenty years. Before his armies, Murad II was forced to retreat and to feign meekness. A truce of ten years was established in July 1444, and actually kept until the following September. Murad II's eldest son, Aladdin, dying at about the same time, Murad abdicated, out of disgust with the double chagrin, and handed on the government to his second son, Mahomet II, a boy of fourteen. He then moved to Magnesia and a retirement of Diocletian watchfulness, his empire having no Maximian.

Mahomet was an exceptionally ambitious and later an exceptionally accomplished young man, but at fourteen he naturally had no beard, the symbol of authority in those parts, and so could scarcely expect to be obeyed. He was, therefore, almost immediately deposed in favor of his own father's restoration. Cardinal Caesarini, the papal legate, had claimed that faith pledged to an infidel, no matter on how many Bibles, was null and void, and that therefore King Ladislas of the Hungarians should undertake a crusade to drive the Turks back into Asia. The army consisted of German and Italian mercenaries under the command of the cardinal, and of 10,000 Hungarians entrusted to Hunyadi.

This troop worked its way to Varna, on the shores of the Black Sea (November 1444), but so did Murad II, the Genoese having found the temptation to transport his troops at a profit irresistible. In the engagement which followed, Hunyadi won the first charge. Murad II, who was in personal command, wished to flee, but one of his beys restrained his horse. King Ladislas rushed upon the Janissaries, one of whom cut off his head and put it on a pike, shouting, "Giaours, behold your king."

Beholding it, the Hungarians fled to their own camp, which

the Turks took the next day, slaughtering, among others, the legate, Cardinal Caesarini. This decisive defeat allowed Murad II to plan the taking of Constantinople. As a preliminary he burned Corinth and sacked the Peloponnesus, with the exception of the city of Mistra, a strongly defended place. The Palaeologi bought him off, and since he was distracted by the sudden rise of Scanderbeg, he consented to retire.

Of the four sons of John Castriot, Despot of Northern Albania (he had only been able to hold the area of Mirdita, however), three were poisoned—at least so it seems—but George, the fourth, was reared as a Janissary. He was a good Janissary, and thus won his name of Iskender Bey (Lord Alexander, after Alexander the Great), which, in its European form, became Scanderbeg.

Not only brave but ambitious, in 1443 he forced his way into the presence of a secretary of the Sultan and compelled him to sign an order addressed to the commandant of Croia, which he had chosen as his future capital, directing him to turn the place over. He then murdered the secretary and fled to Albania where, with 600 partisans, he entered Croia, slaughtered the Turkish garrison, raised a general insurrection in those parts, and in 30 days found himself master of Albania. Between 1443 and 1447 four expeditions were sent against him, and all were defeated. Nor could Murad II put him down, either.

In 1444 Murad II had to deal with a mutiny of the Janissaries —their first—during which they burned down part of Adrianople; in 1448, with the Hungarians again, at the second battle of Kossovo. Though he won out against both, his attention was understandably diverted.

He died of apoplexy, on February 9, 1451. He is the first Osmanli sultan of whose character and pomp we have a detailed Western account, the French pilgrim to the Holy Land, Bertrandon de la Brocquière, having visited the capitals of both the Byzantine and Osmanli empires in 1433.

Though his periods of retirement—he abdicated twice—were spent elsewhere for choice, Murad II kept state most usually at

Adrianople. The pomp of this was considerable. His personal escort was made up of 400 or 500 horsemen who, since he was passionately devoted to hawking, were more apt to be falconers than warriors. He had 2,000 falconers, as such. It was probably good countryside for hawking, since 200 years of invasion, civil war, and counterinvasion had reduced it to an uninhabitable rubble.

Murad II was a short thickset man with a brown complexion, high cheekbones, a round beard, a hooked nose, and small eyes. He was lazy, indolent, generous, and capable of rousing himself when necessary, as many indolent people are, to sometimes, as in his case, startling effect. He had an income of two and a half million ducats a year. When he raised an army, he managed to turn a profit on the transaction, for troops brought from Asia had to pay three aspers each and five for horse transport money to Gallipoli, in return for slaves and booty to come. This brought in a tidy sum, and if the sum proved insufficient, he then had his troops cross the Danube as well, whose tolls were similar.

He had 1,000 hounds and 2,000 trained hawks, loved to get drunk, and also loved drunkards. His own capacity was six to seven quarts a day. Drunkenness made him generous, so whenever he called for wine, he got it. A Moor pointed out to him one day that wine was forbidden by the Prophet. Murad II had him flung first into jail, and second out of the country. He also liked venery, and had 300 concubines. He had about half a million ducats in cash, plate, and slaves, and a million worth of gold jewelry. If he had not been so generous, he would have had far more.

Despite all this luxury, he knew how to maintain order. Occasionally he performed an act of conspicuous justice, which was enough to reassure the people, and he was careful to maintain the army, of which his personal troop alone numbered 5,000.

He governed through three intermediaries, a vizier, or counselor, and two bashaws, or heads of departments. There was a compulsory levy of 30,000 fighting men from Greece, 10,000 from his own dominions, and he could always raise more, though for extra troops it was necessary to pay salaries (five aspers for infantry, eight for cavalry). When he traveled, 100 camels and 250 mules and horses were needed to carry the baggage.

When he received ambassadors, which was as seldom as he could manage, it was his custom to dismiss the troop of boys he kept about him, but to retain a dwarf and two fools as being, perhaps, more appropriate to the occasion. He received seated cross-legged on a divan "as do our tailors when they are going to work," a comparison which would not have bothered him. The Turks had tailors too. He communicated with those he received only indirectly, through the bashaws and viziers.

His palace, says La Brocquière, was cluttered with hostages for their countries' good behavior, including twenty Wallachian gentlemen (the term was then, as always, a comparative rather than an optimum) more or less tethered in the courtyard. These people were well taken care of. Murad II was a blood seeker only when necessary.

His father, Mahomet I, had said to the Emperor Manuel, "Close the gates of the city and rule within it, for I own everything outside the walls." This advice had been followed, and had led, on the whole, at least to a personal amity. Murad II and Manuel sometimes chatted from their imperial barges in the cool of the evening, on the Bosphorus. Diplomatic relations were deliberately hampered, however, so far as the ambassadors went, by the necessity of speaking to an intermediary rather than to the Sultan direct.

One of the sights of Adrianople were chains of Christians being brought through the streets to the slave markets. The sufferings of these, if they showed ability or brought a good price, were seldom profound. A militant, increasingly voluptuous, and until recently a nomadic nation, the Osmanli preferred to put slaves or, after a term of trial, liberated slaves, in administrative positions in both the bureaus and their own households. As for those without ability, they would never have amounted to much anyhow, and almost certainly lived better at Turkish expense than they had done paying the expenses of the Byzantines.

But what all travelers, and most opponents were most impressed by was the army, if only because it was the first regular standing army seen in the Mediterranean basin and in Europe since Roman times (the first regular army in the West was that of Charles VII of France, who established his Franc-Archeurs in 1449). According to Francesco Philelphò, this consisted, on November 14, 1461, which is when he saw it, of 12,000 Janissaries, 8,000 Assabs (regular troops), 25,000 troops raised by feudal levy in Europe and 15,000 levied in Asia. To this 60,000-man force, was added, in time of war, an eddying band of irregulars, mostly shepherds from Thrace, Thessaly, and Moesia, who carried ropes to bind up their captured slaves, who moved ahead of the Sultan, pillaging and burning, and who were tolerated by the Osmanli for the havoc they could always be trusted to create and because they were expendable, so what happened to them was as much a matter of military indifference as what they caused to happen was of military assistance.

La Brocquière was not only French, but also first equerry to Philippe le Bon, Duke of Burgundy. To the natural loathing of his countrymen toward anything not French he added the hauteur of a Burgundian, which was considerable. He was therefore capable of taking a dim view in even the strongest light. The Turks, he reported, were "a tolerably handsome race, with long beards, but of a moderate size and strength. I know well it is a common expression to say 'strong as a Turk'; nevertheless, I have seen an infinity of . . . Christians excel them when strength was necessary, and I myself, who am not of the strongest make, have, when circumstances required labor, found very many Turks weaker than I." He does not specify what circumstances.

"They are diligent, willingly rise early, and live on little, being satisfied with bread badly baked, raw meat dried in the sun, milk curdled or not, honey, cheese, grapes, fruit, herbs, and even a handful of flour, with which they make a soup sufficient to feed six or eight for a day. Should they have a horse or a camel sick without hopes of recovery, they cut its throat and eat it. . . . They are indifferent to where they sleep, and usually lie on the ground. Their dress consists of two or three cotton garments, thrown one over the other, which fall to their feet. Over these, again, they wear a mantle of felt, called a 'capinat.' This, though light, resists rain, and some capinats are very fine and handsome. Their boots come up to the knees, and they wear wide drawers, some of crimson velvet, others of silk or fustian and common stuffs; in war, or when traveling, to avoid being embarrassed by their gowns, they tuck the ends into their drawers, that they may move with greater freedom."

Their horses were good, he said, and were kept on short rations, being fed only at night, and then no more than five or six handfuls of barley and double the quantity of straw. They were never watered before midday, only in the afternoon and evening. Since the horses knew they would get no water until noon, and until the army bivouacked for the night, by a stream if possible, this was one way to keep them moving.

When it came to saddle furniture, the Turks were less canny. Saddles had peaks before and behind, which gave the effect of an army riding in armchairs, comfortably; but with their knees raised so high, they were easily unhorsed.

It was a singularly obedient army, at least by western European standards of the day, whereby at any given moment the leaders would be quarreling about points of precedence while their followers refused to proceed. They traveled light, they were trained to be as noiseless as possible, and they frequently won battles by nocturnal forced marches. Their scouting and espionage were excellent, their manner of fighting closer to guerrilla warfare than anything else, for rather than charge en masse, or even upon bugle, they would attack an enemy line with small raiding forces at multiple points simultaneously, or else, as they preferred, sally out of nowhere to surround small detached forces. They were also much given to ambuscades. If the enemy was drawn up in battle array, they filed their cavalry by rapidly in Indian style, shooting into the ranks but never pausing to be shot at. When pursued, the cavalry dispersed; and dispersed anyway, if faced with an enemy more than a fourth their own number.

Western armies, more cumbersome and less adaptable, did not regard this kind of conduct as sporting, but it saved lives and won battles, which was its point. In addition, the Turkish forces were well disciplined and ready for instant maneuvers, the maneuvers themselves being signaled by a system of coded drumbeats.

They had other underhanded, childish but effective tricks, one of which was to throw fireworks under the bellies of the enemy cavalry. Another was to drive ahead of their own cavalry a herd of dromedaries and camels, undependable and ill-natured animals, which bit and scattered the Western cavalry formations, making their horsemen easier to attack. And as a matter of policy, they never consented to fight at all unless sure that their own armies were at least twice as numerous as those of the Christians.

Personally, however, La Brocquière, who reports all this, was forced to admit that in his own experience he had always found the Turks frank and loyal, and when necessary, infallibly courageous. He adds that the Turkish armies had in their ranks a multitude of impressed Greeks, Bulgarians, Macedonians, Albanians, Slavonians, Wallachians, and Serbians, and that in his opinion all these people detested the Turk who held them in subjection, and should they see Christians, and above all French Christians, marching against the Turk, would turn against the Sultan and do him great mischief. Whether he believed this or wrote it for home consumption, Philippe le Bon being an ardent Christian, we do not know. What we do know is that he was quite wrong. The Greeks, Bulgarians, Albanians, etc. were loyal to the Turk, and if not loyal, sufficiently suborned not to revolt.

There is a supposed speech, extant in two versions, in which Mahomet I tells his troops what he thinks of the Christians. Whether he made the speech or not, somebody obviously wrote out what he thought of the nature of the opposing forces.

"You have heard," says the Sultan, "that the Christians have united against us. But fear not.... You know well the unwashed Gaiours, and their ways and manners, which certainly are not fine. They are indolent, sleepy, easily shocked, inactive; they like to drink much and to eat much; in misfortunes they are impatient, and in times of good fortune proud and overbearing. They are lovers of repose, and do not like to sleep without soft feather beds; when they have no women with them they are sad and gloomy; and without plenty of good wine they are unable to keep counsel among themselves. They are ignorant of any military stratagems. They keep horses only to ride while hunting with their dogs; if one of them wishes to have a good war-horse, he sends to buy it from us. They are unable to bear hunger, or cold, or heat, effort and menial work. They let women follow them in the campaigns, and at their dinners give them the upper places, and want always to have warm dishes. In short, there is no good in them.

"And then, the Christians fight constantly among themselves, because every one desires to be a king, or a prince, or the first amongst them. One says to another: 'Brother, help thou me today against this Prince, and tomorrow I will help thee against that one!' Fear them not; there is no concord amongst them. Every one takes care of himself only; no one thinks of the common interest. They are quarrelsome, unruly, self-willed, and disobedient. Obedience to their superiors and discipline they have none, and yet everything depends on that!

"When they lose a battle they always say: 'We were not well prepared!' or 'This or that traitor has betrayed us!' or 'We were too few in number, and the Turks were far more numerous!' or 'The Turks came upon us without previous declaration of war, by misleading representations and treachery! They have occupied our country by turning our internal difficulties to their own advantage!'

"Well, that is what they say, being not willing to confess truly and rightly: 'God is on the side of the Turks! It is God who helps them, and therefore they conquer us.' "

This of course is propaganda, but it has some truth in it; enough, at any rate, to give Mahomet II the final victory.

XIII

MAHOMET II was at Magnesia when he learned of his father's death. When told of it, he leaped on his horse shouting, "Who loves me, follows me." The anecdote is at least characteristic of him. Those who did not love him usually found themselves driven like cattle before his insurgent armies. "He was persevering as a camel in hostilities against his enemies," says Phrantzes. At the time of his third, and since his father was now dead, final accession to power, the camel was twenty-one. Once he had gotten what he wanted, on the other hand, he behaved with exemplary decorum.

He was considered to be accomplished, unscrupulous when necessary, scrupulous when not, and ambitious. Rumor, in particular Greek rumor, made him the son of that Maria of Serbia who became a nun rather than marry Constantine XI Dragases, his opponent, once she had been widowed. It seems much more likely that his mother was an Albanian slave and that Maria was his stepmother.

He was outwardly a devout Muslim, but brooked no interference from his own sectaries on that account, let alone those of any other faith. He was fluent in Arabic, Turkish, Persian, Hebrew (some say rather Chaldaic, which seems improbable until we remember that he was learned in astrology, of which science Chaldaic was the language—Finlay considers his fourth language to have been Serbian or Croat, in view of how many Serbs and Slavonian slaves there were at Adrianople, and even suggests an Albanian dialect; but the Turks did not consider Albanian a language, claiming that there were 72 and a half languages spoken in the world, and that Albanians spoke only the half), Latin (perhaps a little), and Greek. He disliked games, hunting, arranged entertainments, and sexual indulgence in excess; and he was secretive. "If a hair of my beard knew what I had in mind, I would pluck it out," he said, if only because if the hair of his beard had known what he had in mind, it would have turned white, which would have been unsightly. He knew both the history and the geography of the world he lived in, he believed in and was skilled at astrology, he was fond of Persian poetry and wrote it himself, he was interested enough in the arts to import Bellini from Venice; he was impulsive, astute at dissimulation, fearless, a brave general and, most important, when it came to the logistics of organizing, feeding, moving, and directing an army, he was a genius. He had enough personal authority to put down intrigue, scotch rebellion, inspire his followers, and reward the faithful, though usually not much. In short, he was a conqueror, a Renaissance prince on the other side, and with Suleiman the Magnificent, one of the two most impressive members of his house.

Needless to say, he also had his vices, real and imaginary. He was both bloodthirsty and violent. Impatient of red tape, he took shortcuts, sometimes literally. The story that he once had the bellies of fourteen of his pages slit open in order to discover which of them had stolen and eaten a melon is untrue, but illustrates his pragmatic turn of mind. He was bisexual, indulging himself in what the French call *pédérastie héroique,* but in the Muslim world this might better be called an alternative than a vice. Indeed, his so-called vices seldom amount to much more than the casual whims of a soldier at a loose end between campaigns. Bellini's two portraits—even if one of them is, as art historians say, "school of" and not by the master himself, though they do not seem quite to agree as to which is which—show us a man not only in complete control of himself, but in control of practically everyone else as well.

He had been particularly displeased, upon this third and ultimate accession, to have to pay the Janissaries a donative. Since his father, Murad II, had deposed him twice in order to fight his battles for him, he was generally considered to be a mollycoddle. His own vizier, Chalil Pasha, has gone so far, the second time, as to call Murad back to the throne himself. To dispel this essentially erroneous view of his character, Mahomet II had the leader of the Janissaries flogged and then degraded. He did not propose to see his own best troops turn into a Praetorian guard. Nor, under his reign after this rebuke, did they.

His other definitive act upon his accession was promptly and prudently to have the only other available male heir, a boy of seven, strangled; and then, in order to show that lèse-majesté is not an act that even princes may commit with impunity, had the strangler murdered too. He next made the practice of royal infanticide legal, for though it had been practiced before, he did not believe in unnecessarily offending the law. Despite his precaution, one other male heir survived but was smuggled to Rome where he was baptized as Callistus Othomannus, given estates in Austria by the Holy Roman Emperor Frederick III, lived on and for his prestige as an illustrious convert to Christianity, and, lacking ambition, troubled no one. The only remaining possible claimant to the sultanate was an heir of an older generation who was kept locked up at Constantinople by the Emperor, in return for a yearly stipend of 300,000 gold aspers, paid to him out of the income of property along the River Strymon—the income, not the property, having been granted for this purpose by Murad II.

On his accession, Mahomet was congratulated by envoys from the Emperors of Byzantium and of Trebizond, the Despots of the Peloponnesus, the Dukes of Athens (still in French hands), and of Naxos (Venetian), the Princes of Arcarania, Lesbos, and Chios, the Podestà of Galata, and the Grand Master of Rhodes. They wished to have the favorable treaties granted them by Murad II continued. For the time being, Mahomet II sent them away satisfied. He was, they thought, only a boy. He even retained Chalil Pasha as grand vizier, thus indicating that his father's policy would indeed be continued.

But Mahomet II, to judge by such portraits as exist, all of which show him in maturity, had a bull neck, a hook nose, a prominent, aggressive chin, the set eyes of a hawk, and the general air of a man to whom disobedience was so trivial, impotent, and irrelevant a thing as to be valued merely for its novelty. It is the bust of a predator. His first acts, however, were mild. He turned over Macedonian estates to Maria, his stepmother, and allowed her to return to Serbia. He paid the Greeks 10,000 Venetian ducats (300,000 aspers) to keep Orchan Effendi, the supposed grandson of Bayazid, where he was. He asked the Despot George of Serbia to try to arrange a peace between the Porte and Hungary. The Despot George was a remarkable man, but on a smaller scale than either Constantine or Mahomet, and was remarkable chiefly for the astuteness by means of which he managed to keep his nominal independence, his very real wealth, and his court in a contentious world eager to absorb all three. He was well thought of, Pope Pius II saying he was full of dignity and deserving of the highest respect, though unfortunately belonging to the Greek Church. Since he had large Hungarian estates, was a member of the Hungarian nobility, and was the husband, in turn, of both a Comnenus and of a Cantacuzenos, and also Constantine XI's cousin-german (his son had married a daughter of Constantine's brother, the Despot Thomas), he counted almost as a member of the royal family. As Murad II had married his daughter Maria, he was thus connected to both sides.

A Greek interpreter begged him not to conclude a truce between Hungary and the Porte, because in that case the Porte would be free to attack Constantinople. The Despot George, who thought it to his advantage to act for the Porte in this matter and so preserve his own estates, would not listen and negotiated a three-year truce. This was to make the conquest of Constantinople practicable.

Unlike his father, Mahomet was neither luxurious nor extravagant. In order to sweat his household to fighting weight, he told his inherited retinue of 6,000—one way or another—falconers they could either go hungry or join the army. Most of them consented to join the army. Also unlike his father, he did not always keep his word. Muslim casuists hold that no promise can bind a Muslim against the interest of his religion, a doctrine not unlike the Catholic doctrine of reservation; and since any war is apt to become holy at any moment, Mahomet thus felt at liberty to abrogate not only his own treaties but those of his predecessors as well, particularly that agreement Murad II had made with Byzantium. He wanted Constantinople and waited only upon a pretext.

This the Byzantines were not slow to supply, by means of a blunder so ill-timed and so inane that no one has ever been able to suggest an adequate motive for it, though that Constantine found himself in the horny hands of the moneylenders and bankrupt besides, so that not even the Emperor's personal bodyguard could be paid, seems the most convincing of explanations. Mijatovich, the nineteenth-century Serbian minister to the Court of St. James, says: "Looking at the empty Imperial Treasury, and listening to the reports of the conciliatory disposition of the new Sultan, the Greek Statesmen came to the conclusion that they had not sufficiently turned to financial advantage the evident wish of Mohammed to live in peace." That the wish was more evident than real seems not to have occurred to them. An embassy was sent to Mahomet's camp, not to ask but to demand that the annual payment made to the Emperor for the detention of Orchan, the pretender, should be increased. Otherwise, they were told to say, Orchan would be released into Asia Minor, with sufficient money to raise a rebellion against Mahomet (this alternative was actually put in motion, though nothing came of it). These ambassadors were sent to Brusa, where Mahomet then was, to the grand vizier, Chalil Pasha.

Chalil was not Turkish, but the son of a Serbian father and of a Greek mother, taken prisoner as a child, brought up as a Muslim at a school for Janissaries and then released, fully grown, into the civil service. He combined moderation with decision, and had been Murad's chief and most trusted adviser. Unfortunately he was greedy, and so in the pay both of the

Greeks and of the Serbs as well as in that of his master. Greediness was accompanied by stinginess, so that the military and the people disliked him. Since he had advised his former master to depose Mahomet and return to power in order to deal with those problems of empire considered too difficult for a child, Mahomet did not greatly love him either, but left him in office since he knew his office, for the time being.

Chalil found the combined request and threat of the Byzantines stupefying.

"Oh, you foolish Greeks," he said. "Long ago I learned to know both your falsehood and your cunning! [Indeed he had learned it at his mothers' knee.] While Sultan Murad lived it was possible for you to go on comparatively well, because he was just and conscientious. But Sultan Mahomet is quite another man. If Constantinople escapes his impetuosity and his power, it will be a proof that God does not punish your crooked ways and your sins. The ink on the documents of peace concluded between us has not yet dried, and you come to us with silly threats. You are mistaken. We are not inexperienced and simple children to be easily scared. If you really believe you can do something, you are free to do it! If you desire to proclaim Orchan Sultan of Rumania, go and proclaim him. If you wish to bring the Hungarians from across the Danube, do so. Beg them to come. If you wish to recover the countries you have lost, try. But be sure of this: you will only succeed in losing what little you have left."

The Hungarian question was much in the air, it being the opinion in the Turkish camp that Mahomet intended to take Constantinople before the truce with Hungary expired; which was to say, soon.

Mahomet, when he heard of the matter, was extremely civil. Since he was in Asia, he thought it best to temporize. He received the embassy courteously, listened to its demands, perhaps agreed a little, promised to take care of the matter as soon as he returned to Adrianople, and was as good as his word. As soon as he reached his European capital, he canceled the Byzantine pension, ejected the Byzantine taxgatherers from the banks of the Strymon, made a truce with the Venetians, and proceeded to bottle Constantinople up.

The Sea of Marmora, or Propontis, at whose northern end Constantinople sits, is connected with the Black Sea by the Bosphorus, a channel with steep banks eight miles long, and at its narrowest point a little less than half a mile wide. The entrance to it is directly opposite Seraglio Point, in those days the ancient Acropolis of Constantinople, the administrative and official center of the city. The Genoese suburb of Galata is on the left; Scutari (by now for some decades in Turkish hands) is on the right. On the Asiatic side of this narrow channel, Bayazid had built a fortress called Anatolia Hissar. Mahomet gave orders to build one opposite it on the European shore in order to gain complete control of all shipping which passed to and from the Black Sea, and thus over Byzantium itself, which got its wheat from the Ukraine and whose only remaining wealth, except for the yearly tribute from Mistra, came from tolls levied on shipping through the Bosphorus, though actual control of the trade had passed into Genoese hands. The site chosen was one of the few remaining bits of Greek territory along the Bosphorus, at a place called Loemocopia, where stood ruins of an earlier castle built by the first Palaeologi for the same purpose, the remains of a church dedicated to the Archangel Michael, and where, most appropriately, in classical times there had stood a temple to Hermes, patron of lost articles, travelers, and thieves. Today this fortress is known as Rumelia Hissar. Mahomet himself called it by a Turkish word meaning cutthroat, which had the same play upon the word *gorge* as exists in English.

That a hostile force should build a fortress on Byzantine territory without declaring war and seizing it first, was unheard of. And indeed Chalil, for it never does any harm to keep up at least the appearance of appearances, sent a special envoy to Constantine with a well-worded request to build the fort. It was to be built, he explained, exclusively to protect trade, as pirates would not be apt to venture into the Bosphorus if they knew the Sultan to have a force there. As a matter of fact, the

Sultan had had a force there for thirty years, since by treaty with Murad II the Empire granted the Turks the right to cross from Asia to Adrianople at this place, which was the crossing at which Darius of Persia had also entered Europe to attack the Greeks, though with less success, about 2,000 years before.

Since it was now the winter of 1451–52, the building was postponed until early the next spring; but Mahomet ordered that 1,000 masons were to assemble at Asomaton, five miles from the Greek capital, though on the other side of the Golden Horn and with Galata in between, as early as possible after the thaw.

Both sides knew this to be the penultimate act of aggression on the part of a power which had already taken away everything else, and had been doing so since 1299, when the Osmanli first invaded Nicomedia, and 1352–53, when they had established themselves in Europe with the inevitable onrush of lemmings. There is nothing anyone can do about lemmings, or about a lemming war either. There are too many of them, and they go right on marching in.

As Gibbon says in his history, "Persuasion is the resource of the feeble, and the feeble can seldom persuade." Like most of Gibbon's better remarks, this has the bone-crushing elegance of the inexorable. It is graveling. There is no answer to it, and none is expected. Nonetheless, Constantine endeavored to persuade.

In those stiff but flapping robes which had been already derided in Europe as old-fashioned and outlandish, if picturesque, an embassy presented itself to Mahomet and starchily informed him that though the Empire had graciously permitted his grandfather to build a castle on his side of the Bosphorus, to attempt to build one on the European side was a flagrant violation of previous agreements; also, in cutting off shipping, it would inconvenience the Byzantines. Therefore he should desist. To reinforce this argument, it was pointed out that a Latin army might be prompted to move in a crusade against the Turks, and that though Constantine would have been delighted to oblige the Sultan with the cession of the territory, unfortunately it had long ago been ceded to the Franks of Galata. Ask them.

Chalil replied that the Sultan, unwilling to hurt his good friend the emperor by building without permission, was delighted to learn that the ground belonged to the Franks, since in that case to build there a fortress would in no way impinge upon Byzantine territory; and as for the Genoese of Galata, who cared about them?

The fortress would have gone up in any case, but this turning against them of their own two-edged diplomatic sword did not please the Greeks, who prided themselves on their cunning. It was now remembered that on his deathbed Murad II had urged on his son the duty of taking Constantinople, even though Mahomet had not himself been present at the time. They were now confronted with their nominal suzerain's real purpose, which, though always there, had not previously been so mercilessly unveiled, and they found it about as attractive as a whitened skull.

Mahomet made the matter even plainer. The Turks are, like many taciturn peoples, overwhelmingly voluble when they do choose to speak, and the Sultan enjoyed nothing so much, it appeared, as a really succulent game of cat and mouse. He blustered. He called up historical precedent. He was withering.

He pointed out that the Byzantines had caused considerable difficulties to his dynasty by releasing and financing false pretenders to the throne, particularly after the death of Bayazid. He pointed out other acts of bad faith, the better to conceal his own.

"I form no enterprise," he said, "against the city." And kindly added that they had best behave themselves, as the Empire was measured by the city's walls, and as their strength was not the equal of their malevolence. He went on to say that his father, Murad II, had made a vow to erect a fort on the western shore, a vow was a holy obligation, it must be fulfilled, and therefore, as a filial son, he felt it his duty to carry out his father's wish, as why should he not, since Byzantium had neither the right nor the power to control his actions, on his own ground; and, as he further cruelly pointed out to them, it was his own ground, since he had taken it, had the strength to occupy it, and they had not. He dismissed the embassy with a safe-conduct to the city, but told its members that if another embassy was sent, he would flay it alive.

When this answer was brought back to Constantine, he wished to sally out of the city gates with what forces he had in order to push the Turks back at least from the immediate suburbs. But his forces were feeble and the will of his advisers feebler still. They were afraid to fight and refused to do so. The clergy, which, since it alone could control the half-starving rabble of the city, had more say in the government than it should have been allowed to have, suggested that by patience and long-suffering it would be possible to prove Mahomet the violator of an honorable treaty, and thus a guilty aggressor almost certain to be punished in heaven—theirs, not his—as well as censured by all those with sufficient leisure to investigate the rights of the matter. We must turn the other cheek, they said, and Constantine, who had but two, could do nothing to dissuade them from a quietistic obstinacy as cowardly as it was foolish, since in this case any chance, in being their last, was better than none.

There was only one course of action left: to fulfill the decisions of the Council of Ferrara and Florence, cultivate the Western powers, and reunite finally the two Churches, in return for an army.

Greek ambassadors arrived in Rome at the end of September 1451. The Pope answered them in a letter dated October 5th. He pointed out that the Union of Florence had been supported by all Christian countries, only the Greeks, with whom it had been made, choosing to ignore it. Therefore the Holy See remained irritated and mistrustful. "If you with your nobles and the peoples of Constantinople are ready to execute the decree of the Union, you will find us and our venerable brethren the Cardinals, together with the whole Occidental Church, always willing to work for your honor and your State; but if you and your people refuse to execute that decree, you will force us to make such provisions as may seem fit to us for your own salvation and our honor." The Pope demanded that the Patriarch Joseph, who had been removed from the patriarchal throne as a result of his adherence to the Union, be reinstated. Constantine clearly felt his capital to be worth a mass, but his people unfortunately didn't. Like Mahomet, they were stubborn as a camel, but on even less water. He spent the winter unhappily trying to bring his own clergy and citizens into some semblance of obedience to an inevitable order, and in remonstrating with the Sultan. Mahomet spent the winter more profitably in organizing his forces, in winter dreams, and in contemplation of his future capital.

XIV

THE winter of 1451–52 was passed by those in Constantinople in a state of trapped, impotent uneasiness, and by Mahomet at Adrianople with industrious glee. Certainly his winter was spent far more pleasantly. He had the St. Michael's Church at Loemocopia pulled down for building stone, and chose one among several plans for the fort, settling on a triangular one wtih a cabalistic significance; indeed the site, a steep bank, demanded such a shape.

"Constantinople is a city larger than its renown proclaims," said the Arab traveler Hassan Ali al Haraway, who visited it in the twelfth century. "May God in His Grace and generosity, deign to make of it the capital of Islam." "I believe," said La Brocquière in 1433, surveying its lack of defenses, "that God has spared the city more for the holy relics it contains than anything else."

Mahomet agreed with the Arab, and saw no impediment in the Frankish Christian explanation of its so far impregnability. The city obsessed him. Even as a child, he had dreamed not only of taking it, but of ruling his empire from it; though he had, of course, never seen it except from a distance. Though impotent itself, once backed by his own power its strategic importance would once more be as great as it had ever been; the site was magnificent; and he was not indifferent to the moral effects upon the West of its capture by Islam, even though, so it seemed, the West was. But, good tactician that he was, he seemed in no apparent hurry.

The literature of militant politics is absurdly small, and has produced few classics. Four of the greatest of these, however—Kautilya's *Arthasastra Sutra,* written under the Indian Emperor Chandragupta, Sun-tzu, Machiavelli's *Prince* and *Commentaries on Livy,* and Clausewitz's famous work—all agree that a system of subsidized buffer states combined with a policy of inducing their outer neighbors to attack them is essential to the security of a strong military and civil state. Though they spent a fortune on bribery and were only too willing to finance rebellion in the rear, the Byzantines never grasped the principle of the buffer state, if only because those states which might have been used as buffers were usually engaged in invading them, rather than the enemy on their other flank. Mahomet was more adroit, in keeping with the established policies of his house.

By the end of the winter he was ready, and having dispatched 30 new-built armed triremes and a fleet of transports from Gallipoli, both to cover him and to assist building operations, himself left Adrianople on the 26th of March, 1452, so spacing his journey as to arrive at the site on the seventh day. Everything had been prepared and assembled. A work army of 5,000 consisting of a 1,000 masons, 2,000 masons' assistants, and 2,000 assistants to them, was already in residence, in its turn protected by a professional army of cavalry and foot. Lime had been burned at Cataphrygia; the woods of Heraclea and Nicomedia had been cut for timber; and stones had been quarried in Anatolia and ferried across the strait. The Bosphorus was clogged with the going and coming of barges and small boats.

For him it was a festive occasion. Rams were slaughtered so that their blood might mix with the chalk and mortar of the first courses of stone, both as a binding and for luck. The proceedings were only too visible, for Hagia Sophia, the great palace, the imperial box, and the colonnades of the Hippodrome were tall structures standing on high rocky ground; from Constantinople to Rumelia Hissar, the site, is a distance of only five miles; and though the air shimmered, it was plain enough to see what was going on. Constantinople, whose walls had always kept barbarians out, was now being walled in.

Mahomet laid the cornerstone himself. As was said at the time, Rumelia Hissar (Fortress of Europe) was less a redoubt than a town of sizable dimensions. Since it still stands, and since it does contain a small town, the remark was truthful enough. It was not only an extensive but also a somewhat fanciful building, its layout designed to represent the interwoven Arabic initials both of the Founder of Islam itself and of his namesake, the letter M in Arabic script being roughly the shape of our O with a tail added. There were five large and thirteen small towers, connected by walls, three of these towers, representing consonants, being 25 feet wide. The curtain walls were 100 feet long and 22 feet thick, the towers 30 feet thick, and both walls and towers roofed with lead. Rumelia Hissar was almost directly opposite the Asiatic tower built by Bayazid, Mahomet's grandfather, the distance between them being about half a mile (accounts differ, depending upon whether one measures by the English statute mile of 1,760 yards, or the nautical mile of 2,025). At any rate, the passage was narrow and the current swift, the place also being known as Red Dog because the waves snapped against it like the barking of a dog and because the rocks were red.

Each master mason was supposed to lay two cubits of wall a day, with the assistance of two helpers; and the three viziers were responsible for the rapid completion of the three principal towers, with penalties should they fail of sufficient speed and zeal. Each helper in his turn had hod carriers, mortar mixers, and others to assist him. Together with their guards, camp followers, and commissary, these people in themselves constituted a small temporary town of tents and barracks at Asomaton nearby.

They worked night and day. At night the torches and lamps of the work camp reflected against the sky, a sight which must have been as pretty as it was ominous. Since Mahomet commanded universal terror among both his people and his viziers, and was a master of supply, the work went forward smoothly.

Pathetically enough, there were also abandoned Byzantine

towers on either side of the Bosphorus, but farther on, toward the Euxine, built centuries before for the same purpose and long since fallen into disuse. These Mahomet quarried for stone, but ostentatiously concentrated his efforts upon the dismantling of such churches and monasteries as were in the area, in the hope of provoking an incident. He paid particular attention to the Church of the Asomatoi and to that of St. Michael, from which he took the marble columns. Both these buildings, though ruinated, were considered sacrosanct, and as he hoped, the local inhabitants rebelled and were instantly slaughtered. But even this was not enough to draw Constantine from the city.

There was nothing he could do but send new envoys to remonstrate. "Should the Sultan persist in raising the fort he would practically break peace with the Greeks, and violate the treaties which his predecessors had kept loyally, and which he himself had confirmed by solemn oath." The envoys also complained that they could scarcely enjoy what peace was left to them, if their grain supplies were cut off and starvation hung over their heads. The Emperor even offered to pay a larger yearly tribute, on the condition that the fortifications be abandoned.

"Do you think you can prevent my building it?" asked Mahomet. "This ground does not belong to the Emperor, and why should he come my way? Go and tell your master that I am able to do what my predecessors were not able to do, and that I am willing to do what they would not do. And also, I shall have every ambassador impaled who dares to come to me with such a message in future." This was only what he had said before, even more plainly put, but caused a panic in Constantinople. Some claimed that the days of the Antichrist had come. Others said they would rather die of a pestilence (quite likely, there had been nine in thirty years) than see the fall of their city and hear the enemy ask, "Where now are the saints who protected your town?" A few volunteers were sent to make a sally, but none of them came back. They were either hacked down or sold into slavery.

The Sultan ordered the immediate suburbs laid waste, taking as prisoners not only all Greeks but also all cattle his troops came upon. Constantinople responded by sending the grand vizier, Chalil, the gift of some fresh caught fish stuffed with gold, since he was known to have pro-Greek sympathies. Chalil did indeed try to intervene, less because of the gold than because he had heard of envoys being sent to the West for help, and also the rumor that the West might actually send it.

Mahomet paid no attention, but went on supervising everything himself, not out of a sense of duty or even to get it done, but because he was interested in how everything *was* done. He also vastly enjoyed not chess as a game, though being Persian, that was fashionable enough, but chess as a parable of life, and for the playing of this he liked the best to use living pieces.

By this time, because of the difficulty of getting grain from the Ukraine, the Byzantines had taken to growing it in the environs of the city. Again, Mahomet had his Janissaries harass the farmers, hoping to coax Constantine out of the city. But though Constantine had wished to make such a sally, he had not the men with which to risk the venture, and was in any event talked out of doing so by his counselors. Instead, he offered to send out food to the workers. This was not at all to Mahomet's purpose, and to provide a further incident he had his cavalry pass through the fields at night, so the horses and mules might eat up the grain. Pushed beyond patience, the farmers rose up against the Turkish guards supposedly sent to protect them, and delighted with this, Mahomet set his Janissaries upon them. Most of them managed to flee to the city, but forty who had remained to reap what was left of the harvest were cut down.

As it happened, Constantine had made a sortie from the city, crossing behind Galata since Galata proclaimed itself neutral, but had only been able to capture some personal attendants of Mahomet's household, mostly decorative pages. These begged him either to behead them at once or send them back at once, since their master was not kind to those so foolish as to be caught by the other side. Constantine kept them for three days, and then set them free with the following last message to Mahomet:

"Since neither oaths nor treaty nor submission can secure peace, pursue your impious warfare. My trust is in God alone; if it should please him to mollify your heart, I shall rejoice in the happy change; if He delivers the city into your hands, I submit without a murmur to His Holy Will. But until the Judge of the Earth shall pronounce between us, it is my duty to live and die in the defense of my people." Like many another dignified rebuke from the weaker side, this fell on deaf ears.

Constantine, being a practical soldier, scarcely expected divine intervention, having had a lifetime to perceive, like many a leader before and after him, God's eternal preference for the best troops. His citizenry felt somewhat differently however, mostly abandoned, and asked, "Where are the saints who protect the city?" The clergy seemed to feel the responsibility for their absence lay entirely with Constantine, and John Eugenikos, the deacon of Hagia Sophia, addressed to the Emperor the ultimatum either that he submit to the True Faith and abjure Union, or be omitted from the liturgy, and thus from the obedience of his people. That fortress of the true faith, George Scholarios, who had attacked Constantine's election on religious grounds, attacked him no less now that he was Basileus; while Lucas Notaras, the richest and most powerful member of the court as well as the most reactionary and cantankerous, and therefore called by Eugenikos the (true) Father of His Country, totally rejected aid from the Occident. A turban was preferable, he said, to the papal tiara. The anti-Unionists held a council of their own in Hagia Sophia, in the absence of the Emperor, at which three of the Oriental Patriarchs were present, and at which Gemistos Plethon delivered himself of a lengthy if Neoplatonic diatribe against the Double Procession of the Holy Ghost. The Patriarch Gregory was deposed for Catholic leanings (he went to Rome), and a list of 25 of the chief errors of the Latin Church was drawn up and duly presented to the Emperor, a copy sent to the Pope. Thus did the greater part of the clergy, supported by most of the populace and more than half of the nobility, endeavor to assist the efforts of the Emperor to save himself and them.

The Basileus Constantine was impotent to interfere, but persisted in Union anyhow, and in the same month that Mahomet had begun to build the fortress, sent to Rome for help. The Pope was agreeable, on the condition that Gregory should be restored to the Patriarchate; Gregory himself did everything he could to urge the sending of supplies; the condition was agreed to by the Emperor, though not by the clergy; and in return the Pope promised Isidore, Cardinal of Kiev, Leonard of Chios, and what galleys and help he could send. Learning of this, George Scholarios, now the monk Gennadios, sent the Basileus a severe public reprimand, offered to dispute against the legate Isidore when that prelate arrived, and issued his own alternative proposal for saving the city, which turned out to be prayer. He added bitterly, however, that he realized his advice would not be taken. He then retired to the Monastery of the Pantocrator, did what he could to undermine anything the papal legates might be able to advise, refused to cooperate in any way, and after Rumelia Hissar was completed, in October of 1452, speaking before the Emperor and a courtly audience at the monastery, denounced his sovereign roundly, as much as told him his efforts at defense were damned and therefore futile, and said that in his opinion he thought the truly Orthodox might be trusted to save the city by their own means—which again turned out to be prayer. As it happened, the Orthodox scarcely lifted a finger, but by means of his own intransigence, Gennadios found his reputation for sanctity, and therefore his power over the citizenry, grown larger every day.

Mahomet went about finishing his fortress. Constantine caused the gates of the city to be closed, thus causing additional inconvenience to those wishing to escape from it rather than defend it; and they were to remain shut for the following eleven months, until Mahomet succeeded in prising them open again.

Though artillery had been used by his father Murad II, to

whom the Genoese had most likely sold not only the cannon themselves but also the requisite technical information, Mahomet was the first military leader to use it on an extensive scale. It had first appeared in the Western world during the second half of the fourteenth century, but Murad's models were experimental and did little damage, so he had done little with them. He was not of a modern turn of mind. His son Mahomet II was.

Therefore, at the end of August 1452, when the fortress was completed, he had small cannon mounted on its walls and towers, as well as on those of Anatolia Hissar opposite.

It was not the custom of the Turks formally to declare war if an actual war was about to be undertaken, though they often threatened it for purposes of diplomacy. At any rate, no such declaration against Constantinople is either on record or in existence. It was the custom among them to send a formal offer of peace, usually upon humiliating terms, into any city they were about to sack, both for religious reasons and because it was the practice of the day that if a besieged city formally surrendered, it could not be sacked, but if it were publicly asked to surrender, no matter what its reply (in practice) it could be. This complicated example of casuitry had, with time, become conventional and obligatory.

Early in September, Mahomet appeared on the landward side of Constantinople, accompanied by 50,000 troops, to reconnoiter the ground. He remained three days, inspecting everything, and then on the 6th of September withdrew to Adrianople, where he intended to pass the winter, not wishing to attack the city until the following spring. He did not remain idle in the interim. In October he sent two military units to the Morea, to prevent the Despots Demetrius and Thomas from coming to the defense of Constantinople, a measure which was unnecessary since they had no intention of coming, being too busy destroying each other to have time to save themselves; and to contain Scanderbeg, a costly but successful effort since, though with heavy losses, the Turkish force managed to immobilize him from the early autumn of 1452 until April of

1453, by which time it was too late for him to take any decisive action to intervene, even had he wished to.

There remained two possibly effective sources of succor. One of these, despite the truce, was Hungary. But it was the opinion of Hunyadi, who headed the Hungarian forces, that "Christianity will always be damned, until the Greeks are destroyed. When the Turks take [Contantinople] then the Christians will be able to have victories again." The other was Venice, neutralized for the time being by somewhat shamefaced secret agreements with the Porte, designed to protect its own trade.

On leaving for Adrianople, Mahomet had garrisoned his Bosphorus forts with 400 Janissaries. On November 10th two Venetian vessels—for the Venetians had always passed to and from the Black Sea unmolested—attempted to run the gauntlet with a cargo of grain, and were sunk by one discharge of cannon. The master and 30 of the crew of one of the ships managed to escape the explosion and swim to shore. They did not escape far. They were captured, manacled, chained, and dragged to Adrianople where Mahomet, to show he meant what he had said insofar as shipping through the Bosphorus was concerned, had the captain impaled (the victim was bound and then pulled down over a sharpened stake which entered through his anus into his guts, came out at his shoulder or thereabouts, and held him writhing, the stake then being elevated and stuck in the ground like a trophy until such time as he died of internal bleeding, internal injuries, pain, and shock; all of which took from a few to 24 hours, depending upon the physical condition of the prisoner) and the crew beheaded. According to the historian Ducas the bodies were then fed to wild animals at Demotica. Despite these hazards and deterrents, a few Venetian ships managed to get through the blockade. The Senate of Venice, thinking better of remaining neutral, promised after all to send ten galleys, as did Alfonso, King of Naples, the Pope himself promising ten. Though not empty, these were ineffectual promises, for it was not until April 27, 1453, at which time the siege had been under way for three weeks, that the Pope signed letters permitting Jacob, Archbishop of Ragusa, to take charge of the equipment promised for the galleys but not yet loaded upon them; the Venetian Senate debated the exact amount and type of aid to be sent for an equally long time; with the result that the three separate fleets never arrived at Constantinople, though the Venetian galleys did, according to some reports, appear at Euboea, the chosen rendezvous, a good safe 300 miles away in the Aegean, two days after the city had fallen.

On the 15th of November, five days after the sinking of the Venetian galleys, Gennadios was summoned to the palace, where he delivered himself of an ekthesis, or list of measures which in his opinion would save both town and Church. These still consisted of prayer. And on the 27th of November, when the Osmanli fleet was already blockading access to the Bosphorus and Hellespont, he delivered himself of an encyclical in which he complained of calumnies made against him, and justified his own conduct to his own satisfaction.

Constantine sent embassies to Pope Nicholas V and to foreign courts but, as Aeneas Silvius said, "To our shame be it said; the ears of our princes were deaf and their eyes blind." He also purchased provisions and military stores, called out volunteers, implored his brothers for aid (there was no answer), sent ambassadors to Venice, and again to Rome. Venice, angry at the sinking of its grain boats, though preferring to prolong the debate about sending aid itself, ordered the Governor of Crete to hire mercenaries at the expense of the mother city's treasury and to send them to Constantinople; and Doge Morosini, the following February 2nd, sent letters to Pope Nicholas, the Emperor Frederick III of Germany, Alfonso of Naples and Sicily, and Hunyadi, urging them also to send help. Even Genoa offered, but did not send, men and arms.

It was during this winter that the Emperor Frederick of Germany arrived in Rome, in order to be crowned Holy Roman Emperor. He found the Vatican divided between lamentations for the Greeks and ambitious schemes for reunion. The Cardinals had been assembled, and before them Aeneas Silvius delivered what everyone present agreed was a brilliant oration upon the sufferings and miseries of the Byzantines and other Christians since the arrival in Europe of the Turks. "Unfortunately the Saracens are far more ardent in their infidelity than we are zealous in our faith," said the future Pius II, and concluded by adding that the Holy Roman Emperor had firmly resolved to lead his armies against the Turks. The only thing wrong with this decision was that Frederick returned to Austria and just as firmly did nothing of the sort. He was the last Holy Roman Emperor to be crowned in Rome, for the journey was difficult, the expense great, and the trip unnecessary. Since the Holy Roman Empire was by now largely imaginary, future emperors could be incoronated in the Germanies just as well.

Giving up hope of any civil support, the Greeks repeatedly asked the Pope to do his best. The Pope required that they declare their subservience to Rome. This was agreed to, though the ambassadors must have known that the citizens of Constantinople would never comply. These negotiations took the better part of a year.

The Pope sent out special legates to stir up a semi-crusade. These were not successful. The rise of nationalism had ruined the spirit of the Crusades, even as the Crusades had proved ruinous to those who undertook them. It was the belief of the day that to be successful, such a crusade must be led by the French. But France was at war with England, and its king was not an effectual prince. "It is not at all likely," the publicist (and somewhat of a turncoat) Philelphò advised him reassuringly, "that Englishmen would prevent your entering upon such a sacred enterprise; the English are a religious people, and it is more probable that they will be ready to follow you, after the example of their forefathers, who always followed the French kings and assisted them whenever these moved against the infidels." True, of recent years, the English had merely followed Charles of France deeper into French territory in order to take it from him, but Charles confessed himself willing. The Duke of Burgundy had applied pressure to him in order to get him to say he was so. Unfortunately the English king, Henry VI, also applied pressure, though to different arteries, by telling the papal legate that they could speak of peace, not to mention a truce, only "at some future day when the English had reconquered by arms all the places they had lost in France."

That ended any projected intervention on the part of France; so that, after a fashion, Jeanne d'Arc, who having put some military starch into Charles was at the moment on trial for her life in Rheims, might be said to have contributed, if involuntarily and indirectly, to the fall of Constantinople as well as to the final rise of France.

Constantine, at the last moment, tried to reactivate the imperial factories, a government monopoly which in better days had supplied luxury goods to the royal palaces, liturgical goods to the churches and, more to the point, ships' stores and armaments to the fleet (now almost nonexistent, the shipyards on the Golden Horn were in hopeless disrepair), and armor and weapons to the armies (no longer existent either, but still he tried to provide weapons to anyone who would consent to use them). But he had not much by way of raw materials, or workmen either. He did the best he could. Tombstones, for example, were uprooted from the graveyards for use in repairing the walls.

Isidore, Cardinal of Kiev, the papal legate, and Leonard of Chios, his assistant, arrived on a Genoese galley at the beginning of November 1452, bringing with them 200 soldiers, a little money, and a demand for an immediately proclaimed union between the Churches. The deposed and now reinstated Patriarch Gregory had also arrived in the city, and Gennadios had again retired to the Monastery of the Pantocrator, to fulminate. The 200 soldiers represented more a personal guard than an addition to the city's forces, for Isidore knew the temper of the Byzantines when it came to religious dispute; even so, they were welcome.

Cardinal Isidore's advance had been leisurely, as he had stopped off at various islands in the Greek Archipelago in an unsuccessful attempt to raise volunteers. He was a Greek who had when young, as many Greeks then did, gone to Russia to make his career. In this he had been successful, soon becoming both Archbishop and Metropolitan of Moscow. Since he had subscribed to and been a delegate at the Council of Ferrara and Florence, both his Church and the Russian court had repudiated him and driven him out of Russia. Taking refuge at Rome, he had been made Cardinal of Kiev.

He found Constantinople not to his taste. Commerce was paralyzed, everyone expected catastrophe, grain shipments had been shut off since the summer so that there was a good deal of hunger, and the people, left idle, had nothing to do but show off their hatred of everything Latin. A prediction had recently been resurrected to reassure them, to the effect that Constantinople would not pass to foreign masters until such time as ships were seen sailing under canvas across dry land; in other words, never. In view of what was consequently to happen, though most predictions are made retroactive to the event, one cannot help wondering if occasionally they do not provide incentives to the ingenious to fulfill them.

Constantine XI, driven to the expedient of pretending Union possible on any but the court level, though he knew better from his own experience, let alone historical precedent, greeted Isidore warmly, and was met by a demand for a ceremony of Union to be performed at once. Isidore was not unsympathetic. His cardinalate title dated from Polish attempts to introduce the Latin Rite into an area that was firmly Orthodox (and Russian), the efforts had failed, and though he had himself never seen Kiev he knew what Constantine was up against. But his orders were to insist, so insist he did.

The matter was first agreed to privately, at court. The Patriarch Gregory signed a declaration accepting the Union, though with the reservation that once the present danger was past, the whole problem should be re-examined and revised on all doctrinal points before a final settlement was agreed to. This was merely to save face. A follower of John Hüss, the Bohemian reformer, circulated inflammatory and scandalous stories about the obscene sexual practices of the Pope and Roman clergy. Lucas Notaras refused to enter Hagi Sophia. The Union was proclaimed anyway, with a solemn *Te Deum,* on December 12,

1452, in the presence of Constantine, Isidore, Leonard, the Patriarch Gregory, and 300 more or less forcibly constrained priests, while the congregation alternately and severally sighed, wept, booed, and hissed, and the clergy wished many years to Pope Nicholas. Gennadios had made certain preparations of his own.

Constantine merely let the crowds shout themselves hoarse, but the consequences of this ceremony were violent and disastrous. Since the congregation, even while it was going on, had been restive, noticing that the language of the mass, though as usual slurred, was Latin not Greek; that the rite was also Latin rather than Orthodox; that Isidore was wearing foreign rather than native robes; and that, worst of all, he had consecrated an unleavened Host and thus clearly belonged to the Azymite heresy, and poured cold water into the sacremental cup rather than wine—the instant the mass was over, the mob rushed out of the church and poured through the deserted state avenue, or Mese, through the forums of Constantine, Theodosius, and of the Tauri, the several miles to the Monastery of the Pantocrator, in the Venetian quarter of the city near the inner side of Constantine's wall, to consult the monk Gennadios.

Gennadios, to put it bluntly, wished to be patriarch. His temper was terrible, so was his learning; contumacy had made him sacred; and when it came to the politics of the mob, he was astute. So he was not there. Rumor had it that he was lost in meditation, possibly even divine rapture, somewhere in the building, but he had left on the door of his cell a lettered tablet.

"O miserable Romans!" it read: "Why will ye abandon the truth? and why, instead of confiding in God, will ye put your trust in the Italians? In losing your faith, you will lose your city. Have mercy on me, O Lord! I protest, in Thy presence, I am innocent of the crime. O miserable Romans! Consider, pause, and repent. At the same moment that you renounce the religion of your fathers, by embracing impiety, you submit to a foreign servitude."

This seems to have been composed at leisure, with thought and psychological insight, well before the fact. At any rate, it was effective. In Hagia Sophia, those lamps not smashed were allowed to go out, even before the miraculous ikons. The place was denounced, now that it had been sullied by a Latin mass, as "nothing better than a Jewish synagogue or a heathen temple." Priests who had assisted at the *Te Deum* were not allowed to offer communion, to bury the dead—who therefore went unburied—or to baptize children. The nuns attached to the Pantocrator abjured all communion with the present and future associates of the Latins, and following their example, both clergy and people did the same. The nuns were particularly obstreperous, one of them declaring that "she would not fast any more; she would eat meat, wear Turkish clothes, and offer sacrifices to Mahomet." She was shortly to be seen, as publicly as possible, doing exactly that. And since, under these conditions, the nobles, led by Lucas Notaras (whose wealth was both portable and well concealed in his own palace), refused to contribute one groat to the city's defense and the treasury was empty, Constantine, on the advice of his privy council, forced the churches and monasteries to give up their gold and silver plate, in return for scrip to four times its value, redeemable after the city had been saved.

Constantine next ordered a house-to-house census, discovering, as a result, that out of the 18,000 monks and clergy and the 42,000-odd inhabitants, only 4,970 were willing to man the walls. Of this 4,970-odd, about 4,000 were mercenaries, the 970 alone being citizens. This was so demoralizing a percentage that Phrantzes, who had directed the census, and Constantine resolved to keep the results to themselves.

The authorities for the siege—and they are few, being mostly Greek—are given to hyperbole, and so exaggerate the nature of the odds. However, everyone agrees on the number of the defenders, for that a city defended by so few should hold out so long against so many redounds to its credit. The two most responsible recorders of the siege, Nicolo Barbaro, a Venetian ship's surgeon of noble birth little given to exaggeration and experienced in war, and Tedardi or Tedaldi, a soldier who helped to defend the capital, usually roughly agree, however, and their accounts have been followed here. The historian Phrantzes, though in the city and constant in attendance upon the Emperor, was not a soldier, and of course had no accurate knowledge of the exact extent of the Turkish forces. Besides, he seldom bothered to climb the walls to look. Tedardi and Barbaro did. Their estimates are also compatible with reason.

When the Emperor rode through the streets he was jeered at, and sometimes assailed, by the people he was trying to save. "Better we turn Turk than Latin," the crowd shouted after him, and one historian of the period adds that if an angel had descended from heaven to promote the Union so that the city might be saved, the people would have sent him back.

Under the circumstances, Constantine, a firm-minded and practical prince, set himself to the study of gunpowder, but could produce nothing more effective than small ordnance and shotguns capable of scattering five or ten lead balls the size of a walnut. He had also, though his brothers in the Morea would do nothing and Galata had made a secret and, as it turned out, inoperative treaty with the Turks to remain neutral, obtained supplies from the Archipelago, the Morea, and Sicily, some of them at the last moment. But gunpowder was in short supply, could not be bought, and the materials for its manufacture were not sufficiently to hand.

Toward the early part of December, six Venetian vessels somehow got through the Bosphorus, despite the two forts, on their way home from a trading voyage, and their captain, a man named Gabrielli Trevisano, consented to stay *"per honor de Dio et per honor de tuta la Christianitade."* The crews of three Cretan vessels were also persuaded to stay on, and on the 13th of December a meeting was held to determine on what terms additional aid might once more be asked of Venice. This went on for several days, with Trevisano and a Captain Diedo as advisers.

On the 29th of January, Giovanni Justiniani (or Giustiniani), a Genoese condottiere of great and deserved reputation, arrived with two vessels and 400 cuirassiers, and since he had also rounded up men in Genoa, Chios and Rhodes, 300 additional soldiers. He had not been sent by Genoa, but had come of his own accord. The Emperor made him as liberal a donative as he could round up and promised him the sovereignty of the island of Lesbos, should they survive the siege. He was named, by consent of the war council, commander in chief of the defenses and given dictatorial powers. As a member of a family syndicate which had controlled Chios for some time, he knew the fighting methods of both Byzantine and Turk as well as any man.

At the end of March, Trevisano, his crew, and Alexis (or Aloysius) Diedo with his, reopened a trench which ran from the Golden Horn southward in front of the land walls until it reached higher ground, in order the better to defend the poorly built defenses of the Blachernae quarter. They also strengthened the walls as well as they were able, the two monks originally commissioned to see that this was done having done little, and that badly. Diedo had come from Tana, the Genoese trading city on the Sea of Azov, but proved more reliable as a defender than did his fellow citizens at Galata.

On April 2nd, shortly before Mahomet appeared with his armies, a chain or boom was put in place to defend the entrance to the Golden Horn. This consisted of large wooden links heavily covered with metal and supported from piles or by large floating logs. An embargo had been put upon all ships in port as early as the 26th of January, though during February and March some Venetian vessels had managed to make their escape. Of those remaining, ten large ones—five Genoese, three from Crete, one from Ancona, and one imperial—guarded the boom, with their bows toward it and supported by triremes and smaller vessels. The garrison for these was Genoese, though the Genoese at Galata refused to break their treaty with Mahomet, giving as excuse that to keep it would enable them to aid the city secretly, though Leonard of Chios denounced them for this dishonesty, and though they made no effort whatsoever directly to aid the city.

Fortunately, the Byzantines still held control of the Tower of Galata, within the walls of the suburb, and had manned it.

The boom stretched from this through the wall, across the water, to the Tower of Eugenius near Seraglio Point.

These were the entire defenses Constantine had been able to make.

At Adrianople, Mahomet had naturally enough done much better. Among other things, he amused himself with having a pleasure palace built for him. Should he win the city, though enormous it was only a toy (it was in the shape of a tower), and so could be dispensed with. If he did not take the city, he could live in it.

Encouraged by the intelligence that Pope Nicholas V was more devoted to his hobby (the collection of good book bindings) than to warfare, he went his way. A well-rounded Renaissance prince, though on the opposite side, he consulted both his astrologers (whose calculations he himself checked) *and* the best military experts available (whose calculations he was also in a position to be able to check), discussed the coming campaign, and himself drew up sketches of troop dispositions. Indeed, he worked so hard he was unable to sleep.

One night he sent for Chalil Pasha, who never having been sent for at so late an hour before, feared the worst (and he had much to fear). Chalil arrived carrying above him, with arms upstretched, a bowl of gold coins after the fashion of a slave. Mahomet was in bed, but completely dressed.

"What does this mean?" asked Mahomet (who knew perfectly well what it meant, having spies to spy on spies and so always knowing a little bit more than everything that was going on, spies being an inventive lot, to earn their pay), but called Chalil "Lala" (my uncle), a term of affection, to show that this was not to be a fatal interview.

"Sire, it is an old custom that dignitaries of state, when the Padishah calls for them at unusual hours, should not appear before his Majesty empty-handed. I have not."

"Put the bowl down," said the Sultan. "I have gold. What I want is Constantinople. Look at this bed. I turn on it all night long, from one side to the other. I wish only to remind thee that thou must not allow thyself to be softened by gold or silver. Let us fight the Greeks, let us work to win the residence of the Caesars."

This gentle rebuke ended any hints of temporizing with the Greeks. Since he was as usual on both, it could not exactly be said that Chalil shifted sides. But he did at least shift the greater part of his bulk onto one foot and leave it there. The outcome of this midnight meeting was an ultimatim, of which we do not know the text, sent to Constantine. We do have the answer.

"As it is clear," wrote Constantine, "that thou desirest more war than peace, as I cannot satisfy thee either by my protestations of sincerity, or by my readiness to swear allegiance, so let it be according to thy desire. I turn now and look alone to God. Should it be His will that the city be thine, where is he who can oppose His will? If He should inspire thee with a desire for peace, I shall be only too happy. However, I release thee from all thy oaths and treaties with me, and closing the gates of my capital, I will defend my people to the last drop of my blood! Reign in happiness until the All-Just, the Supreme Judge, calls us both before His judgment seat."

This is merely a variant upon Constantine's earlier pronouncement while the tower of Rumelia Hissar was being built, but is reported by the various historians of the period, now as delivered at the one time, now at the other. Since until recently most of the speeches attributed to great men have been almost entirely in form, and sometimes in substance, delivered by the historian rather than the man whose life he was chronicling, constituting a sort of rhetorical set piece, naturally versions vary, and only their substance can be believed.

Mahomet, always secretive, had waited until Rumelia Hissar was finished before telling his advisers and army the purpose for which it had been built, but now, feeling more confident, he assembled his pashas at Adrianople and delivered himself of an harangue. This is reported by Critobulus, a Greek who was brought up in and became an official at the Osmanli court and wrote an extensive history of the career of his master.

Mahomet recapitulated the progress made by the Turks in

Asia Minor, Thrace, Macedonia, Bulgaria, Serbia, and Selymbria. The only barrier to their advance was the city and army of the Basileus, who had always resisted whatever the Turks had wished to do, often by treachery. This barrier must now be removed, and the work begun by his forefathers completed. It was only a single city, which was impoverished, underinhabited, defenseless, and could not resist their attacks. Indeed, it was merely a city in name, since the greater part of it was given over to cultivated land, orchards, and vineyards. Nonetheless, it alone was to blame for the attacks of Tamerlane, the inconvenient invasions by the Hungarians under Hunyadi, and for opposing the sacred ambition of the Turks. He was now determined either to have it or to see it destroyed; either to possess it or to lose his empire, as not worth having without it. He also claimed that the Italians in the city would do nothing to aid the Emperor because of the religious differences between the two peoples; and concluded by saying the attack must be made soon, before any aid could be sent from the West. He voted for war, and naturally his entourage followed his example. As a preliminary, he ordered Selymbria, Perinthos, the Castle of San Stephano, and other small Byzantine enclaves to be taken, which was done during February and March, and all the lands around the capital to be cleared, which was also done. Turachan Pasha was left with a large auxiliary army to hold Scanderbeg under control in Thessaly, and his son Achmed to make sure Demetrius and Thomas did nothing in the Morea.

During the winter, Mahomet concentrated upon his experiments with cannon. These engines, though in use for a hundred years, were still unreliable pieces of machinery. At the siege of Zara by the Venetians in 1346, Francesco dell' Barchè threw balls weighing 3,000 pounds into the city, but unluckily perished by his own invention which, going off too soon, catapulted him into Zara and dashed him to pieces on the pavement. The Genoese, undeterred by this example, had used balls almost as large at the siege of Cyprus in 1373; Murad II brought some into place before Constantinople in 1422. But they were unreliable, not only because they had a tendency to explode, but also because it was almost impossible accurately to direct their fire.

Constantine had had in his employ a Wallachian cum Hungarian gunnery specialist named Orban or Urban, but had been unable to pay his demanded salary, or indeed much of any salary. Half-starved, the man had defected to the Turks, who paid him better. Mahomet asked if he could cast a cannon capable of flinging a stone large enough to batter the walls of the city. Orban said that he could, for though neither the Turks nor the Byzantines possessed the art of casting large guns, he did. He claimed to be competent to batter Babylon, but added cautiously that the effectiveness of the result would depend upon the postion and management of the guns, a matter he would leave to Mahomet's own siege engineers.

Mahomet, who never left anything to anybody, gave Orban all the metal, assistants, and material he might need; a foundry was established at Adrianople; and within three months Orban had produced a cannon, cast in pieces so it could be dismantled for transport, with a bore of 96 inches (12 palms), and capable of hurling a stone weighing 1,456 pounds. This sounds outlandish, but several such cannon cast later still exist, one of them at an emplacement above the Dardanelles. They had other than offensive uses; in later times, a tailor successfully concealed himself inside the bore of one for several days to escape his creditors, and passed the time comfortably enough. Small balls were also used. Some two feet in diameter, made of granite, are still imbedded in the walls of the Jewish quarter of Constantinople. The balls were quarried and polished on the European Black Sea coast, and from there sent by barge to the Sea of Marmora, probably being unloaded southwest of the city, for delivery to the artillery corps.

To discharge Orban's giant cannon required from 150 to 330 pounds of powder. The cannon was hollow cast, bound with hoops, and liable to burst, while the passage of the stone balls ground away the inner surface of the bore. The gun was water-cooled, water being poured into the bore after each firing and then drained off. It could be fired at most only seven times a day, and at that, even larger balls flung by ballista had been in use during earlier times. They had not had, however, the same impact.

This monster armament was christened by Mahomet, Basilica, in graceful allusion to the Basileus, against whom it was soon to be pointed, though by extension the name may also be made to mean "judge." Basilica had a length of 26 feet 8 inches, the hollow-cast bronze of which it was made a thickness of 8 inches. The half of the barrel through which the ball was blown was 30 inches in the bore; the other half containing the powder, 10 inches, with stronger walls. The ball which this monster flung forth, says Tedardi, was big enough around to reach to his waist. On its first trial, a vacant field before the new pleasure palace was chosen for its position, and a proclamation issued announcing what was about to happen, to prevent miscarriages, terror, and a stampede. The explosion, when it came, could be heard for over 12 miles, and the ball, after having traveled more than a mile, buried itself 6 feet deep in the ground. Mahomet was delighted, and promptly ordered more, both in the large size and in sizes smaller. One of the larger size subsequently exploded during the siege, killing Orban, but the others greatly contributed toward the fall of the city. Another, when tested during the eighteenth century, drove a stone ball 600 yards across the Dardenelles, whereupon it split into three pieces which ricocheted out of the water, and still had enough force behind them to bounce up the opposite hill.

In February Basilica was moved from Adrianople to Constantinople, a distance of some 150 rocky, hilly miles. The journey took six weeks. The barrel was loaded on a frame made up of 30 wagons linked together, drawn by 60 oxen, and supported by 200 men on either side of it to balance the weight. Two hundred and fifty workmen marched ahead of it to smooth the way and repair the bridges. This must have made a slow, glittering, ominous spectacle. The big cannon was followed by the smaller, which were more numerous, and by its sisters.

The first divisions of the army left Adrianople at the same time. In March, armed bands led by the Timar and Ziyamet beys, or chiefs of the military fiefs, began to assemble on the plains of Adrianople; and during the second half of the month, the Sultan held a grand review of his troops while the most popular ulemas, sheiks and white-robed descendants of the Prophet preached up the coming siege and battle. At the end of the month a party of 1,500 cuirassiers was sighted on the road between Philipopolis and Adrianople. These were Serbians, sent by George, Despot of Serbia, who was a vassal of the Sultan and had been forced to contribute them toward the siege of the city, though they were not told until their arrival of the purpose for which they had been summoned. At the last moment, Mahomet had the tiny enclaves of Anchialos and Bizya wiped out, but the citadel of Selymbria, though not the town, against all expectation had defended itself so successfully that it did not fall until shortly after the capital had done so. He ordered it to be blockaded and, having himself left Adrianople on the 23rd of March, marched on toward Constantinople. His progress was leisurely. Estimates of his forces vary, but the number is best set at 70,000 picked troops because, according to a prophecy popular among the Turks, the Prophet is supposed to have asked one of his disciples, "Hast thou heard of a city of which one side looks to the Continent and the two sides to the sea?" "Yes, Envoy of God." "The Day of Judgment will not arrive until that city is taken by seventy thousand of the sons of Ishak." The sons of Ishak were, of course, the Osmanli Turks.

At any rate, he had with him at least 20,000 cavalry, and prophecy or not, his entire force probably numbered 150,000 men, not counting an additional horde of Bashi Bazouks, or lawless "thieves, plunderers, hawkers, and others following the siege for gain and booty," to quote Tedardi. The main troops were stationed between the Marmora and the Golden Horn, and the Bashi Bazouks were also foregathered there. The hard core of this army was the 12,000 Janissaries, who were used as reserve troops throughout the siege and as shock troops at the end of it.

Mahomet overlooked nothing. The cannon had been moved

into their preliminary positions at the end of March, reinforced by 14 batteries of smaller artillery; and at the same time the Sea of Marmora abruptly blossomed with the approximately 140 ships of the new-built Turkish fleet, moving up the Marmora from Gallipoli and down the Bosphorus from the Black Sea. There may have been as many as 320 boats, all told, most of them half-decked coasters, and even the largest inferior to the galleys and galleasses of the Greeks and Italians. The Turks were no better sailors and navigators than the Arabs had been before them, the ships being largely manned by Genoese and other Christian seamen, under the direction of Admiral Baltoglu, a Bulgarian renegade. The effective part of this armada probably consisted of 18 triremes, 48 biremes, according to Phrantzes; 6 triremes, 10 biremes, and 70 single-banked boats, according to Leonard of Chios.

Since Constantinople was surrounded on three sides by sea, a fleet was indispensable to the taking of it, if only because it could spread the defenders away from the land and onto the sea walls. The Constantinopolitans, who had never been besieged so heavily on land and sea walls combined, therefore felt the city was all the more likely to fall. However, the Venetians who had been able to throw ladders from their boats to the walls had done so from the Golden Horn, which was now chained off. And since 1204, the shore had changed its shape, the tidal flats being wider and higher now than they had been then, the Horn having partially silted up, so that even if they succeeded in getting into the Golden Horn, the Turkish ships would be unable to make use of the same landing device.

The fleet left Gallipoli at the beginning of April, but was not in place at its mooring at the Double Columns of Diplokynion, in the Bosphorus just beyond Galata, until April 12, six days after the commencement of the siege.

Mahomet arrived before the city most probably on April 5th. Shortly before this, Justiniani, according to Critobulus, had led a sortie against such troops as had already arrived, at first with success, but when Mahomet arrived with the main part of the army such countermeasures were no longer practicable, and the temporary bridges placed over the fosse outside the walls were broken down and the gates permanently closed.

The Turkish army had been set to digging preliminary trenches and defenses about the 2nd of April, before Mahomet's arrival. These were completed by the night of the 5th, and on the morning of the 6th the entire army slowly and methodically advanced three-quarters of a mile closer to the city, to Maltepe, a district facing the Blachernae quarter, and a position slightly in advance of that the Crusaders had taken up in 1203–04. From here, it spread out from Blachernae and the Adrianople Gate into the district known as Mesoteichion, which was the valley of the Lycus; and the artillery, at first concentrated at Blachernae, was partially shifted to a position in front of the St. Romanus Gate, and the line extended to the Golden Gate and the Sea of Marmora.

Mahomet spread his prayer rug on the ground and prayed publicly for the success of his enterprise. He then, in compliance with the custom mentioned earlier, sent a formal offer of peace, which was refused, and, the ceremonies proper to the occasion having thus been completed, the thirtieth or thirty-first (the numbering varies) and final siege of the city began.

XV

IN the late eighteenth and early nineteenth centuries, the schoolboys of Westminster School, in London, had a derisive song which it was their habit to chant whenever it was proposed to restore the fabric of the building.

" 'Twill cost you nothing to remove that wall," they shouted. "You need not pull it down, but let it fall." This was somewhat the case with Byzantium, but by no means entirely. The walls before which Mahomet was now encamped, and to whose strength and weaknesses he had devoted so much and, as it turned out, successful study, had a history as old and complicated as that of the city, and on the landward side had not been successfully taken from without during the entire occupation of the site.

To put it simply, they consisted, looking at them from the outside, of a low wall, a wide treacherous glacis, a deep fosse, another glacis equally exposed to fire, another low wall, a cleared area, a first wall, an inner courtyard, an inner wall, and a mile behind that, what remained of the original walls built by Constantine—all these walls defended by strong towers. But the matter cannot be put both simply and clearly, for they were much more elaborate and complicated than that, representing the continual building and rebuilding of some 1,100 years, always in accordance with the latest military science of the day.

Those of the original Megaran Greek city were still standing. Constantine had incorporated them into his own and strengthened them, between 330 and his death in 337. Almost every emperor after that either repaired them, elaborated them, or extended them. Those on the land side were the most formidable, but those on the sides of the city bounded by the sea were not neglected either. Whatever happened to the Empire, the walls were always kept in repair.

In 439 Theodosius II completed and extended the sea walls to meet his new land walls, which made the city a mile wider and gave it new limits at Blachernae on the Golden Horn and at the Golden Gate on the Sea of Marmora. These were double walls with a defensible space between, the inner walls being higher and stronger than the outer.

The city had greatly expanded, but between the Constantinian and the Theodosian walls the area was never really built up, and remained semirural. The main open cisterns of Constantinople were in this section. They were superfluous. Near Hagia Sophia was the Great Cistern (Yeri Batan Serai), which has 300 columns 12 feet apart, in 28 rows, each column 40 feet 9 inches high, the whole 336 feet long and 182 feet wide. This, which had been built by Justinian not far from his preferred church, had long been virtually forgotten, its entrance through the trapdoor in the basement of a private house, whose owner kept a skiff and did his fishing there, it being well stocked with fish. Wells let down through the roof made the water itself accessible. When completely full, the reservoir was flooded to within a few inches of the vaulting. There was more than enough water there to supply what was left of the city indefinitely.

The location of a good many things had been forgotten in the course of 1,100 years of incessant and superimposed building, one of them a small door in the ditch, called the Kerkoporta, which was to be of some importance later.

During the arctic winter of 763, the ice floes in the Bosphorus and Golden Horn formed pressure ridges massive enough to break down the wall at what is now called Seraglio Point. This had been repaired, and further strengthened by Theophilus in the ninth century and Leo the Wise a little later.

After the recovery of the city from the Franks in 1261,

Michael Palaeologus built an inner sea wall, and in 1351 this system of defenses was once more set in order and all houses between the sea wall and the sea were destroyed. The strip of land there was narrower then than it is now.

Along the Golden Horn was a series of landing stages: one at which the Emperors were received by the Senate when they came around to Blachernae by water; one from which hunting parties customarily set out; one for the fish market; one for the ferry to Galata; then the pier where the imperial navy had a shipyard; and finally, at the entrance to the Golden Horn, the dock used only for the reception of imperial brides, when they entered the city by sea. It was from here (the Tower of Eugenius) that the chain was stretched across the Horn to Galata on the far shore in times of danger. All these stages had gates into the city.

Byzantium was impregnable from the sea side. Therefore, its strongest fortifications were concentrated to the landward, from the Marble Tower on the Sea of Marmora, to Blachernae on the Golden Horn. These were formidable. The only reason the walls ever were breached is not because of any weakness in their design or structure, but because all told there were 16 double miles of them, four and a little more on the landward side, and they were in consequence difficult adequately to man.

Looking out toward the enemy, from the point of view of the defenders, the Theodosian walls consisted of an inner wall, 13½ to 15½ feet thick and about 50 feet high, with a battlement 4 feet 8 inches high. This inner wall was guarded by 96 towers 60 feet high and about 180 feet apart, which projected out from the main wall 18 to 34 feet. Though connected to it, these towers were detached from the wall, access to them could quickly be shut off, so even if you captured a tower you were still no closer to taking the wall itself. Greek fire, a substance whose constituents were kept a closely guarded secret, but which most probably had a napalm-like chemical as a base, was flung down from the parapets onto the besiegers. This inner wall was the stronger of the two.

Between the inner and the outer walls was a terrace 50 to

64 feet wide where the defenders of the outer wall could take shelter, and in which anyone who succeeded in breaking through the outer wall could be shot down. The outer or little wall, now, in its ruined state, about 10 feet high but probably originally about 20, was from 2 to 6½ feet thick, and rose about 27½ feet above the terrace leveled between the outer wall and the moat.

Beyond this wall was an embankment 20 feet wide leading down to the moat—more a fosse than a moat since it was seldom if ever flooded—which even today, after 500 years' accumulated detritus, is about 22 feet deep. The moat had both a scarp and a counterscarp, each 5 feet thick, steeply canted, and bearing breastworks with battlements 5 feet high.

The outer wall was equipped with about ten gates (some were walled up, a few had been altered out of existence) which ran through both walls. Some of these merely gave onto the fortifications. Others formed public gates to the city, temporary bridges being placed across the moat in front of them. The first of these gates, the Porta Aurea, or Golden Gate, otherwise the Marble Gate, had three arches, was elaborately decorated, and was the imperial and state entry into the city. It had been built by Theodosius the Great, rebuilt in recent times, was heavily fortified, and under Mahomet II became the Prison of the Seven Towers. It had been little used since the death of Michael Palaeologus. Next, reading from Sea of Marmora to Golden Horn, came a public gate, then another military gate, then a second public gate, now called Seliviri Kapoussi. Civil and military gates had been planned in alternation.

Behind Seliviri Kapoussi is that sacred well where, so the story runs, a priest sat frying fish over a campfire, on the day the city finally fell. A friend told him it had fallen. The priest refused to believe it. He would as soon believe it as that the fish in his pan should leap back into the spring, he said. The fish then leaped back into the spring.

The third military gate came next, then the Rhegium; after the Rhegium, the Gate of St. Romanus, known to its defenders as the "Civil Gate." In 1453 it was the most frequented gate in the city, but it was the weakest, even if the most strongly defended, part of the defenses because it sat low in the valley of the Lycus. Here the main attack was to be concentrated.

Beyond was the Pempton Gate, in which the Turkish cannon made their first breach of the siege, and near which the Janissaries were to make their entrance into the city. Beyond this stood the Adrianople or Charisius Gate, now known as Edirne Kapoussi. Beyond this the walls turned eastward and became irregular, but were strong enough to withstand a siege, even so. This was the quarter of Blachernae, where Diedo had irrigated his moat.

It should be added that there has always been some confusion about the identities of the St. Romanus and Pempton gates, their being often taken for each other. The defenders themselves make the matter no clearer. This book follows the order given above, for though various authorities claim one to be the other, and the other the one, this seems inconsistent, since there *was* a Romanus Gate coexisting with a Pempton Gate, and the main fighting is almost always said to have occurred at the Romanus Gate, which in its present condition certainly looks as though it had been fought over.

As for the city behind these defenses, it was empty; the defenses were no more than the large exoskeleton of some now dying shriveled animal. As recently as a century before, a law had been in effect whereby private house owners had the right to direct views of the sea, gardens, or public monuments from their houses, though persons claiming the right to enjoy the historic prospect unobstructed by new buildings had first to prove themselves sufficiently educated to appreciate what they were looking at. This law was no longer necessary. Nothing had been built. The view was now unobstructed, though sometimes the monument so to be viewed was no longer there, having been carted off by the Venetians 200 years before, or else sold for ready money since.

One also wonders if, at this time, Hagia Sophia still maintained its skeleton staff (even the Patriarch had at times endeavored to retrench) of 8 priests, 150 deacons, 40 deaconesses,

70 subdeacons, 160 lectors, 25 cantors, and 75 doorkeepers. It seems unlikely. Besides, the populace had deserted the building since its, to their eyes, pollution on December 12. What had been the sumptuous display of a triumphant and religious people, a glittering hosannah full of gratitude and pride, had become, these last few years, an anxious, sincere, but increasingly abandoned cry for help.

Unfortunately the repairs to the walls had been placed in the hands of two monks skilled in engineering but also, it seems, in peculation, so that the repairs were not well done, and after the city fell, the money intrusted to them for this purpose was found where they had buried it.

Some of the walls were so tottery that the Greeks were afraid to put cannon on the towers of them, lest they collapse. But the outside wall had been repaired by John VIII Palaeologus between 1433 and 1444. And George Brankovič, the Prince of Serbia, who had as feudatory been forced to send the Sultan troops for the siege, as an ally of the Emperors had reconstructed, in 1448, two towers, one on the Marmora at the gate now called Koum Kapou, the other in the wall along the Golden Horn.

There were, all told, 112 square towers on the land side, most of them dating from the ninth and tenth centuries, though the tower Anemandra, near the Xyloporta, had been restored as late as 1452 by Cardinal Isidore; and the ditch dug by Diedo and his men behind the Palace of the Hebdomon, the weakest part of the walls, had been inaugurated March 14, 1453, with much ceremony, in the presence of the Emperor and the court, though just how you inaugurate a ditch is not made clear. On the 31st, seven days before Mahomet's arrival to invest the city, this was completed. The Diedo Ditch was 104 yards long, with a scarp of 15 feet and a counterscarp of 13. While it was being finished, the Emperor himself mounted guard with a few troops on a neighboring hill to prevent Turkish outriders from cutting down the workmen.

Armies had once marched out the landward gates, accompanied by special orators to rouse their spirits, by members of the clergy to sing both morning and evening mass, before and after every battle, and the marching songs had been hymns. But now, every night, those in the city could see, if they wished, the flares and torches of quite a different army moving on the landward side; they could see the lights of a hostile fleet moving up the Sea of Marmora, and that cry from the hills around the city was not a hymn but the muezzin.

There was now no army to march out. At the highest estimate, which is undoubtedly exaggerated, Constantine could not dispose of more than 8,000 or 9,000 men all told, to patrol 16 miles of wall and to make sure that the crossbars of the great closed gates were thick and heavy and in place, that no informer touched them, and that the barricades against them had been properly bricked up.

His effective fighting force was much smaller than that. Therefore, it was decided to defend only the outer wall and to leave the inner wall unmanned, an unwise but inevitable procedure. The inner wall had not been kept in such a good state of preservation as the outer; and so would have been, in any case, probably indefensible. It was this inner wall which the monks Jagarus and Neophytus had particularly neglected in order to save those 70,000 gold pieces which the Turks subsequently found. Phrantzes has nothing but praise for Jagarus, but passes over Neophytus in silence, so perhaps only one of them was an embezzler.

Lucas Notaras, the richest man in the city, contributed not one ducat to its defense. We do not know exactly how great his wealth was. It was certainly greater than that of the unnamed woman who had jewels and cash to the value of 150,000 ducats about her, and of the man who had 80,000, reported by the Superior of the Franciscans as having been unwilling in any way to assist at their own defense. As a matter of fact, two towers bear an inscription to the effect that Jagarus repaired them. Two out of 112, however, is not many.

The civil gates in the inner wall were closed, and the defenders encamped in the space between the two walls.

Mahomet moved his troops up. Before Pera he placed Zagan

Pasha with an army to keep an eye on the Genoese and to patrol the northern shore of the Golden Horn, and the southern from the suburbs as far as the Xyloporta, or wood gate. He was directed to build a bridge across the upper Horn so that his troops might be summoned at any time.

Between the Xyloporta and the palaces of Blachernae and Porphyrogenitus and as far as the Adrianople Gate, the armies were controlled by Caraja Pasha. This was the European division of the troops. Guns were placed here at first, this being the weakest section of the walls. From Top Kapou to the Marmora, the Asiatic troops were stationed under Isaac Pasha.

The most important position was before that part of the city known as the Mesoteichion, between the Adrianople and Top Kapou gates, and facing the Romanus Gate. Here Mahomet had his headquarters, in a red and gold tent pitched on a small knoll some quarter of a mile from the walls. His quarters were ringed by those of the Janissaries. A trench and a wooden palisade protected them from any forays made on the part of the defenders. The palisade had intervals through which cannon could be fired, and was closer to the fosse than to their own encampments.

The seaward walls were to be patrolled by the Turkish fleet.

It is difficult to determine how many batteries of cannon Mahomet had, since he moved them about from time to time. Phrantzes says fourteen; Barbaro, a more dependable witness, nine. Montaldo says they consisted of in all 200 guns or "torments." Each battery was strengthened by one larger gun. Their fire was concentrated on the weak wall between Tekfour Serai and the Adrianople Gate; near the Romanus Gate; and on the third military gate, between the Seliviri and Rhegium gates.

Basilica was kept near the tent of Mahomet. He had a fondness for it.

These guns were called bombards, machines, skeves, helepoles (takers of cities), torments, and teleboles. Archbishop Leonard of Chios once measured one of the balls, and found it 88 inches in circumference. They were reinforced with culverins. The culverins were on wheels. The great guns were not, but were carefully pointed at the target, lowered into place, and wedged there with lengths of wood.

Against these, Constantine could offer what was, in effect, a force of 3,000 competent Italians, Genoese and Venetians, the rest of his men being highly dubious and not always too competent Greeks. The Italians were fighting, they said, for God, but also because if the Turks once took the city, that would mean the end of all trade east of Cape Matapan (the southernmost cape of the Morea).

The Greeks, also fighting for God, felt hampered by a natural reluctance to cooperate with schismatics and heretics. The livery and armaments of the troops on both sides were irregular. Of Justiniani's 700 fighting men, only 400 had body armor.

Each side had a curious medley of ancient and modern weapons. The Turks had dolabras, wooden turrets, and sometimes locked their shields in a position over their heads as ancient as the Greek phalanx. The bow was the principle weapon on both sides, but mangonels threw stones almost as well as did the cannon. Both longbows and crossbows were used. Their archers, according to La Brocquière, were the best troops the Turks had. Wooden shields were used. A fourth of the Turks had body armor, hauberks and quilted cotton and leather-padded tunics. Some had iron helmets, some did not. Because of the nature of the battle, the Turkish cavalry, which was numerous, fought as infantry.

But the deciding factor was the cannon. They were still a novelty. There being no name for them in ancient or even in demotic Greek, Critobulus, in his history, was the one to christen them "helepolis," or "taker of cities." "When fire is applied to the touchhole," he wrote, "the powder lights quicker than thought. The discharge makes the earth around it tremble, and sends forth an incredible roar. The stone ball passes out with irresistible force and energy, strikes the wall at which it has been aimed, overthrows it, and is itself dashed into a thousand pieces." He was writing for the information of those who had not, as yet, seen one in operation. It was, in other words, the feeble but horrendous commencement of the admirable technological advances made in recent times.

Shortly before or just after the siege began, Mahomet sent troops to clear out any small centers of possible resistance previously overlooked. There were only three of these. At Therapia a small fortress surrendered, and its 40 defenders were impaled. Another fortress, the Studium, also surrendered, and its 36 defenders were led up to the walls of the city and also impaled, as an example of what was to come. And in the Sea of Marmora, on the island of Prinkipo, the most important of those islets called the Islands of the Princes because the imperial family liked to take monastic retreats there, unable to batter down the strong walls of the monastery with cannon, Baltoglu, sent with part of his fleet to destroy it, was forced to smoke out the garrison with brushwood fires on which straw and sulphur had been flung. Some smothered, some surrendered; those who were armed were killed, and those who were not armed were sold into slavery.

All pockets of possible resistance, except Galata, whose disloyalty could be depended upon, now being wiped out, the siege began. Mahomet had his troops in their final positions by the morning of April 7th.

XVI

WHEN told that a good many of the nobles had slipped out of the city, taking their valuables with them, the Emperor "said nothing, but sighed deeply." He then held a council of war. The chief question discussed was the defense of the St. Romanus Gate, where the Turks obviously intended to concentrate their heaviest attack, having moved their bigger ordnance there from its first station, at Blachernae, opposite the Cynegium amphitheatre used for wild beast fights, though not recently.

Neither the Greek nor Latin captains present volunteered until Justiniani rose, bowed to the Emperor, and said, "Trusting in God's help, I am ready to stand there with my men and to the honor of Christ's name defend the gate against the attacks of the enemy." The others then cheered, and the Emperor himself decided to make his headquarters at the Church of St. Romanus, near the threatened gate, and took 3,000, or roughly almost half his total troops, there with him.

The Charisius Gate, to the north, was defended by a small company of Greeks under the archer Theodore of Karystos. The next gate after that was the Polyandrium or Milyandrium. This was defended by three Genoese brothers, Paolo, Antonio and Troilus (appropriately enough) Bocciardi, with a small band of fellow countrymen, and at their own expense. From this point the wall swerved east toward the Golden Horn and the Blachernae quarter. This position was given to the Venetian bailo (the resident minister of the Venetian quarter), Girolamo Minnoti, who had a mixed corps of Venetians and strangers under him. Beyond Blachernae, the walls had no ditch to defend them. This was the Calligaria district, and it was expected that the Turks would try to breach the walls here. With this in mind, Constantine turned this part of the walls over to a German mining engineer named Johannes Grant. The last part of the walls, at the northwestern angle where they met the Golden Horn, was under the command of Cardinal Isidore, who had repaired them at his own expense.

To the left, or Sea of Marmora side of the St. Romanus Gate, looking out toward the Turks, was another small band of Venetians, under Dolphino. This gate had been walled up, and its name is forgotten. At the Seliviri Gate, a Greek mathematician and member of the royal family, Theophilo Palaeologus, was supported by Maurico Cattaneo, a Genoese, and Niccolo Mocenigo, a Venetian. The next gate over was also under the command of a Venetian, Fabrucio Cornero.

The southwestern angle of the fortifications at the Sea of Marmora, called Cyclobyon, where the Golden Gate was, was under the direction of the Venetian N. Contarini and the Genoese Emanuelo N. (his last name has been lost), who had 200 Italian archers to support them.

On the seaward side, between the Golden Gate and Hagia Sophia, the next gate, the Hypsomatia, was in the hands of a group of young monks extracted, one way and another, from various monasteries in the city, no serious attack being expected on this gate. Giacomo Contarini and a group of fellow Venetians had charge of the Contoscalium, next on, and the one after that, which was near Hagia Sophia and therefore called the Basilica, or Chodegetria, was held by the Spanish consul, Don Pedro Giuliano. This was the easternmost gate of the city.

At the tip of the peninsula (the old Greek Acropolis), that pretender to the Osmanli throne, Orchan Effendi, was stationed with a small group of Turks loyal to himself. They had every reason to be loyal; if Mahomet took the city, he would also take their heads. As for the imperial quarter, the consul of the Catalans defended the Bucoleon and the port of Contoskolium.

From the Acropolis to the Cynegion, along the Golden Horn,

where no real assault could be expected, since the Golden Horn was shut off by the unbreakable boom and his loyalty was amply assured by a plentiful supply of water between himself and anyone with whom he might be tempted to treat, Kyr Lucas Notaras was stationed. The grand admiral of the non-existent navy, he had the highest military rank in Byzantium, and the shortest temper. However, he was considered brave and an experienced commander and in that spot, since no one had to depend upon what he might do, sufficiently dependable.

At the entrance to the Golden Horn the Venetian Gabriello Trevisano had been posted with 50 men to guard the chain and the 15 galleys and the smaller boats set to guard it. The boats themselves were under the captaincy of the Venetian, Antonio Diedo. All told, the harbor held 26 galleys: 5 Genoese, 5 Venetian, 3 Cretan, 1 Anconan, 1 Spanish, and 1 French, the remaining ten being Greek.

Of 12 military divisions into which he had divided his forces in order to defend the 14 zones of the city, Constantine had dared to entrust only two to direct command by Greek officers, though as underofficers others of his staff could be trusted well enough.

Within the town, in the square surrounding the partially dismantled and totally ruinated Church of the Holy Apostles, parts of which John VIII Palaeologus had used to strengthen the walls, a corps of about 700 men were stationed, most of them impressed monks, as a reserve. These were under the command of Demetrius Cantacuzenos and his son-in-law, Nicephorus Palaeologus.

Each body of men on the walls had a group of monks and priests permanently in attendance upon it, to say mass and offer up prayers for divine intercession, and also, no doubt, to administer last rites and to hear confession, should there be time. Services were performed day and night in the churches, with the exception of the desecrated Hagai Sophia, and according to different rites, without pause, the morning services being followed by religious processions through the streets and along the walls, their members carrying banners, images, relics, and ikons. No doubt they made excellent targets. In short, while only at the very most 6,000, and undoubtedly much fewer (4,000 operatively) of the 60,000 citizens were willing to defend the city themselves, or could be coerced into doing so, the other 54,000 were quite willing to implore God and the saints to do so for them—a novel, not to say an overwhelming, division of labor. Miracles were many. Ikons were given to sweat. There were portents in the night sky. Oracles were handed about as soon as received. Feeling against the defenders, most of whom were followers of the Latin Rite and therefore heretics, ran high. Lucas Notaras complained.

The Emperor Constantine himself usually attended morning mass at whatever church happened to be closest to his early morning visits to the walls, and often looked in again just before noon. Between these devotions, and followed by a small retinue, he made the rounds of the fortifications on a small Arab mare, to exhort the soldiers to their duty "of enduring everything for God's glory"; and also to prevent them from deserting. In the afternoons he returned to his headquarters, a large tent pitched between the inner Gate of St. Romanus and the church, to take a short rest before making the rounds again in the evening. His invariable companions were George Phrantzes and a distant cousin, the Spaniard Don Francesco di Toledo, an ancestor of the present Duke of Alba.

At Galata, the virtually independent Genoese suburb on the other side of the Golden Horn, against Pera hill, defense was scarcely undertaken. The inhabitants petitioned Genoa for military assistance and sent envoys to Mahomet to impress upon him that Galata was independent of Byzantium, owed the Emperor no allegiance, and therefore proposed to pledge itself neutral if Mahomet would agree not to molest them. Mahomet, who had them prudently under military observation, so agreed. He, too, knew his Genoese.

Thus while, a few hundred yards away, Byzantium was struggling for its life, the merchants of Galata were able to turn large profits by selling both belligerants comestibles and luxury goods at outrageous prices, making more in the last 53 days of the city's life than they had been able to take in during the past several years.

Should Mahomet take the city, the arrangements was, according to the Janissary Michael, one of the few of those fighting on the Turkish side to leave a memoir, that the Galatans were to be recognized as loyal subjects of the Osmanli, in return for this profitable neutrality.

For the first few days of the siege nothing much happened. Justiniani made an ineffectual sortie, which was not repeated. The Osmanli fleet, under Baltoglu, moved in to the foot of Pera Hill, and then on to its anchorage in the Bosphorus. Since it was said at the time that 10,000 Turks made less noise than 100 Christians, Constantine hoped to profit by the din, so at the Emperor's request the crews of Trevisano's and Diedo's galleys came ashore, numbering a thousand men, and marched along the entire length of the landward walls, to prove to the observant Turks that they would have to fight Italians as well as Greeks.

Mahomet's reply was to move his entire line, which had been 2 kilometers from the city, to within 1,200 meters.

At morning and evening, he made it his particular task pointedly to unroll his rug, turn toward Mecca (also roughly the direction of Hagia Sophia) and pray. He also made a point of sending tellahs, or criers, through the camp with ulemas to visit each regiment in turn in order to incite the true believer.

From his tent flap to Basilica was only a short stroll. There were 9 other great cannon, 56 of lesser dimension, and many of a standard size. Catapults stationed between the cannon were useful for picking defenders off the walls.

Apart from his troops, he had tailors, pastry cooks, artisans, petty traders, and others who follow an army in hope of profit or plunder. There were no prostitutes. Mahomet frowned on this type of diversion during campaign, though he had no objection to it once the campaign was over. He also had a good many Greek troops, the author of the *Lament for the Fall of the City* informing us they were there to the number of 30,000.

"But who in fact besieged the city?" wrote Leonard of Chios

afterward. "And who has taught the Turks the military art, if not the Christians themselves? I have seen with my own eyes that the Greeks, the Latins, the Germans, the Hungarians, and men of every other Christian nationality were mixed up with the Turks, and with them together stormed the walls."

As has been often pointed out, disintegration of character is the cause, not the result, of the fall of a state, and is first shown in the demand for material goods growing stronger than the demand for the appurtenances proper to pride. This being so, even in its depleted state the former capital of the former Empire would yield much booty.

XVII

THE Turkish bombardment began on the 11th of April, a signal being given for the first salvo from Basilica (though she could be fired only seven times a day, she was also to be fired once each night as a reminder of the next seven salvos to come). This made a flash of white fire, much smoke, an uproar, a heavy whistling sound, a bang, and a heavy thud which seemed to jar the whole city. Men, women, and children rushed out of their houses, crossed themselves, and cried "Kyrie Eleison. What is going to happen now?"

What happened was eight days of continuous bombardment. Nor were the citizens pleased by the size of the balls. The Greek cannon could throw nothing heavier than a 150-pound ball. The smallest Turkish discharged a 200-pounder, the heavier, 500-pounders, while Basilica could fling almost three times that amount of granite against the Romanus Gate. At first the low velocity of the balls seemed to make the bombardment ineffective. It was believed at the time that the longer the gun, the greater the effect produced by it. Nor did the Turks at first know how to calculate a trajectory, so their aim was bad. But by repetition they managed to shake the walls. The inhabitants hung down bales of cotton, tapestry, anything, as padding, and much of their efforts were expended in repairing the breaches with house timbers and what lay to hand, whether from a church or not.

Their own artillery they dared not mount on the towers, for the land walls were too narrow to permit of their recoil, and besides they shook them to their foundations when they went off.

Early in the siege Basilica blew up, killing its founder, Orban. This caused less inconvenience to the besiegers than one might suppose, for Mahomet, who foresaw everything, had had several more cast to the same size, and one of these was moved up. Orban, however, proved more difficult to replace, and it was not for some time possible to obtain such good advice about the cannon's nature and abilities.

Mahomet also released sappers into the fosse in an effort to mine the walls (the cannon had by now been advanced almost to the fosse). Johannes Grant, the most experienced artilleryman on the Byzantine side, though advising that the walls would not support the Greek cannon, did manage to deal with the sappers in his own experienced explosive way. They were not, among other things, though determined, very competent sappers; the ground under the walls was mostly bedrock; and Grant, who had been trained as a miner, knew all there then was to know about tunneling.

On April 12th, at about one o'clock in the afternoon, the Turkish fleet came in sight of Constantinople but attempted nothing, and moving toward the Bosphorus, stood off Diplokynion. Barbaro counted 145 ships. Diplokynion, beyond Galata and Pera, was about two miles up the Bosphorus on the European shore, but clearly visible from the walls and towers of the city. For the time being, the fleet hovered there, except for small patrols sent out into the waters around Byzantium.

Between the 12th of April and the 18th nothing much happened. The bombardment went on continuously each day but had little effect, since the Turks had yet to learn how to aim, and Orban was dead. He had strengthened Basilica, shortly before it blew him up, with iron hoops. Basilica's replacement was also strengthened with iron hoops.

The Greeks tried to lessen the effect of the impact of the balls by cushioning the walls with a mortar made of brick and chalk dust. Flights of arrows arched each way, and sometimes clattered in the sky and fell to neutral ground. There were a few rifles with long, cumbersome barrels, a recent innovation of which the Greeks, for once, had more examples than the

Turks. What they lacked was saltpeter. Most of the rifles were given to the defenders of the Romanus Gate.

Ambassadors from John Hunyadi, the now Regent of Hungary, arrived at the Turkish camp to announce that he had resigned the regency and surrendered power into the hands of his ward, King Vladislas, and that therefore, in order to permit the new king freedom of action, he was returning the three-year truce signed by him with the Turks and wished his own copy of it, deposited with the Turks, back. This action, inspired probably by agents from the Vatican, was a diplomatic hint that the Hungarians might possibly be induced to march against the Turks if the siege continued (Hunyadi had already offered to do so, if Constantine would cede to him the at present reduced city of Selymbria, and a few other properties).

The ambassadors were allowed, and indeed induced, to watch the bombardment of the walls. They found the way in which this was being done so ludicrous that they laughed out loud. The Turks would never be able to make so much as a dint in the walls if they persisted in firing the guns the way they had been doing, said the ambassadors, forgetting the purpose of their embassy in absorption in a technical problem, for some of them were military officers, and in a fit of nonsectarian ballistic enthusiasm taught the Turkish artillery officers how to level their guns properly, how to fire in volleys, and how to aim to cut the wall in triangular sections, in order to produce a practicable breach, one ball at each point. The Greeks attributed another motive to these impromptu lessons. Phrantzes, Ducas, Chalcochondyles and Barbaro all report that the Hungarians *wished* Constantinople to fall, because a Serbian hermit had allowed himself to say that Christendom would not be rid of the Turks until it did.

It seems a strange prophecy for a Serbian to deliver himself of, Serbia being more Orthodox than given to the Latin Rite; however, perhaps he was himself a heretic.

Their aim corrected, the Turks battered away with a will, and the Hungarian ambassadors took the road back to Buda, along which before many years the Turks would follow them;

Buda, like Constantinople, was esteemed by the Osmanlis an excellent site for a capital.

The 18th was a fine day, warm and balmy and clear. The moon being full and there being no clouds, that evening the Bosphorus looked like a pewter platter; the city itself was washed in deep blue shadow. Bombarding and sniping had gone on as usual, but fallen off at dusk.

The constant firing of the past week had badly damaged the outer wall, and partially collapsed the two towers of the inner, near the Romanus Gate, in the declivity of the Lycus valley. The walls of the fosse had also been crumbled at this place, and the fosse partially filled in. It had been necessary for Justiniani to supervise the building of a stockade, for which crates of vine cuttings, old beams, and timber were used, the whole being topped by barrels of earth, to be used as sheltering crenelations.

At nine o'clock that night big drums began to roll on the hillsides, followed by cymbals, horns, and pipes. This music passed through the entire Turkish line, echoing on the soft air. Then, supported by archers and slingers, the Turks charged the wall en masse, but only at the Romanus Gate, flickering through the deep shadows in the moonlight, yelling and shouting.

Though unwilling to risk his entire force in a general attack, Mahomet wished to see how weakened the defenders were.

Inside the city, vigils were being held in most of the churches, and these were well attended. The congregations held lighted tapers in their hands. When they prostrated themselves, the flames of these wavered. Since it was so balmy an evening, a good many people were sauntering through the streets. But a distant yelling could now be heard, and the alarm sounded from the walls five miles away was taken up by the church bells. The noise was deafening. The congregations, terrified, rushed out of the churches and into hiding. Smoke from the bombardment drifted over the walls and into the city. It was acrid and tickling. It grew so thick on the walls that the combatants could not see one another.

Supported by cuirassiers, archers, ballista, and lancers, the attacking Turks tried with hooks and secateurs to bring down the barrels which formed crenelations, so the defenders could be picked off by archers. They also tried to fire the stockade, but could not do so, and to scale the wall itself.

The Emperor began to believe this was the beginning of a full-scale attack, since "we Christians were not yet ready for it." Fortunately he was wrong. After four hours of fighting, the Turks were beaten off and retired, leaving about 200 killed and no one counted how many wounded, to moan and scream on the glacis. The final attackers, however, lingered, and did not take their last departure until three A.M. The defenders were so exhausted that when the Emperor went his rounds of the positions just before dawn, he found several of the sentinels and guards had fallen asleep at their posts. The Greeks and Italians not only had to fight, but also to repair the wall. It was this double duty which wore them out. No one in the city offered to help.

When dawn of the 19th came, and during the morning, the Turks removed their wounded from the glacis and then burned the bodies of their dead, this being their usual practice during a siege, probably for reasons of sanitation. Their fires looked pale but constant in the morning air.

Inside the city a *Te Deum* was celebrated, to offer thanks for divine assistance given during the successful repulse of this attack. After it, the Emperor held a council with all his commanders and some civil state officials present. The latter of these held to the opinion that the attack of the previous night was connected with Hunyadi's cancellation of his truce with the Osmanli, being a last attempt to take the city before Mahomet raised the siege. In order that Mahomet might raise the siege without loss of face, it was decided to send an embassy to him to ask for peace on any conditions he might make, short of surrender of the city to him.

On this day, most probably, but perhaps a day or two before, the Turkish fleet, under Baltoglu, sailed from Diplokynion and attempted to force the boom at the mouth of the Golden

Horn. Torches were fired at the defending ships, also arrows tipped with burning cotton flares. Others tried to cut the anchor cables of the Greek vessels. But even at this late date, the Greeks were superior to the Turks in the arts both of navigation and of shipbuilding. The Greek vessels rode higher in the water than the Turkish, which gave them the advantage when it came to hurling weapons down upon their attackers. Large stones had been taken up into the rigging, out onto the yards and bowsprits, and the dropping of these staved in many bottoms. Fires were extinguished quickly. To do him justice, Kyr Lucas Notaras—though the only real way to do him justice is to condemn him out of hand—was in charge of this defense and conducted it ably. The Turkish fleet withdrew.

If it was beaten back on this occasion, the events of the next day were to prove how useless it was, 350 accumulated small boats or no.

April 20th saw the only victory the defenders were decisively to have, as well as the only succor they were to receive.

Because the Act of Union had finally been proclaimed, both the Emperor and all the inhabitants of the city, whether defenders or not, lived in daily expectation of the appearance of a Western fleet (even Mahomet's advisers were nervous about its probable advent). As it happened, no fleet had been sent. But during March and the first half of April, three Genoese galleys, loaded with soldiers, arms, and bullion for Constantinople, had been held at Chios by northerlies. The Emperor had handed down an order allowing all Genoese ships bringing provisions to the city to enter the port duty free, as an inducement to the greedy. On the other hand, Critobulus and Leonard Archbishop of Chios claim they had actually been sent for the defense as well as the supply of the city. At any rate, for whatever reason, they were freighted and they came. About April 15th they reached the Dardanelles, having been joined on the way by an imperial transport commanded by Flantanelas, on its way from Sicily with a cargo of grain. On the 16th the wind strengthened, carrying the ships into the Sea of Marmora, and on the 20th, at about ten in the morning, their crews could see the dome of Hagia Sophia on the horizon.

When this tiny armada of four was first sighted from the city, the Turkish fleet was anchored at the Double Columns, or Diplokynion. Lookouts posted at the Marmora mouth of the Bosphorus soon brought the news. Mahomet at once rode the two miles from his camp to Diplokynion, crossing the Golden Horn high up, and gave orders that the boats were to be prevented from reaching and entering the boom. So the Turkish main fleet raised anchor and sailed to meet them. This was the first real naval engagement of the Turkish navy, with the odds 145 large boats to 4, and those 145 crowded with the best fighting men procurable. It seemed an easy enough task.

There is some doubt as to where exactly this engagement took place. It seems, however, to have been fought in the triangle between Seraglio Point, Pera (in the modern sense of that term; the area behind Galata), and Scutari on the Asiatic shore.

The walls of the city were lined with spectators.

Baltoglu, according to Critobulus, believed the matter was over before it had begun, as who would have not with those odds. The Turks rowed forward with shouts of incipient and amused victory, their oars making a continuous splash, their trumpets sounding over the waters. Leonard says that drums were also triumphantly beaten, but these may merely have served to give the stroke to the oarsmen. The only thing against the Turks was the wind, which is why they used their oars.

The four Greek ships held to a steady course, aiming for the Tower of the Megademetrius, which stood on the ancient Acropolis as a beacon and navigation point. They were well supported by a brisk southerly. Ships attended by a southerly had to stand well out from the point if they were to enter the Golden Horn without mishap.

Seldom has a battle had a better-seated audience. The maintenance galleries of Hagia Sophia, the walls, and the roofs of the palaces, of the Sphendone (royal box) of the Hippodrome, even the columns of the ancient Emperors—any high points, in short—were crowded with spectators, all shielding their eyes against the morning sun, which made the ships black blobs on the magnesium flare of the water.

Boats entering the Horn did not attempt to tack until they were opposite Seraglio Point, where they had to make a curve into the mouth of the Bosphorus in order to round the land and current configuration of the northeast direction of the point, and so reach harbor. The Genoese boats had short strong hulls, high bows, and extremely high poops, and carried enormous mainsails.

As the Genoese and imperial boats approached the straits, and so came into full view of those crowded on the roof of the Sphendone, the Turkish admiral, on the poop of his own trireme, ordered them to lower their sails. When they did not do so, he gave the orders to attack. This was done, but not only was the wind blowing against the Turkish boats but they were ill designed, and a heavy sea was running at the time. Since the Greek and Italian vessels rode higher in the water and were built with higher sides, and the Turkish had lower sides and rode heavily, boarding attacks were easily beaten off with axes and boathooks. The attackers then shot arrows and fire darts, but in a heavy sea, on uncertain decks, against the wind, could achieve little.

The relieving vessels bore on to Seraglio Point, where, unfortunately, the wind abruptly fell. The sails flapped idle, directly opposite the Acropolis. Having the advantage now, the Turks closed to the attack. The Turks had oars. The Genoese did not. But the Genoese were not quite sitting ducks, for after a southerly in those waters, the current sets in the direction of the Galata shore of the Golden Horn, so, though without propulsive means of their own, they were nevertheless carried to their destination. Also, they might hope to depend upon those few sudden gusts which always come thereabouts when the southerly has dropped. The battle was therefore fought between Seraglio Point and Tophana on the shore east of Galata, outside of the walls of that uncooperative suburb. At one time, says Phrantzes, the ships were within a stone's throw of the harbor walls. The Byzantine ships inside the boom were, because of the calm, unable to give assistance.

Not only did everyone of any importance in Byzantium watch the battle. Mahomet and his suite watched it, too. They had no more doubts than Baltoglu of its outcome.

The admiral first ordered the four ships surrounded but in a wide circle, and proposed to pellet them to the bottom. But the Genoese were expert sailors and not only extinguished fire arrows and such, but fired in their turn on the Turks. Seeing his tactics to be useless, Baltoglu ordered his own ships to advance and board, himself making for the imperial transport, the largest of the four. He ran his bow against her poop and tried to board. For the between two to three hours the fight lasted, there he stayed, but he did not succeed in boarding her.

Neither did his forces fare any better. The Genoese had body armor against lighter missiles, and simply chopped off any hands appearing over the rails. The sea became a detritus of spent arrows. Five triremes surrounded one Genoese ship, 30 large caiques the second, and 40 transports the third. But the sea was high and the ships packed so closely that, the Turkish vessels being lighter built, a good many of them were damaged by being smacked against the good sound Italian hulls, as well as against each other.

The imperial ship, of course, had Greek fire, a material little used at sea, since it was as dangerous to the user as to the recipient. Small boats, however, were sent up in flames by means of this, though Baltoglu could not be dislodged.

The imperial ship was weaker, if only because so much older, than the Genoese; therefore, despite the seas, all four ships were lashed together. Thus lashed they moved, says Pusculus, like four towers.

Mahomet became so infuriated that he spurred his horse into the sea from the Galata shore and forced it so far out his saddle was awash, in an effort to shout commands and directions at the fleet even while he struggled with the horse. When nobody would pay any attention, he stood in the stirrups and cursed. Turkish is a language excellently adapted to cursing, the vocabulary is rich, and his knowledge of it extensive. Many of his suite followed him, endeavoring to ride through the water to the ships.

The Turks made a final effort. It was now late afternoon. The sun was beginning to go down. At this time the wind suddenly freshened, became a gale, and the four ships, their sails suddenly filling, lashed together as they were, smashed through everything in front of them. At the same time the wind, being against them, beat the Turkish boats back. Mahomet went on shouting orders at Baltoglu but could not make himself heard. The Genoese and imperial victors reached the boom. Baltoglu retired to Diplokynion.

After darkness had fallen, three galleys went outside the boom, with a blowing of trumpets to make their force sound the larger, since they feared attack. The three galleys made the noise of twenty. Also fearing attack, the Turkish fleet remained on the defensive, at anchor. The four ships were safely towed inside the boom, which was closed again. Flantanelas and the three Genoese captains, Cantaneo, Novara, and Balanere, received a heroes' welcome. And they had brought supplies.

While this battle had been going on, the bombardment on the landward walls continued, and on the 21st an important tower near the Romanus Gate, the Bactantinian, collapsed with an adjacent part of the outer wall and slid down into the fosse and the courtyard behind. Had the Turks stormed with 10,000 men then and there, said Barbaro, they could have taken the town. The Turks, not expecting any such result from their fire and not prepared for an assault, held off. Mahomet, who might have been there to spur them on, had gone shortly after dawn to Diplokynion with 10,000 troops, to have his way with Suleiman Bey Baltoglu, his admiral. He cursed him out and threatened to have him beheaded or impaled. The admiral explained his conduct, of which he had no reason to be ashamed. His own men spoke up for him, pointing out that he had been severely wounded in the eye. After some hesitation, Mahomet decided to be merciful and merely had the man given a hundred lashes, stripped of all honors, degraded, and whatever he possessed given to the Janissaries.

The naval defeat had whipped Mahomet into a fury. It was at this inauspicious moment that he called a council to debate upon the Emperor's peace offer, which had arrived the previous evening.

Chalil Pasha, the vizier, who was known but not trusted for his Greek sympathies, argued that the peace offer formed an excellent pretext for withdrawing honorably from the siege, an action he advised insofar as the unsuccessful assaults on the walls (another had been made after Justiniani had fired some of his small cannon to great effect, though five of the battlements had been knocked down by it and one of the balls had buried itself in the walls of St. Kyriake, near the Pempton Gate; though spurred on by Mahomet himself, shouting "Jagma, jagma!" ["Pillage, pillage!"], the Turks had again been beaten back) and the ridiculous result of the naval battle had shown that there was no telling how long the siege might go on, and that with each day the chances of a Christian army appearing to Mahomet's rear were increased. Chalil therefore suggested that the taking of Constantinople be put off until some more favorable time, and that peace be made with the Emperor on terms which would drain every last ounce of force or financial power from the city. As a beginning, he suggested a Byzantine tribute of 70,000 ducats a year.

Mahomet was one of those people who see in defeat nothing but a further incentive to victory. It is a trait common enough to young men, before their elders grind them down into a conformable maturity. Inspired by his naval defeat and the sight of a Genoese cargo ship captured at Sinope, he ordered a monster vessel to be built of 3,000 hogsheads displacement. It was to prove too unseaworthy to float, but he did not know that yet.

The war council was divided; which is to say, under so strong a commander, no more than that one group jockeyed for favor anticipating his decision in one way, and another group in another. The ulema Ahmed Kurani and Zagan Pasha, both military men, disagreed with Chalil Pasha. They had been trained for war, therefore war was what they wanted. Because of the difficutly of holding together troops and of keeping them supplied, nothing was feared more during the medieval and early Renaissance period than a siege. Men were impressed for at the most not more than three months. At the end of that time armies drifted away. But Mahomet having solved both these problems, they were therefore no problem. It was decided to continue the siege.

With this decision in mind, the Emperor's envoys were told that peace would be acceptable only on the condition of the city's surrender, in which event Mahomet would cede the entire Peloponnesus to Constantine, guarantee his sovereignty during his lifetime, and undertake to compensate the Despots Demetrius and Thomas with place and pensions elsewhere. The offer was made only to be refused, and was refused; so the siege might continue. All Chalil had succeeded in doing, in exchange for a few fish stuffed with gold, was to convince the Turkish commanders they must take the city as soon as possible, without dawdling.

So far it had been attacked only from the landward side, which permitted the Greeks to concentrate their small forces. The siege would have the greater chance of being over the sooner if the town could be attacked from the seaward side as well, the defenses on the Golden Horn being the weakest; but the Golden Horn was shut off by its chain.

Mahomet had his own possible solution to this problem. Even though the Turks were so numerous before the landward walls as to make nothing visible from above except the white headdresses of the Janissaries, the red fezzes of the others, he drew off a sufficient labor force to effect his design.

So elaborate were (and so smoothly worked) his plans, that it is impossible to believe that they were so suddenly arrived at as the chronicles of the day would have us believe. Since he could not force the boom, he proposed to move part of his fleet overland from the Bosphorus to the Golden Horn, and there launch his own boats.

This would give him three advantages. The defenders would be forced to spread their forces even thinner; he could communicate with his fleet the more easily, apart from perhaps defeating the ships defending the boom from within the harbor; and he could terrorize Galata. Galata, dominated by its Tower of Christ on the hill behind it, might be neutral, but was as much concerned to preserve the privacy of the Golden Horn as were the Byzantines, though for different reasons. If he attacked Galata, the Duke of Milan and Genoa itself would probably send fleets against him. If he could bring ships overland and thus by pass Galata entirely, the neutrality of the place would no longer have any strategic or tactical significance.

As things stood, the only way he could communicate with his troops and fleet stationed behind Galata was to pass a difficult and somewhat dangerous ford across the Golden Horn, inconveniently at its farther end, near Cydaris. With Turkish ships in the estuary, he would no longer have to do this, but under their guard a pontoon bridge could be built from shore to shore.

Fourteen years before, the Venetians had set a precedent for such a maneuver by moving part of their fleet overland from the Adige to Lake Garda. In ancient Greek times a like feat had been performed across the Isthmus of Corinth. The Byzantines themselves had transported their fleet into Lake Ascanius in 1097, in order to retake Nicaea.

Mahomet had noted that behind Galata and in front of Dylokynion a small valley opened southward from the Bosphorus, on the eastern side of that hill against whose western side Galata had been built. This ravine debouched at the Golden Horn and was about five miles long. In it was the cemetery of Galata. It was known as the Valley of the Springs.

Several thousand men were sent to clear out the bush and underbrush. Timbers had been amassed, cradles had been built for the ships. Obviously preparations had been taken well in advance. But nothing had been allowed to leak out. While a narrow channel was dug all the way through the valley (actually two ravines connected) and paved with strong beams, and the beams smeared with tar, tallow and lard, Mahomet bombarded over Galata as a covering measure, perhaps to conceal the noise of his preparations. The guns were placed on the hill of St. Theodore, north of the eastern wall of Galata. Presumably the guns were trained on the ships guarding the boom. If a few cannonballs fell in Galata itself, which was also choked with black clouds of their smoke, that was not Mahomet's fault. One of the Byzantine boats was sunk by a successful shot. The others moved out of range. A hundred cannonballs were discharged anyway; they fell commendably short and destroyed houses in Galata, as well as one woman. The Galatans were thus decoyed into ignorance of what was being prepared in the valley to their rear. For the same reason, fire was also stepped up before the Romanus Gate, continuing during the night.

An army was stationed to protect the coming transit, even so. Rollers 16 feet long were placed on top of the greased planking, and a small ship was eased onto its cradle as a first trial. It was drawn by bullocks and guided, or rather supported and pushed, by soldiers, while gangs of workmen put more rollers ahead of it. The system worked better than expected. The boat moved quite easily.

So, on the night of April 21st–22nd, between 30 (Michael the Janissary), and 80 (Tedardi, Ducas) boats were moved overland. Some were pulled by hand, some by bullocks, some manipulated by pulleys, but there being a favorable breeze, Mahomet ordered the sails unfurled and flags and pennants hoisted, and could not resist the impulse to put a band of musicians on each vessel, who played martial airs and gaily piped the fleet overland. The billowing sails caught the air, the pennants flapped, the rollers creaked, the oxen flicked their tails and strained, and at the stern of each vessel men pushed, while at the sides others stood to correct any list. Anyone who has ever played with one of those silver and gilt galleons on wheels, seventeenth- or eighteenth-century trophies pushed around the commons table with the port and often containing it, must have some idea of what this spectacle must have been like, though here on the scale of life.

If the citizens of Galata knew what was going on, they gave no sign. Their motto seems to have been: See no evil, hear no evil, and sell more lard; the stench of which must have been all-pervasive, even if the sound of the fleet's moving was not. This land-borne flotilla also neatly fulfilled that prophecy from which the Turkophil Byzantines took comfort, that the city would not fall until ships were seen moving under full sail across land. Though this display of billowed sail and oars that rowed at the air was probably designed more to keep the men in good humor than to assist the passage of the boats, it did keep them in good humor, it did assist the passage of the boats, and Mahomet, who never neglected propaganda, must have been pleased to see the prophecy so exactly carried out. All night long, Zagan kept his batteries firing into the Horn to prevent any hindrance on the part of the Byzantine boats moored there.

Two or three hours after midnight, the first Turkish ship accelerated on its rollers, sped downhill and swooshed through the night into the Golden Horn, wobbled, splashed and righted itself. The others followed smoothly after.

On the other side of the city, Justiniani and his men worked feverishly to repair breaches in the wall, to such effect that they could therefore face the dawn with confidence. They were not only busy but five miles away, and therefore had no idea what was happening.

Tradesmen and fishermen are early risers. So are those who attend morning mass. The garrison on the harbor walls, which was under the command of Notaras, began to wake up. What they saw was the Turkish fleet in their own harbor. A pontoon bridge from shore to shore was already under construction. Zagan Pasha's batteries fired a minatory shot from time to time. Whether Turkish bands struck up a mocking air, we are not told. The citizens rushed to the walls, which were low on the harbor side and thus harder to defend, and a good many of them lost all hope that day. The Emperor was chiefly troubled by the new need to spread his forces thinner over the defenses; and about Notaras, who refused to cooperate with any troops not strictly Orthodox, which meant with practically nobody, since the effective troops were all Genoese or Venetian and hence Latin.

The pontoon bridge was being constructed rapidly. It stretched from the Galata shore to the angle of the city walls, near the ancient amphitheatre, and was supported on large oil and wine storage jars, their mouths in the water, to form a series of buoyant air traps. Work had also been begun on a raft for a floating battery.

A meeting was hastily called at the Church of St. Mary, probably in the Venetian quarter, since the Venetian bailo appears to have convoked it. Only twelve men attended, only twelve being found who trusted one another. Justiniani was, of course, one of them. It was thought that the Christian ships in the harbor should attack the newly arrived Turkish fleet, but this idea was abandoned because it would have meant getting the consent of the Genoese at Galata, who were unwilling openly to resist Mahomet. The next notion was to destroy the Turkish batteries on Pera Hill, and after they could no longer protect the Turkish boats, to destroy the latter with Greek fire. Cocco, the captain of a Trebizond galley, suggested ignoring the Genoese at Galata and making a dash to burn the Turkish ships. He himself volunteered to attempt to do this, and his offer was accepted. In order to be successful, the attempt must be kept secret and it must be done at once.

Cocco chose two 500-ton transports, armored them against cannon fire with bales of wool and cotton, and chose two large and two smaller and swifter galleys to accompany them. The smaller boats were rowed by 70 oarsmen. Each was accompanied by a large boat. The large ships were to screen the smaller, which at the last moment were to dart forward and set fire to the Turkish fleet.

These ships were to collect together one hour after sunset on the 24th, in order to attack at midnight. Late that night the captains met for the last time in Diedo's cabin. Some Genoese captains, who had got wind of the scheme, asked that it be postponed so they might join. Since to refuse would have been to show jealousy of an ancient trade rival, Cocco and the other Venetian captains agreed to the postponement. The Genoese needed four days for their preparations, during which time Mahomet became aware of what was going on and strengthened his batteries, some of which had been moved down to the Galata shore.

During the 25th, 26th, and 27th of April, the bombardment of the landward walls continued, but the Greeks and Latins still managed to fill the breaches at night. Nonetheless the defenders were growing tired, they had too much to do, the odds were at least 20 to 1 against them, and the Turks could replace their troops with fresh men whenever they chose. A rumor began to circulate in the city that food was running short.

Meanwhile a man called Faiuzzo, a Genoese, finding out that something unusual was going on on the defenders' ships in the Horn, slipped over to the Turkish camp and betrayed the Venetians' plans. No doubt he was scrupulous, at the same time, to preserve the neutrality of Galata.

Since Ducas, Critobulus, Pusculus, Archbishop Leonard and, most importantly, Barbaro, who says that the Podestà of Galata himself sent a man to inform the Sultan, all agree that this happened, later historians profess to doubt it. However they found out, the Turks knew what was planned, and the Greeks and Venetians did not know that they knew.

Two hours before dawn of the 28th, two galleys, commanded by Trevisano and Zacharia Grione, put out from anchorage. Three fustae, or swifter smaller galleys, accompanied them. These were laden with gunpowder, Greek fire, tar, and anything else that would burn. The two great galleys covered the others. A beacon fire surprised everyone by suddenly flaring up from the top of Galata Tower. Cocco, growing impatient and in command of one of the swifter fusta, drew ahead of the others. The Turks fired, and on the second volley destroyed his boat. "Before you could say ten paternosters, she had sunk," says Barbaro. This completely disrupted the attack. Because of the darkness and the smoke of the Turkish bombardment, nothing could be seen. Trevisano's ship was also struck and, filling rapidly, had to be abandoned. The remaining 70-odd Turkish boats now moved out to attack. The fight went on for an hour and a half. At the end of that time each side retired. The Greeks and Venetians had lost 80 or 90 men. The Turks had lost one ship.

Trevisano and most of his men managed to save their lives by swimming for the Byzantine shore, which was lined with spectators, while the one Turkish boat destroyed, having been hit by Greek fire, lit up the harbor while it burned to the waterline.

Some of those who tried to save themselves by swimming unfortunately in the confusion swam the wrong way, hauled themselves out of the sea on the northern or Turkish shore, were captured by the Turks, led back down to the shore, and decapitated to the number of 40. Their heads were allowed to float into the harbor, where they bobbled about like cabbages among the flotsam until they sank.

In reprisal for this reprisal, a large number (Phrantzes says 260) of Turkish prisoners were taken from the city prisons and hanged from the highest part of the city walls on the harbor side, while the Turks watched in their turn.

April 29th was devoted to recriminations and to a rest period on both sides. The Venetians, who had lost 90 of their best soldiers and sailors, charged the Genoese with treason. The Genoese blamed Venetian ignorance of navigation and Cocco's foolhardiness. Accusations were followed by threats, the Venetians and Genoese guarding the walls were about to attack each other, and the Emperor was compelled to assemble all his commanders of both nations and to say to them: "I pray you, my brethren, be of one mind and work together. Is it not enough of misery that we have to fight against such fearful odds outside the walls? For God's sake let us not have any conflicts among ourselves within them!"

This proved effective for the time being. But only for the time being. Meanwhile Basilica II went on firing at the Romanus Gate and shook the wall badly, carrying away the upper part of it to make a breach five feet wide. Since night was coming on, and since the gun had to be cooled for at least an hour after firing, another shot was not attempted, and so repairs could once more be made before dawn came.

Mahomet had his bridge finished by the end of the month. It rested on 1,000 wine casks, lashed together and planked. It was about 2,000 feet long, and five soldiers could walk on it abreast quite easily. Floating batteries on pontoons were moored to the bridge here and there along its length.

The Emperor found it necessary to shift part of his troops from the landward walls to the point where the bridge reached the city shore.

On May 1st, the Turks concentrated the fire of several inferior cannon on the earth- and wood-filled breach in the walls which Basilica II had made the day before. The gun was fired. Its ball went too high, sailed over the wall, and smashing against the side of the nearest church inside the city, shattered its brickwork to a powder.

At noon, just as Basilica II was about to be fired again, Justiniani let off a shot of his own which hit the big cannon and knocked it off its mount. This infuriated Mahomet, who ordered an assault on the walls. The alarm bells of the city were rung at once, and the Emperor came in person to encourage the defenders. The fighting went on until shortly after dark, at which time the Turks retreated.

The Turks had noticed that the defenders left their stations on the towers to go home for their noon meal, and had taken advantage of this lull to go down into the moat and attempt to pull down with hooks and secateurs the bundles and earth-filled bales used to stuff the breach. The storm troops had followed.

On May 2nd the Emperor called the Greek troops together and scolded them for exposing the city to the danger of being taken by surprise, the Turks not necessarily taking dinner at the same hour.

The soldiers replied that they had had no choice, since nothing was brought them to eat. Organization was bad and supplies, as rumor had it, were running low. Even in the city, they had to fight to get food for their families.

Shocked to hear this, the Emperor ordered that among those unwilling or unable to defend the city, some at least should be compelled to carry food and drink to their defenders on the walls, whose families should also be fed at the public expense. A sort of canteen was set up, and a relief committee. At the same time, Constantine ordered Demetrius Cantacuzenos, the commander of the reserve forces, to inspect the position several times a day, to make sure the men were at them and that they were being fed, and to make a house-to-house search for men who, though capable of bearing arms, had preferred to remain indoors until there was no longer any necessity of their doing so. In their defense, it may be said that the armor of those days weighed 40 pounds, and few of them had the musculature to support it—or, for that matter, the practice required if one was to move about freely in it—and that the torsion of a bow was beyond them.

On May 3rd, the Greeks placed cannon on the harbor walls and opened fire on the Turkish flotilla, which obligingly moved out of range. The Turks moved guns down to the foreshore and fired back. This went on for ten days, to little purpose on either side, though at first the Greeks managed to destroy a few of the Turkish ships. The effective range of the guns was not so great as the width of the Golden Horn at this point, which according to Barbaro was half an Italian mile.

In the city it was well known that Venice, Naples, and the Pope had promised to send relief, and that an agreement had been made with the Venetian bailo to this effect on January 26th. As a result the western horizon was watched 24 hours a day for the appearance of the first sails. They did not appear. They did not exist.

Twelve men in a brigantine were sent out, disguised as Turks and flying a Turkish flag, at midnight from the boom, to search for this illusory fleet, as far as Euboea if necessary. Envoys were also sent into the Morea, to the islands and to Europe.

A general council was again held. The military commanders said it was clear that the Turks were preparing for a general assault, and that since the walls were weak and their defenders weary, they could not speak confidently of being able to hold it off. The senators and prelates, together with the Patriarch, advised the Emperor to leave the city and to retreat to some secure place, saying that so soon as the people of the provinces heard that the Emperor was alive and safe, they would volunteer to defend him, and that these imaginary volunteers, together with the armies of his brothers Demetrius and Thomas, and the Albanians under Scanderbeg, would force the Sultan to lift the siege. Even Justiniani supported this suggestion, placing his ships at the Emperor's disposal.

The Emperor knew better. There were no provinces. He also knew his brothers. He listened patiently and quietly, and then thanked his leaders for their advice.

"I know that my going out of the city might be of some benefit to me, inasmuch as all that you foresee might really happen. But it is impossible for me to go away! How could I leave the churches of Our Lord, and His servants the clergy, and the throne, and my people in such a plight? What would the world say of me? I pray of you, in future do not say anything to me but, 'Sire, nay, do not leave us.' Never, never will I leave you. I am resolved to die here with you."

At this, he turned his head aside, and the Patriarch and the others wept. Everybody wept. Besides, those at the top cannot escape. They are too prominent. They can only suicide themselves or be caught and killed. Exile, poverty, and the condescension of the Latin states did not appeal to Constantine. Death did. On this or some other occasion like it, he also expressed his willingness "to follow the example of the Good Shepherd who lays down his life for his sheep." What he did not propose to do was lay it down because they were sheep.

On May 4th, at night, another attempt was made to destroy the Turkish ships in the bay, this time undertaken by the captain of one of Justiniani's ships, but the Turks were on the alert and sank the attacker with one broadside.

On the 5th, the Turks, who had moved their guns onto the slope of Pera Hill, opened fire on the Venetian ships guarding the boom. It must be remembered the Galatan Genoese ships were also in the bay, anchored neutral in front of Galata. The Turks fired over them, but a ball of 200 pounds hit a Genoese merchant ship of 300 tons' burden, laden with luxury silks, and sank her. Firing continued all day, and the ships at the boom sought shelter at a Galata anchorage.

The merchants of Galata went at once to complain of this attack against a neutral. They said that they had not destroyed the ships transported overland, and wished to be left in peace in consequence. According to Ducas, the grand vizier apologized and promised full compensation once Constantinople had been taken. According to Phrantzes, the Sultan himself replied that it had not been a merchantman but a Genoese pirate vessel, and to return home at once. Whichever answer is the true one, they returned home at once, and they did not receive compensation.

On the 6th, the Turks moved still more cannon up opposite the Romanus Gate, and fired steadily until dusk. By evening, a wide breach had been opened near the gate itself. To prevent its being filled, the guns went on firing all night long. Justiniani made no attempt to fill it, but instead built a stockade and tower on the inner side of the wall.

On this day, fighting broke out between the Venetian and Genoese defenders, chiefly because of the anomalous conduct of Galata. Each accused the other of being poised to flee on his own ships at any moment. The Venetians replied that they had unshipped their rudders and deposited both rudders and sails within the city. The Genoese said that though they had not done this, it was not because they planned to desert, but only because they had wives and children at Galata, and so had no intention of abandoning the city. This is the sort of tight reasoning that can only be made convincing by shouting. Fighting came next, but once more the Emperor managed to make peace between them.

On the 7th the Turks went on widening the breach by means

of concentrated fire, the cannonballs either shattering, or else bounding against each other to accumulate on the other side of the wall. These were a godsend to the Greeks, who were running low on ammunition. They gathered them up and, if the balls were small enough to fit the bores of their own cannon, promptly fired them back. It was expected that a combined assault by land and sea would take place on this day, for there had been both troop movements and naval movements on a large scale. No naval assault was made, but at dusk the firing ceased and at eleven that night Turks raced across the glacis, swarmed down into and up out of the moat, and hurried toward the breach. Barbaro says there were 30,000 of them. The siege was now entering its second month.

The Greeks and Latins, under the command of Justiniani, went from their stockade to the breach and fought off the attackers, though Justiniani was almost cut down by a Janissary. Reinforcements were brought up from inside the town, and the Turks finally withdrew. The next day the twelve Venetian leaders who formed the Emperor's council decided that Trevisano and his 400 men should leave the boom and defend the walls at that point where the pontoon bridge reached the Byzantine shore. The men were unwilling, and it was not before the 13th that they took up their new positions. Their ships were partly disarmed so that the cannon could be moved to the walls and left in the imperial harbor, near the Constantinople end of the chain. Trevisano's place as commander of the fleet was taken over by Diedo.

Bombardment continued. The Turks were now using smaller balls in larger numbers, though between the 8th and the 11th of May, 100 or 120 of the 800- to 1,200-pound size were flung against or over the walls.

The defenders were too busy to give way to despair, but the citizens of the city were becoming more and more depressed. Services in the churches were increasing. They were according to the Greek Rite. Hagia Sophia was still deserted, and that the defenders held to the Latin Rite was noted and held against them, since it probably explained why the Turks would not go away—at least to the minds of the extremely pious. Of the ikons in the city, that of Mary Mother of God was the most popular, and there were queues to kiss it. It was reputed to have saved the city once already and might do so again, despite the Act of Union. It was exposed to the donations of the pious in Our Lady Chodogetria Church, near the Acropolis. The only persons to use Hagia Sophia were the Emperor and those of his suite who were either compelled to attend or else did not care about the Union one way or the other.

Mahomet's tactics were to bombard the Romanus Gate incessantly but at the same time make unexpected assaults in different quarters at different hours, in order to weaken the defenders. On the 12th his cannon made a breach in the walls near the imperial palace of the Hebdomon, to the south of the Blachernae quarter, in the district known as Calligaria, near the so-called Palace of the Porphyrogenitus, which dominates the walls there. Before the Greeks could repair the breach, several thousand troops had stormed it. The Greeks fell back, but were supported by Nicephorus Palaeologus, in command of the cavalry and reserves, who was stationed not far away. Theodore Karystos, who commanded the Charisius Gate, and the indispensable Justiniani also came up, other troops were called from their more distant stations, and the worst assault yet attempted was beaten back vigorously; but the Turks by weight of numbers began to gain. Though the section of wall before the Porphyrogenitus was double and the fighting thus presumably went on in the area between the two walls, defenses immediately to the north became a confused nightmare of less well-built walls and discontinuous abutments, the imperial palace at Blachernae itself being put in a state of defense, and partially bricked and shored up to form a double wall.

The Emperor and his entourage were at Hagia Sophia, at a night service, which took two to three hours. This could not be interrupted, but as soon as it was over, the Emperor hurried into one of the halls nearby and conferred with his commanders. Phrantzes recommended a sortie, first as a moral rebuke, second to capture much-needed provisions. Notaras objected to this, as did the prefect of the city. They felt it would be too dangerous. "We may well say," said Notaras, "that we have been fighting already for five months, and if it is God's will we can fight as many months longer, but without God's help, whatever we do, we shall all fall, and the city will be lost." He dated the siege from the previous November, and does not seem to have believed in hampering God's will by anything so trivial as assistance.

While this disagreement was going on, a messenger arrived to say that the Turks were at the Hebdomon. Without pausing to argue with Notaras, the Emperor galloped through the streets, against crowds of frightened people, and met some soldiers fleeing from the walls toward the Acropolis. He stopped them and ordered them to their posts, but his bodyguard had to force them back with swords and lances.

Arriving at the Hebdomon, Constantine found that the Turks had penetrated the city itself and were fighting Greek and Latin volunteers in the streets around the palace. He had a few soldiers with him, his presence was inspiriting, and he managed to drive the Turks back through the empty disused halls of the palace, through the breach in the wall, and into the moat. He was so excited that he spurred his horse into the breach, and would have pursued the Turks into the moat itself if his German guards had not grabbed the reins and talked him into riding back inside the city.

The Turks by this assault lost more than 10,000 men. Nikola Goudeli, the prefect of the city, had their bodies flung outside the fortifications.

On the 14th the Turks were observed to be moving cannon from Zagan Pasha's battery on Galata Hill down toward the Cynegium. But they only paused there to rest, and then moved on to reinforce the battery opposite the Romanus Gate, an additional indication that the main attack, when it came, would come there. Therefore Justiniani's forces were reorganized and added to, chiefly from the ship crews and from less exposed positions on the walls. This gave him 400 well-armed men.

On the 15th there was another lull, but on the 16th, Mahomet, who seems to have learned that Trevisano's men were now ashore, ordered his fleet down from the Diplokynion, or Double Columns, to make one last attempt to force the boom.

No effort was made to use the Turkish fleet inside the Golden Horn for this purpose. Mahomet was afraid of any open war with the Genoese of Galata, just as much as the Galatans were afraid of war with him. As the Turkish fleet moved up to the boom from the Bosphorus, Diedo moved his ships out from the shelter of the Galata walls to defend it. He could do this safely, since the heavy artillery on Galata Hill had been removed on the 14th. But after inconclusive firing, the Turkish fleet retired.

On the 16th or 17th, the Greeks had discovered that the Turks were trying to undermine the walls. Zagan Pasha had imported professional miners from Novo Brodo in Serbia, Germans who had come there to work the silver mines. They concentrated on the Calligaria quarter, where the walls were single rather than double and where there was no ditch. The German, John Grant, found and entered the mines, and so contrived matters that the tunnel fell in, burying the Turkish workmen. John Grant was an efficient counterminer, the ground was too rocky to permit of the successful digging of tunnels, and so mining never accomplished much more than the destruction of the miners themselves and of one tower. We do not know what tower.

On the 18th of May something more dramatic was attempted. Just as dawn was breaking, the watchman at the Charisius Gate saw an odd structure on the other side of the ditch: a high wooden tower, built of beams and boards covered with oxhides, which had been wheeled up to within ten or twelve yards of the fosse. Barbaro says that the Byzantines could not have built it in a month. Mahomet had had it assembled, to plan, in one night. It was sufficiently high to overlook the outer wall. It had two stories, the lower double-armored with double boards, between which earth had been rammed down; the upper accessible from inside from the lower story by ladders. Scaling ladders could be flung from the upper story onto the wall. It was on rollers, and had three openings facing the city from which archers and riflemen on a level with the battlements could easily pick off the defenders. Its other purpose was to allow the ditch to be filled in in safety. From the rear of the tower a covered way led back to the Turkish camp.

Laborers came down this and flung down brushwood, earth, and other material to close up the fosse. Fighting went on all day, and another section of the wall of the Romanus Gate and one of its towers collapsed. During the night, Constantine and Justiniani succeeded in having the breach in the wall filled, and incredible as it may seem, built a new tower to replace the old. They also induced some volunteers to climb the counterscarp and set charges in the dry moat. The brushwood caught from the explosion of these, incinerating the guards in the siege tower, and burning it down.

In the morning there was nothing left of the siege machine, and there was a new tower, built in the night. This feat evoked admiration from the Turks. "If yesterday all the thirty-seven thousand prophets had told me that such a feat was possible, I would not have believed it," said Mahomet.

For the next few days, the Turks redoubled their efforts at undermining the city. On the 21st, with a beating of drums and sounding of trumpets, the Turkish fleet left its anchorage at Diplokynion again, two hours before dawn, and sailed toward the Golden Horn and its boom. An alarm was sounded in the city, the soldiers rushed to the seaward walls, and the citizens, trembling from a prudent distance, expected a general attack. But at about seven in the morning, the Turks changed their minds and went back to their original position. This was the last attempt to force the boom. Whether these attempts were genuine or were merely designed further to fatigue the defenders, they accomplished nothing.

During the afternoon of the same day, Grant found another Turkish mine and blew it up. The Turks brought down part of another tower, but this too was restored. On the 22nd, two more mines were detected and destroyed. In one of them, it was necessary to fight hand to hand with the Turkish workmen and soldiers in the tunnel itself before it could be caved in. On the 24th another was found, built from a dummy wooden turret outside the walls, disguised as a siege machine. The last effort to dig a mine was made on May 25th. This, a very dangerous one, actually led under the walls into the city, and if it had been detonated would have brought the walls down. But it was found in time and stopped up.

Tedardi says, "Zagan Pasha, with his men accustomed to gold and silver mines, had undermined the fortifications at fourteen different points, having commenced digging at a great distance from the walls. The Christians, on their side, by listening, discovered the positions and made countermines. By smoke, sometimes by bad odors, they suffocated the Turks in their subterranean galleries. In some places they drowned them by admitting water, and at others, fought them hand to hand."

The Greek defenders went into the ditch during the night, and through the brickwork of the counterscarp laid countermines. The explosions were spectacular, again according to Tedardi: "It was as if the lightning had struck the place, for the earth shook and with a great crash a greenish whirlwind carried the Turks into the air. Fragments of men and timber fell into the city and into the camp. The besieged ran away from the walls, and the besiegers fled back from the ditch."

On the 23rd of May, a few Turkish cavalry approached the Gate of St. Romanus, accompanied by trumpeters and flags, to make clear to the guard that they had a communication to make. A special envoy of the Sultan desired to deliver a message to the Emperor personally. After waiting some time, they were told the envoy might enter the city.

The envoy's name was Ismail Hamza, and he was Lord of Sinope and Kostamboli and related by marriage to the Padishah himself. His family were independent princes who had resisted absorption into the Osmanli Empire, but at last had been obliged to recognize the overlordship of the Sultan. They had been on friendly terms with the Greek Emperors for generations. Hamza was therefore received amicably.

He said that Mahomet said the situation of the city was hopeless, so why should the Emperor prolong the miseries of war and expose his people to the consequences of a sack of the city? He sincerely respected the Emperor, and would allow him to withdraw unmolested, with his court and his treasures, wherever he wished to go. Indeed, he once more offered suzerainty of the Peloponnesus. The inhabitants of the city would also be allowed to depart with their portable property, if they chose to go; and those who wished to remain would be guaranteed the security both of their persons and their possessions. This was the Sultan's last offer of surrender. If it was rejected, the horrors of a sack would follow.

Hamza, less as an envoy than as a confidant, tried to persuade Constantine to accept these inflexible terms. By now the walls on the land side were broken through in several places, four towers had been blown to bits, and the small garrison was exhausted. There was no hope of help arriving in time. All of which was quite true.

Worse than that, food was getting scarcer by the day, the citizens were in despair and blamed the Emperor and the government for their sufferings, and for the still greater sufferings they might now expect. The Virgin Mary had not been responsive, and had not appeared on the walls to disperse the enemy. This the Orthodox Greeks blamed entirely on the desecration of Hagia Sophia on the 12th of December.

"We have sinned, our forefathers and fathers have sinned, and it is right in God's providence that we should be punished. All these misfortunes are God's punishment. Why seek to escape punishment? Is it right to continue to fight, and to oppose God's manifest will?" Such ran the argument of the Orthodox.

Constantine would have been justified in surrendering. But he did not propose to do so. He sent the following message back to the Sultan:

"I should praise God if thou wouldst live in peace with us, as thy forefathers did; they treated my predecessors with filial respect, and this city with the greatest consideration. Whoever of them was persecuted by misfortune and came to us was safe; but whoever raised a hand against our city never prospered. Retain as thy rightful possession the territories which thou hast unjustly taken from us, and settle the amount of the tribute, which we will do our utmost to pay every year, and then go in peace. Remember, that grasping the possessions of others, thou mayest thyself become the prey of others. To surrender the city is neither in my power nor in the power of anyone here. We are all prepared to die, and shall do so without regret."

This answer was all the more firm, insofar as either on the 23rd or the 24th, early in the morning, a small boat had approached the boom closing the harbor. The crew looked to be Turks, but the Turkish patrols had given chase to it, so it was let into the boom, after an exchange with the Venetian ships set on guard there.

This was the brigantine which had been dispatched some twenty days earlier to search for the allied fleet. It had called at a good many isles of the Greek Archipelago but found the fleet nowhere, and had heard no news of it.

At first it had seemed to the commander futile to return to the doomed city, but then he and the crew had conceived it was their duty to return, at least not to leave the Emperor in uncertainty. To fear the worst is not the same as to be certain of it. The Union of the Churches had accomplished nothing. They now knew they would die, and that the city would fall.

We are not told how Constantine took the news. We do know what he did. He went on as before. There was nothing else to do.

The Turks bombarded the city all day without intermission, and when night fell, the Turkish camp was illuminated as though for a celebration, while numerous lanterns were hoisted onto the masts of the fleet at Diplokynion. There were sounds of rejoicing, Turkish music, the booming of drums, striking of cymbals, and shrill nacaires. In the city there was scarcely any sound at all but the moaning in the churches. Constantine rode out as usual to visit his outposts. At several places, he dismounted and went onto the walls to watch the fiery crescent which encircled the city. It was clearly a relaxation before the final assault.

The Emperor, in a cloak against the night breeze, said nothing, but tears ran down his cheeks. He let them fall. Then he went down and continued his rounds.

Because of the size of the city and the height of the walls, the Byzantine citizens were not aware of what was going on in the Turkish camp. But some of them, returning from the churches, noticed a red light at the base of the cupola of Hagia Sophia which crept slowly up until it reached the gilt cross on top. They thought at first it was an afterglow of the sunset, or perhaps a divine sign. It filled them with foreboding. As the light flickered away, it was like an eclipse of the moon. Someone promptly remembered another old prophecy to the effect "that the city would fall in the days when the moon should give a sign."

The monks made this quite clear. In order to calm the people, they told them, "The Holy Light which dwelt in the church of Hagia Sophia, and the angel whom God had in the time of the Emperor Justinian appointed to watch over his holy church and over the city, had that night departed to heaven in the pervading brightness so many people had seen.

"It is a sign that God meant to deliver the city into the hands of its enemies."

Constantine's answer to that was to send messengers through the half-deserted streets to summon all heads of government and the armed forces to a conference the next morning.

There had been other portents at this time. During a solemn procession, a statue of the Virgin slipped from the hands of its bearers and fell to the ground. It proved to have become so heavy that it took several prayers and a good body of men to raise it up again. The procession continued, but ran into a violent thunder and lightning storm, followed by a torrential downpour. This was taken to mean the downfall of the city was at hand, and since it was followed the next day by an unusually thick fog which hung in the streets until evening, everyone was certain of defeat. Fog in May is of rare occurrence at Constantinople. Critobulus says in his history of the event: "The Divinity hides his presence in the clouds when He descends upon the earth." This was the general belief. Millennialist doctrines had been popular ever since the year 1000, when they had proved to be untrue. It was merely a matter of accurately fixing the Last Day of His Wrath.

However such events may be taken, the weather that year was certainly unusual. And the great light that had hovered over the dome of Hagia Sophia put a panic into both sides. The followers of Mahomet wished to lift the siege (they wished to lift it anyway). Mahomet turned the prophecy against the city, instead of against the besiegers. It is impossible at this remove to determine what this light may have been. It was not just the glow from the campfires. There had been an eclipse of the moon on either the 22nd or 24th of May, but this could scarcely have produced such an illumination. All authorities testify that such an illumination took place. But their accounts differ. Flames ran around the dome and streamed upward into a single oriflame over it. Considering the previous electrical storms, it may have been St. Elmo's fire. At any rate, it so impressed the Patriarch that he and the chief dignitaries of the Church, together with members of the Senate, waited on the Emperor and advised him to leave the city and to take the Empress with him. "God has deserted the city," he said. The light fulfilled an ancient prophecy. On hearing this, the Emperor, exhausted by his own efforts not to desert it, fell into a faint, and was restored with rose water. He was again urged to flee. "If it is the will of God, whither can we fly before His anger?" he asked, and refused.

This scene, of course, is myth. There was no Empress. She had prudently never left Trebizond or Georgia. Nonetheless there was some kind of light, the Patriarch did wait upon the Emperor, and the Emperor did refuse to leave.

The siege was now at the end of its sixth week. By degrees, men, women, girls, old men, and even the priests had been persuaded to work in gangs at night to repair the broken walls, which were being bombarded in three places, but most heavily in the Lycus valley. The constant impact shook bricks loose from the walls of buildings in the city, which seemed to be in tremor continuously. The reverberations could be felt even by ships in the Golden Horn.

Constantine's council met early on the morning of the 25th of May. Some of its members were tired out from a night on the walls; the rest looked despairing. They were now absolutely certain that the end could not be far away, and that few of them would survive it. The Emperor, if he could not command the cooperation of most of the citizens, had at least earned the respect and devotion of the heads of state. It was again proposed that he might slip out of the capital, for as long as he survived there was at least hope that, even if the capital were lost, it might be recaptured.

The Patriarch Gregory had resigned his office. No new patriarch had been appointed, but the Prelate, the titular head of the clergy, supported this suggestion.

"The servants of the altar," he said, "saw unmistakable signs that it was God's will the city should now fall; but God's providence was unsearchable, and it might please Him to remember His people in mercy. If the Imperial City could not be saved, let the Emperor be saved. The Emperor should live, because in his person are centered the hopes of his people. We must all bow to the decree of the Almighty, whose mercy might return to our people as it had returned to Israel in olden times."

His auditors found this speech moving. The Slavonic Chronicler says that the Emperor, being told that the Church also believed the fall of the city to be unavoidable, fainted, and "it was necessary to use perfumed waters to revive him." He was worn out. However, he was himself again as soon as he revived, and when everyone had had his say, told them:

"My friends, if it is God's will that our city shall fall, can we escape His wrath? How many emperors, great and glorious, before me had to suffer and to die for their country? Shall I be the one to flee from it? No, I will stay and die here with you."

Phrantzes, describing this last government council, is less flowery and more laconic. "The Emperor could have left the place, but he would not," he says.

It was decided to send away the Princess Helena, the highest-ranking female Palaeologus, with the ladies of her court; and this was done.

It was also decided that all men, without distinction, must assist in repairing the walls, though there were scarcely enough troops to round them up. Justiniani complained bitterly that the citizens of the town had refused to do so, saying that it was the duty of the Latin troops he commanded to do that, not theirs. Justiniani said it was imperative that he be reinforced by additional artillery, and suggested that some guns might be brought from positions along the Golden Horn, which was not much exposed to danger. When Kyr Notaras refused to do so, Justiniani said, "You traitor, why should I not cut you down?" In reply, the Greeks refused to carry wooden mantles to the walls to help defend the soldiers, unless paid by the piece. This led to a long argument, so that though the mantles did eventually reach the walls, it was already nightfall and a good many of the defenders had been cut down, for want of them, in the interim.

If the Latins regarded the Genoese as half heathen because of their long parasitic relations with the Greeks, the Greeks on the other hand regarded them as half devil because they were given to the Roman Rite, and Notaras would cooperate with them in no way. The two men began to quarrel, and would have gone further than that, but the Emperor intervened. "My friends, this is not the time for quarrels; rather let us bear with each other, and pray God to save us from the mouth of the Turkish serpent."

Justiniani returned to his post, and with impressed labor succeeded in repairing his walls within 32 hours. Seeing this, the Sultan is reported to have said, "Why have I not such men?" Apparently he had made attempts to bribe Justiniani over to his own side. They had not worked, but they did give the Venetians and the Greeks a further pretext for indulging in spite and interracial, international, and ecclesiastical hatred.

The true flaw in Notaras' character lay not in his contumacy, for which however he was later to die, but in his greed, which was ungovernable.

Notaras and Gennadios worked in agreement to scream down, since they had not the strength to destroy it, anything or anyone involved in the union between the two Churches. They were supported by most of the citizenry, which showed its bravery by, for example, shouting down the priests when they mentioned the Pope's name during service. To the mutual contumely of Greek for Greek was added the universal hatred of all Greeks toward the Latins.

In addition, the Venetian and Genoese defenders were, since they had been at each other's throats for more than a century in their eternal trade wars, also suspicious of each other. The Venetians, who lived within the city walls, were compelled either to defend it or flee. The Genoese, with Galata supposedly neutral, were in a stronger position. Each side once more accused the other of treachery. Leonard of Chios, himself a Genoese, speaking of the inhabitants of Galata, said, "I will keep silence, lest I should speak ill of my own people, whom foreigners may justly condemn." He then went on to condemn them himself, ending that they "did not lend help to the Lord against the mighty." Which of course was true. However, soldiers came over to the city privately to fight for Justiniani, and some of the Galatans functioned as spies, under cover of selling provisions to the Turks. The truth of the matter is that merchants are seldom ready to fight, and soldiers are. The Podestà of Galata sent the soldiers but could do nothing with the merchants, an anarchic group chiefly concerned to do each other in the eye. The result was rather as though the inhabitants of Staten Island, at the time of the War of Independence, had victualed the Hessians, even though some of their younger sons were with Washington (they did and were).

The Greeks in the city were equally divided. "What does the capture of the city matter to us if our families die of starvation?" one of them asked Archbishop Leonard. When they could, they stole away from their posts in order to tend their fields and vineyards in the city. And quite a few managed to make their way out of the town, mostly by sea in small boats.

Under these circumstances, it is astonishing that the defense should have proved so effective, the siege so long. And the perils of a long siege in that day were greater for the besieger than for the besieged. Epidemics broke out in the camps. Supplies failed. Men drifted away. But Mahomet had prepared well. His sanitation corps was efficient, so was his supply; and best of all, his discipline was severe and effective.

He went on making his final preparations. So far his armament, turrets, and mining operations had failed. For the assault itself he gathered together 2,000 scaling ladders, secateurs and hooks in like number, and went on with his bombardment. In these last days, he had five cannon firing against the walls between the Palace of the Porphyrogenitus and the Adrianople Gate; four, including Basilica II, against the Romanus Gate; and three against the Third Military Gate. These were at last proving effective. The Bactatinian Tower was gone. Its stones had helped fill the fosse. The breastworks had been employed to the same purpose. Much of the outer wall near the Romanus Gate and of its towers had gone to the same use. Two towers of the inner wall had fallen. And according to Tedardi, a breach 1,200 feet long had been made opposite the Sultan's tent.

Justiniani and the 2,000 men under him, of whom his own 400 Genoese curassiers were in armor, defended less a wall than an opening, but had gradually managed to build a large vallum, stauroma, or stockade. This was made of anything that came to hand, cemented with earth and clay, and faced with hides and skins as a protection against fire arrows. Vats and barrels were used for crenellation, and the clay scooped up to cement it had been taken from a defensible trench.

This stockade was about 400 yards long, and was a substitute for the destroyed outer wall. It was entered in the middle by the military gate of St. Romanus, and from the ends by two small posterns, one at the Adrianople Gate, the other at that now called Top Capou. There was also, it appeared, a new postern opened in the wall by Justiniani, but its exact position is unknown.

This stockade had been begun about April 21st, when the outer wall was still mostly standing, and had been added to almost every night since. Between it and the inner wall most of the defending army was stationed.

Justiniani was, and justly, admired. He was the one person, even more than the Emperor, upon whom the entire defense of the city depended, the only person who was always obeyed. So on him the defense turned.

XVIII

ON the 26th of May the Sultan held a diplomatic reception for the embassy sent by the new king of Hungary, Vladislas. The ambassadors expressed the desire that the Sultan should raise the siege, since otherwise Hungary would be forced to join the league which the Pope was endeavoring to form against the Turks. A Venetian squadron, it was said, was on the way. A rumor was spread to the effect that the Hungarian ambassador had arrived with a declaration of war, and that Hunyadi had already crossed the Danube and was marching on Adrianople. The Vizier Chalil's agents, according to Phrantzes, attempted to incite the soldiers to revolt, lest they be caught by the city on one side and the Hungarians on the other. Even if these rumors were set in motion (they are reported only by Greek historians) nothing came of them.

Within the city, most of whose inhabitants were, after all, women, monks, and nuns, the religious processions were continued. The brigantine sent out to search for the as yet unassembled Venetian fleet had sighted some Italians near Chios, who said they were on the way to the capital; they might arrive; the Venetian fleet might arrive too, though not one of the defenders seriously believed this. "If the Venetian army," says Tedardi, "led by Loredano, had arrived at Constantinople even a single day before it was taken, there is no doubt but that it would not have been taken." But it did not arrive.

The citizens were encouraged by yet another prophecy—this one authentically ancient—that if the city ever were taken, the insurgents would be pushed back (by divine intervention through a single human instrument) at the column before Hagia Sophia. The desperate will believe almost anything.

Celebrations in the Turkish camp began on the 24th, according to Barbaro. The entire Turkish lines were illuminated at night. Three days' feasting had been decreed, followed by one of fasting, before the main attack.

On the 27th, Mahomet held a war council in his tent. There was some hesitation as to whether or not to lift the siege, because of rumors of western European intervention on the way.

Chalil Pasha presented his own view of the situation. Though known as a friend to the Greeks, Chalil Pasha was no traitor to the Turks. He sincerely believed that the risk was greater than the chances of success, and had the courage to say so. According to report (false) all Europe was rising to the assistance of Constantinople. If the Franks did arrive, they would not stop merely at driving the Turks from the walls. The Hungarians were ferocious fighters. He spoke with humility but decision. "Raise the siege lest worse evils befall us," he said.

The Sultan was impressed, convinced of his loyalty, but not persuaded.

Zagan, the head of the Turkish forces, felt the crisis that had come upon him. If the siege were lifted, since he had advocated it he would certainly be banished, and might well be strangled, for failure. Also, he was a Turkish patriot and a man of resolute will and, as such, well informed about the political situation both in the Balkans and in Europe. He said that he did not believe that the Franks would either ally or come, and that the Latin fleet did not seem likely to arrive soon either. Italy was torn by political dissension, and France was no better off. The Christians were incapable of uniting against the Turks (which was true enough). The European rulers never kept a peace among themselves long, did not let treaties of alliance prevent their seizing each other's territories, lived in terror of each other, and existed to intrigue against each other. They spoke, thought, and explained much, but did little. Also, they were slow to act, badly organized, and were apt to fall into quarrels among themselves before carrying any concerted action out.

There was therefore no need to fear them. And besides, what if the fleet did arrive, even so their whole force would not be equal to half, to one-fourth the Turkish force. There was therefore no present danger, unless God should send one. Therefore, he advised storming the city at once.

By age, temperament, and ambition, Mahomet was in sympathy with Zagan, and besides it was what he had meant to do anyway. However, being a wise man, he decided to compromise. The city would be assaulted in the early morning of Tuesday, May 29th; if the storm succeeded, well and good; if it did not, the siege would be raised at once.

It was Sunday. That evening the Turkish camp and fleet were again illuminated, for the third time. The Padishah had sent runners through the camp to tell the faithful that they might enjoy themselves as much as they liked, for tomorrow they must fast and pray so that those predestined to enter Paradise should be ready to be gathered to the martyrs for the faith next Tuesday morning. This created a great deal of excitement. Ulemas and dervishes went the rounds to inflame fanatacism, making fantastic gestures and even more fantastic speeches. Zagan Pasha himself, on the Sultan's orders, went about in disguise, eavesdropping on the soldiers to measure their enthusiasm.

That night an informer came from the Turkish camp to the city to tell the Emperor what had been planned and when, during the council in the Sultan's tent, and to advise him to hope for the best, place picked troops on the land walls, to be on the alert, and to fight firmly.

On May 28th, Zagan Pasha reported to Mahomet that morale was excellent. Early on the morning after that, trumpets sounded through the camp, giving the signal that all troops should take the positions assigned to them and that no one should leave his company. The squadron in the Golden Horn thinned out into a line facing the walls across the way. The fleet at Diplokynion left its anchorage and formed a crescent around the sea side of the city, stretching from the harbor entrance to the Gate of Theodosius (Vlanga Bostan Kapoussi).

The Turkish batteries went on firing as usual until four o'clock in the afternoon, when they abruptly became silent. Shortly afterwards, an enormous cheering was heard from the Turkish camp. The Sultan, elaborately costumed and accompanied by a suite only slightly less so, visited each troop in its position, speaking here and there to the soldiers. Finally a manifesto was read to the army as a whole:

"During the assault many soldiers, according to the immutable law, must fall. But bear in mind that it is written: He who falls fighting for the faith will enter directly into Paradise. They who survive after the conquest of the city will for life receive double pay. If the city is taken, you will have license to pillage it for three days. All its wealth, its silver, gold, silk, cloth, and women, will be yours; only the buildings and the walls will be reserved for the Sultan."

This benevolent announcement, as might be expected, was received with enthusiasm, particularly among the ill-disciplined rabble which accompanied the army with just such a purpose in mind. It was received with an exultant shout, and the sounds of this reached the city just as the sun was going down and touching for the last time the cross on top of the dome of Santa Sophia.

That evening the Turks had good reason for their prayers. And so, in the city, had the defenders. Fires sprang up in the Turkish camp, but toward midnight had burned out, and then all was quiet and dark.

No attempt to attack the city had been made from Saturday, the 26th, to and including Monday, the 28th, but the bombardment was kept up. On Sunday Justiniani was wounded by a splinter from a cannonball, and had to be taken into the city. However, by Monday morning he was sufficiently well to supervise the repairs to the stockade. Sunday was spent by the Turks in filling in the fosse. Their mood was one of jubilee. According to Barbaro, they had been told that they would have so many Christian slaves, that two of them could be bought for a ducat, and that they could have enough hair from the heads of Christian priests to make ropes and leashes for their dogs.

On Monday morning, Mahomet with a large cavalry escort rode over to Diplokynion to consult with Admiral Hamoud, Baltoglu's successor, about the disposition of the fleet. This was to be deployed along the sea walls, from the Eugenius Gate on the Golden Horn to that of the Psamatia (or Theodosian) on the Sea of Marmora, either to enter with scaling ladders, or if that proved not possible (it did not prove possible), to occupy the attention of as many of the defenders as were on those parts of the wall. Mahomet then returned to his camp opposite the Romanus Gate, had the Genoese leaders of Galata brought before him, and told them not to interfere.

In the late afternoon he inspected his landward troops—what with irregulars, about 150,000 men. His strategy was to send in wave after wave of fresh troops, until such time as the city fell.

That evening, he once more summoned his commanders to his tent to explain his assault plan, give final orders, and repeat his inducements to the capture of the city. He repeated that everything in the city was theirs to sack for three days, except its fabric, which was to remain his.

This speech, according to Critobulus, was made at sunset on the evening of the 28th.

In the city no one felt triumphant. The silence before the landward walls, while the Turks rested, was unnerving. Inside the city an alarm bell rang continuously, summoning everyone to their posts. The Venetian bailo issued a final appeal for more defenders. Barbaro and others spent the day making more wooden mantles to shield the defenders. The result of this was that the Emperor, who had been personally supervising the strengthening and repairing of the walls, was obliged once more to soothe a quarrel between his Latin and Greek troops. The Venetian bailo had built some movable wooden shelters for his archers, and had asked a number of Greeks to carry these to the Venetian posts. The Greeks once more refused to do so, unless paid in advance. There was a brisk skirmish, the Venetians naturally feeling disgusted and blaming the refusal on the hatred of the Orthodox Greeks for the Latins. Though of course they did hate them, they had merely wanted the money for food. The Emperor stopped the quarrel somehow. This was the third argument on this subject. The rest of the morning he spent gathering and reviewing his troops on the walls. There were now not quite 4,000 fighting men left.

Early that afternoon, a religious procession started out from Hagia Sophia, while the warning bells rang, to visit the more celebrated churches on its way to the city walls. The priests wore full vestments of gold brocade and carried ikons, relics, and jeweled crosses containing "particles of the Holy Tree [or cross]." The citizens, old men, women and children, turned out to follow them, most of them barefoot as a penance, weeping, sighing, and beating their breasts. The men joined the clergy in chanting the psalms (women were not allowed to sing religious hymns).

The procession halted at each important or holy position while the priests read special prayers asking God to strengthen the walls of the city and grant victory to His faithful people. The bishops raised their croziers and blessed the soldiers, sprinkling them with holy water from bunches of dried basil.

In the afternoon, before Vespers, the Emperor gathered around him the commanders and the chief citizens. He asked them not to spare themselves, and not to regret the shedding of their blood in defense of the city. Turning to the Venetians, who were standing at his right, he reminded them that Constantinople had always welcomed them (except when attempting to fling them out) as sons. "I pray you now," he continued, "show us in this difficult hour that you are indeed our companions, our faithful allies, and our brethren."

To the Genoese, on his left, he spoke of their glorious past and asked them to prove once more their celebrated courage. He then asked all those present: "Let us work together, my companions and my brethren, to gain for ourselves liberty, glory, and eternal memory. Into your hands I commit now my scepter. Here it is. Save it. Crowns await you in heaven, and on earth your names will be remembered honorably until the end of time."

This is what is usually said under such circumstances, and he believed it. "Let us die for faith and Fatherland. Let us die for the Church of God and for thee, our Emperor," shouted his audience enthusiastically. This is also what is usually said, at any rate it is what Phrantzes, who was there, has seen fit to write down. And any ultimate moment is moving. Phrantzes says, "The defenders of the city embraced each other, and through tears kissed one another, asking and giving mutual pardon; no one thought more of wife, child, or property, but only of the glorious death which all were ready to meet for the sake of the Fatherland." The bells rang for Vespers. The Emperor went in formal procession to Hagia Sophia, and the church was crowded for the first time since December 12th (for the last time by Christians ever). Having gotten rid of the compromising patriarch, no doubt the congregation felt unsullied again.

Constantine prayed with fervor. He left his imperial chair, a thing unheard of, and approaching the screen separating the altar from the nave, prostrated himself before the great ikons of Christ and of the Madonna which were fixed on the left and the right side of the central entrance to the alter beyond. He then went the rounds of every prelate in the church, asking them to pardon him if he had ever offended any of them, embraced each one, and then went to the altar to receive Holy Communion. As a Christian Emperor, he was solemnly preparing in the presence of his people to say good-bye.

It is perhaps worth remembering that, among other things, a mass is a symbolic rite of passage to death and to rebirth. In this case, it was a memorial service said over the not yet dead.

When he turned to leave the church, the congregation burst into tears, and the women wailed from the arcades of the upper floors. Obviously deeply moved, Contantine walked slowly out of the church into the night air, through the ruined courtyards, and then went on to the imperial palace at Blachernae, where he had ordered his entire court and its servants to await him. There he told them that no one could tell what the night would bring forth; he asked from each forgiveness for any harshness or injustice; and then he took his most touching leave of all, from his intimates and his enemies, whereas before he had merely said farewell to God and his people.

There was more weeping and sobbing. It was, said Phrantzes, a scene to melt the heart. Later in the evening, Constantine left the palace, mounted his horse, and with his usual suite rode toward the walls to inspect his troops again. Notaras went back to the Golden Horn, to guard his cannon against the Venetians who wanted them and to save his neck.

It did not help that the evening of the 28th was sultry and gloomy. Clouds gathered, grew heavier and darker, formed into sagging sheets, and hung there endlessly. The humidity was high enough to make one itch. So did the waiting.

Mahomet, also awake and restless, looked out of his tent and saw the clouds gathering. He called one of his ulemas who had knowledge of the mysteries of astrology and meteorological portents, and asked if the heavy dense clouds meant anything. "Yes," answered the ulema. "It is a great sign; it forebodes the fall of 'Stamboul."

At this, the clouds let loose, not ordinary rain but large drops of water almost as big as a bull's eye, says a witness, the sort of rain you get from a cloudburst. Those in the city said it was a shower of blood.

Just before midnight all fires in the Turkish camp were put out.

The atmosphere was oppressive. Except for an occasional shout in the city and a religious mumbling in the churches, there was no sound, and only a few dim lights. Occasionally a clatter of horses' hoofs skittered over the cobbles near the Romanus Gate walls.

The defenders of the city had deliberately shut themselves off from it by having the gates in the inner wall closed behind them. This was done, says Cambini, in his history published some sixty years after the event, so that they should not be tempted to weaken in their resistance to the besiegers. They were shortly to be confronted with the consequences of this irremediable act.

At about midnight, Phrantzes and the Emperor climbed a tower in the Calligaria quarter. They could not see much. The night was dark. But all around them they could hear the creak and rattle of armaments being moved up, and the movement, hushed but all the more sinister for that, of troops advancing. No doubt some wind stirred at that height. There would have been some light on the Sea of Marmora and the Bosphorus and Golden Horn. The sails of the Turkish fleet moving into position, at any rate, would have been visible as a purposeful blur.

At about one o'clock they separated. Phrantzes never saw the Emperor again.

Constantine rode back to St. Romanus Gate. Everyone seemed determined. The outlines of the broken battlements darkened and then seemed to grow lighter in silhouette. The cocks crowed early in the open spaces of the city and beyond the walls, in the Turkish camp and from the hills. It was between 2 and 3 A.M.

Basilica II fired; as the echoes died away, 50,000 yelling troops swept down into the moat, up the other side, and planted 200 ladders against the outer walls of the city. The assault had begun.

The storming columns, as was the Turkish practice, were arranged in three lines, the poorest irregular troops, as being the most expendable, being thrown in first, accompanied by the followers of the Ziyamet and Timariot beys. The mercenaries or professional soldiers came next. The third line consisted of the even better trained companies of Janissaries and Sipahis.

After an hour, the defenders managed to beat off the attack, not so much by bullets, stones, and arrows as by pouring broad floods of Greek fire down on the Turks, who screamed, tried to beat the fire out, ran mad with the pain, stifled, and fell charred into the ditch, setting fire to others behind them, who had no space to draw away. The Turks in the moat grew frightened, stampeding back the way they had come, across the glacis. The smell must have been dreadful, the hiss and crackle of burning flesh no better. The flames burned for a long time.

The fleeing troops were halted by a line of guards who forced them back into the moat by flaying them with chain whips and beating them with iron maces. Those who escaped the guards ran onto the scimitars of the Janissaries, and having no other choice, turned back to the attack.

The second line moved up, quickly and in good order, to drums and trumpets. One death was certain, the other merely probable. The expendable troops stumbled over the still smoldering and burning bodies, and up the ladders again. This time they were fighting for their lives, always the best way to get troops to behave themselves. Smoke billowed everywhere, for the bombardment went on, cutting through the Turkish irregulars to reach the walls and thud them down. The uproar was overwhelming. At the same time all the bells were ringing in the city, all the drums were being beaten in the camp, and Basilica II and her battery fired regularly, not to mention the screaming and shouting of the troops.

At about 3 A.M., a cannonball took away a piece of the outside wall near St. Romanus Gate, at a point where the Venetians were posted. It was here that the Turks concentrated their attack. The Venetians, with the aid of a few Greeks, repulsed it.

The Janissaries were right behind, and spurred their horses through the hole, into the space between the outer and inner wall, planted their ladders, and scaled the stockade.

The Venetians had already been fighting hard for two hours, had not had much rest for days, and began to give way. The Emperor sent for reinforcements. Theophilus and Demetrius Cantacuzenos hurried their men up to the breach, and again the Turks were beaten back. Seeing this, the Emperor shouted, "Bear yourselves bravely for God's sake; I see the enemy retires in disorder. If God wills, ours shall be the victory." But while he shouted, Justiniani was hit by a rifle bullet which shattered his hand or chest. Accounts vary. At any rate he was severely hit. He also suffered shock, and saying a few words to the two Genoese with him, asked one of them to take over and turned to leave.

The Emperor, who was close by, tried to stop him, apparently saying the wound was not dangerous, for if he left, the life would go out of his troops. Justiniani said he was going to have his wound bandaged up. The Emperor repeated it was not serious. Justiniani was bleeding profusely, and demanded to be given the keys to a small postern gate so he might retire. They were given to him. He had himself carried away and taken to his ship.

This was the most controversial moment in the siege. It was also the most catastrophic. Phrantzes denounces Justiniani as a traitor, which seems unfair. Ducas gives the account above. At any rate he was worn out; he was, as it turned out a few days later, mortally wounded; and he did retire.

Seeing confusion among the Christians, Hassan Ulubadli, a Janissary of enormous stature, called to his companions to follow him, ran up a ladder with some 30 Janissaries right behind him, shouting the name of Allah and giving their war cry. Half of them were flung off the ladder by showers of stones and arrows, but Hassan made it to the top and mowed those around him down with his scimitar. He was struck and staggered by stones and arrows, a second shower toppled him in a heap of rubble, but rising on one knee, he went on fighting until, stuck with arrows, bruises and stray shots, he went down, bled to death, and died. But he had proved the stockade could be surmounted, and urged on by Janissaries, a rabble swarmed up after him. Yet the Byzantine lines still held.

What finally forced them to give way was a panic-stricken error of the Greeks. In the wall near the palace and suburb of Hebdomon was an old gate, low and on a level with the bottom of the moat, called the Kerkoporta. It was half utility door and half emergency exit. It had been closed up long ago, legend has it because someone had prophesied that the enemy would enter the city through it. The Byzantines had a prophecy for everything. The Greek general staff had decided that a large body of troops could easily pass through this door to make a sortie against the left wing of the Turks, thus coming on it by surprise. As preparation for this, the gate had been unbricked and reopened, and a guard posted there. The sortie had been abandoned, but during the confusion of the last days everybody forgot that the gate had been opened.

As the attack was going forward against the St. Romanus Gate, a group of Turks going down the moat came upon this low-lying gate and saw it was open. They rushed in, killed the few guards, found the gate connected with the nearest tower, and hoisted a lance with a horsetail at the end of it as a signal.

Other Turks followed them, shouting as they ran, and soon a thousand had gotten into the city. Notaras, to his surprise involved in actual fighting, did his best to beat them back, but his troops were overpowered, and he was forced to retreat and shut himself up in his own palace, which was nearby and strongly fortified, to await the outcome. The Turks at once took possession of the deserted Hebdomon Palace, and others hurried through side streets toward St. Romanus. Ahead of them, a Greek rode to the Emperor and shouted that the Turks were inside the walls, and would soon assail the Emperor's position from the rear.

As a matter of fact, the Turks were not in the city yet, but within fifteen minutes 30,000 of them poured over the stockade at the Romanus Gate and occupied the space between the two walls. The defenders, with the gates behind them locked, ran north to the Adrianople Gate, and suffocated trying to crowd through the small postern left open there.

The city was more than four miles across and six miles deep. Despite its broad avenues, it was a labyrinth. The news spread along the walls, however, and many Italians at once left their posts and fled toward the harbor, where a good many of them succeeded in getting aboard the Venetian and Genoese galleys. The uproar began to make itself heard, men could be seen fleeing, and crowds of people began to rush away from the Turks, toward Hagia Sophia. Others ran about aimlessly. A group of women was seen walking with burning tapers in their hands, to morning mass at the Church of St. Theodosia, whose feast day it was. They were overtaken by the fleeing citizens from the outer suburbs, joined them, and some thousands of half-dressed women and children—for it was still early morning—raced through the streets, shrieking and screaming, though most had not the breath to be other than silent, all toward Hagia Sophia, irrationally—and yet not so irrationally, since it was the palladium of the city.

There the great bronze doors were closed, barred and bolted, even while other refugees beat upon them and then turned back and tried to conceal themselves as best they could. The prudent descended to the cisterns, cast loose in a skiff, and lurked safely in the underground darkness of those enormous storage tanks. The even more shortsightedly prudent buried what valuables they had not buried already, before taking thought that, sold as slaves, they would themselves be valuables, after a fashion.

The news staggered the Emperor. Someone suggested, as the Italians fled toward the harbor, that he might still be able to reach it safely himself. Those who had horses galloped past the defenders on their way there. Constantine came to himself and said merely, "God forbid that I should live an Emperor without an Empire. As my city falls, I will fall with it." When the crisis comes, one can only repeat what one said before. There is nothing else to say.

One cannot rise from eminence, and neither can one hide from it. It is better to die than be degraded. So he felt, and right he was. From the neighboring streets, the cries of the approaching Turks became audible. Constantine turned to his suite and said, "Whoever wishes to escape, let him save himself if he can; and whoever is ready to face death, let him follow me!" He then swiftly removed any clothing that might identify his body—with one exception, which he unfortunately forgot—and spurring on his horse, rode forward sword in hand to meet the Turks at the end of the street. He was followed by about 200 Greek and Italian nobles and volunteers. Don Francesco di Toledo rode on the Emperor's right hand, Demetrius Cantacuzenos, whose progenitor a hundred years before had usurped the throne, on his left. The Turks engaged them almost at once, and a good many of them were killed. Theophilus Palaeologus was mortally wounded, fell from his horse, and was trodden underfoot. Don Fransesco di Toledo lasted a little longer. The Emperor was separated from his followers, and his horse fell under him. He went on fighting on foot. An Assab struck him in the face. The Emperor cut him down, but fell forward himself, mortally wounded. None of the attackers knew who he was. As Theodora, the consort of Justinian, had said when there was more of it, and to encourage her husband not to flee the Nika riots, the Empire would make an excellent winding sheet; and now, at last, it had.

Such is the Turkish account; it is also a popular tradition among the Greeks. The street fighting continued for some time, until the dead lay in heaps, thus concealing the body of the Emperor.

The Turks mowed down everybody they could find, but as the light became stronger they could see that there were no more fighting men left, but only a crowd of terrified civilians. They therefore stopped fighting, got out their ropes, brought along for the purpose, and began to take people as slaves, linking men, women, children together by means of the ropes until the more enterprising soon had strings of them, valuable salable property even in a glutted market.

The Janissaries, not wishing so to encumber themselves just yet when there was more profitable looting to be done, and three days to do it in, and having heard and believed legends that the cellars of the church were heaped with gold, silver, and precious stones, galloped to the Forum Bous and thence down the deserted Mese, through the squares of Theodosius and Constantine, around Constantine's column, and out with a great clatter into the Augusteum, and so on to Hagia Sophia, whose vast doors were barred and from which came an enormous wailing. There was no time now either for services or prayers. But the lamentations were loud. The church had probably not been so crowded for centuries. Of the 60,000-odd people left in the city, almost a fourth had made their way there. Some had gone higher and higher into the building, to the back service passages, storage rooms, and even to the roof.

These were the more enterprising. Most merely took their proper places, the women above, the men below, or crowded the floor.

At the time the Turks entered the city, the clergy had been reading morning service at the altar. These men were not found in the church when the doors were battered down. Legend has it that one of the church walls near the altar miraculously opened to admit the priest carrying the chalice and closed after him, and that this priest will reappear from the same wall on the day when an Orthodox emperor reconquers the city from the Turks. It seems more likely that the clergy stumbled out through the old passages connecting the church with the residence of the Patriarch nearby, and so made their escape.

The Janissaries galloped into the courtyards, and finding the nine doors fastened against them, battered down the main one, which happened to be the door reserved for the passage of the Emperor and Empress only.

Bursting in, they pillaged what was in the church, which despite so many despoilations was still crammed with gold and silver ornaments, hacked down the ikons as idolatrous, smashed the lamps and altar screens, helped themselves to whatever they could find, passing it out of the building to be heaped up and divided later. They then turned their attention to the equally profitable taking of slaves, each man choosing out what seemed to be either most desirable or most salable, binding the men up like chickens while their wives, mothers, and sisters wailed and wept, and then making the women secure with their own scarves and girdles. Thus nobles as haughty as Notaras (though not Notaras himself; his punishment was to be slightly different) found themselves tied to their own bondsmen, and Orthodox to Latin, in what was indeed a final union of the two Churches.

The storming of the walls had begun at about two in the morning of May 29th; by eight o'clock the city was completely in the hands of its conquerors, though in the outlying streets and around some churches and strongly fortified houses and palaces, fighting still went on. It could scarcely be successful, and those were lucky who knew the secrets of their own cellars sufficiently well to go down into the sewers of the city and make their way through wet and slimy tunnels to the sea, where a few Venetian and Genoese galleys hovered offshore, ready to take them aboard if that proved possible.

Tedardi and some of his companions fought the Turks for two hours after they had entered the city, and then, by hazardous ways, managed to reach the harbor and throw themselves into the sea, as a good many did—in fact too many, for not all could be taken aboard. Tedardi was. The captains kept their boats in the Golden Horn for several hours after the city had been taken, and the Turks did not try to molest them while they picked up survivors. But a good many could not swim, and even of those that could, the fighting to get aboard drowned more. Many fugitives crossed in small boats to Galata, among them the three brothers Bocciardi, who had been on the Charisius Tower.

Cardinal Isidore stripped off his robes and disguised himself as a common soldier. The body of a Latin volunteer was then dressed up in the Cardinal's clothes and left in the street, where the Turks, coming upon it, spitted it on a pike and carried it triumphantly down the Mese.

The Cardinal was captured anyway, but his captor took him as a common slave. He seemed so unpromising for the market that he was allowed to buy himself free again for a small sum, and managed to get away in a skiff.

Orchan Effendi, the pretender to the Turkish throne (the demanded enhanced payment for the detention of whom had given Mahomet his excuse to attack the city), knowing what he might expect if caught, let himself down to the beach from a tower of the Acropolis, disguised as a Greek monk. There he and some Greeks wandered about, trying to hail a boat to take them off, and a boat came, but it turned out to be Turkish. One of the Greeks, to buy his own freedom, explained who Orchan Effendi was, and he was instantly murdered and his head dispatched to Mahomet.

Turkish chronicles say that on this day some 300 Greek

monks, seeing what true faith had triumphed and which side God was on, declared themselves ready to embrace Islam. It is possible.

At any rate, many were killed during the siege and sack, and 50,000 sold as slaves. Only the poorest physical specimens were allowed their liberty, so they might perform the menial work required to keep the sanitation and hygienic functions of the city going.

There was great confusion. Those who fled to the harbor found the guards had locked the gates and flung away the keys. Some Cretan sailors who had defended the walls on the harbor side took refuge in three towers named Basil, Leo, and Alexis, which they defended so well, until the afternoon, that the Sultan allowed them to leave the city with all their belongings. These were the last defenders. Over 400 Christians were taken aboard boats in the harbor. The shore outside the walls was crowded with men, women, monks and nuns, and there was practically no one to take them off.

Any attempt at massacre was over by noon, the Turks realizing that live slaves were better than dead Christians. The city was systematically divided up into areas, and the sack proceeded from house to house. One body took the wealthier houses, a second the churches, a third the smaller houses and shops.

When a house was plundered, a small flag was raised over it to show it had already been taken care of. Movables were, by and large, gathered together for future division among the conquerors.

No angel had descended, as prophecy had claimed it would, from heaven to the column of Constantine, to point out the single man sitting at the foot of it who would, with divine aid, beat back the invaders. Though the city was poor, the Church was not. It was as though the treasures of the Vatican and St. John in Lateran had been dumped out into the street together.

And as for the libraries, the sale of these was to prove profitable for the next hundred years; Busbeck, the ambassador of the Holy Roman Empire to Suleiman the Magnificent, having only a little difficulty in buying "whole wagonloads, if not shiploads, of Greek Manuscripts, and about 250 books which I sent by sea to Venice. I intend them for Caesar's library," so late as 1555.

Despite the sack of 1204, and the selling off of treasures for the next 250 years, the literature of Byzantium was enormous. As for its quality, that was another matter. Though pious to preserve the literature of Greek antiquity, the Byzantines were not, in literature, a creative people, and little of their writing has entered the mainstream of world culture. They had some excellent epigrammatic poets, most of them imbedded in the Greek Anthology, which they preserved and enlarged. They wrote novels on the late Greek pattern, of unexampled tedium. Only the story of *Barlaam and Ioasaph,* a Christianized version of the life of the Buddha, can really be said to have had much influence. They had no higher drama, and what survives of their religious morality plays is not the equal of European examples of the same genre. They wrote epic poems in archaic style, which are today, if not unreadable, at least unread. In philosophy, they preferred Aristotle to the pre-Socratics, Plato to Aristotle, the Neoplatonists to Plato, and the earnest if elevated vaporizings of George Gemisthus Plethon best of all. They excelled in commentary, copying, and the collation of texts. The vast bulk of their literature was devoted to jurisprudence, a field in which their accomplishments were lasting, to history, and to theology. They prided themselves on continuing the tradition of Herodotus, but in point of fact, their history is either stiff archaicizing or else more in the nature of annals and anecdote. Like many peoples who lack a lyric gift, they had a passion for gossip. Procopius's venomous if probably mostly accurate *Secret History* is much more readable than his public ones. Nicephorus Gregoras is one anecdote after another, and no over-all grasp of what was going on anywhere. Anna Comnena's *Alexiad* is interminable, if shot through here and there with a bright ray of malice and ambition. Theology seldom reads well so much as fifty years later, but here, oddly enough, the Byzantines produced a few great mystics; St. John Climacus, for example, whose works soar far above the recriminations and hairsplitting of theological debate, being indeed the equal of the best in this field produced by any people.

At the time of the sack of the city, ten volumes of Plato and Aristotle sold for a nommus, about sixpence, or seven cents. Later, of course, the price rose again. With this in mind, not all books were burned. And meanwhile the slaves were collected together for eventual distribution. Critobulus says that 4,000 of the defenders were slain during the siege. Five hundred of them joined the slave chains. The rest escaped.

The Venetian and Genoese galleys were able to escape the city because the crews of the Turkish fleet had deserted and come ashore for plunder. Diedo went over to Galata to ask the Podestà whether to flee or give battle. The Podestà suggested that they wait to see what the wish of Mahomet might be—that is, whether he wanted war or peace with Venice and Genoa. The gates of Galata were closed, much to the disgust of Barbaro, who was one of the Venetians so locked in. Despite this, the galleys made ready to sail, seeing which, the Podestà allowed the Venetians and such of the Genoese as wished to do so, to leave. Trevisano, unfortunately, had been captured by the Turks and could not join his men. A strong north wind was blowing, so some galleys were able to get away. The nineteen ships which remained in the harbor were seized by the Turks. A great number of the citizens of Galata begged and bribed for passage. Few of them could be taken aboard without swamping the already overladen ships.

The gates of Galata, though closed temporarily to the Venetians who had wished to get out, had been opened to the Turks who wished to get in. Zagan Pasha, to prevent a general exodus, guaranteed the safety of the citizens. He was afraid of provoking war with Genoa.

Nonetheless, as many left as could; but Hamoud, the Turkish admiral, had his sailors in hand again and soon entered the harbor and destroyed the remaining nineteen galleys. Mahomet and the Podestà, as escapes still went on, reached an agreement. The walls of Galata were to be dismantled. Apart from that,

Galata was to be left alone, and even its churches protected, on the condition that they did not ring their bells.

The refugees had taken asylum at Chios. The Podestà sent to ask them, under these terms, to return. Few did.

At about noon, some say later, on either the 29th or the 30th, Mahomet himself entered the city by the gate of Pliandrium in state, accompanied by viziers, pashas, ulemas, and bodyguards, men selected for the uniformity of their strength and for their good looks. He rode straight to Theodosius Square, and then evenly down the middle of the Mese, looking about him, for he had never seen the city before though he had often dreamed of it, and being saluted by such Janissaries and irregulars as had time to look up from their looting. His destination was Hagia Sophia. Riding through the Hippodrome, he saw that column composed of three serpents which had once supported a tripod at Delphi. He broke off the underjaw of one of the serpents with his mace as he passed by, perhaps for luck. When he reached the courtyard of Hagia Sophia, he dismounted, stooped down, and picking up a handful of dirt, let it fall on his turban as an act of humiliation before God (his, not theirs) who had given him this victory. Then he rose and entered the edifice, pausing at the doorway to peer into the silence. The enormous size and wrecked splendor of the building—though the lapis and gold mosaics remained, as did the four great angels in the pendentives and the porphyry columns and the circumambient light—seemed to subdue him.

But that silence was inhabited by a loud, maniacal clatter. Stepping forward, he saw a Turk taking an ax to the mosaic floor.

"Why dost thou do that?" demanded the Sultan.

"For the Faith," yelled the fanatic; for, of course, the floor undeniably contained graven images, which the Koran prohibits to an even greater degree than the Ten Commandments do (which after all say nothing about our admiring them once they are there).

Mahomet was angry and struck the man, saying, "You have

got enough by pillaging the city and taking the citizens for slaves. The buildings are mine."

It is possible he had been struck by the numinous, for some churches hum with it, no matter what the doctrine or successive doctrines preached in them, and Hagia Sophia is one of these. For one thing, it was even then so immeasurably old; and then, it was a masterpiece; and the Turks, though not particularly creative above the ornamental level, have a taste for architecture of a massive sort, and for elaborate but simple-seeming ornament.

As the Sultan advanced toward the altar, he passed groups of his soldiers leading out their Christian slaves. The upper rooms and corridors of the building were still being flushed. Ahead of him a door in the rood screen opened and six priests, those who had not managed to flee, came to meet him, fell on their knees at some distance from him, no doubt waggled their beards, and cried "Aman," which is Turkish for "Be merciful."

With a sign of his hand Mahomet told them to rise, and said, "Be not today afraid of my wrath, neither of death nor of pillage." He then told his followers to send public criers through the city, to prohibit further molestation of the people —after all, if Istanbul was to be his capital, it would need a population—and to the people left in the church he said, "Now let every man go to his own home."

Such is the account of the Slavonic chronicler, and it may well be true, for once he got his own way, Mahomet was not unmerciful.

He waited for the people to leave the church, wishing to be alone again, but since they took a long time to leave he went first, after having ordered one of his ulemas to mount the pulpit and deliver a prayer, while he himself climbed on the marble table which had been the altar of Hagia Sophia, and there made his Rika'at, his salaam to accompany the prayer being said. Thus was Hagia Sophia transformed into Aya Sophia, the mosque.

Coming out of the mosque, Mahomet asked his suite, among

whom were now several Greek dignitaries, whether any of them knew what had become of the Emperor.

No one had any certain information. Some thought he had died in the fight. Others suggested that more probably he had been taken off by an Italian ship. They had not, as courtiers, been near the fighting, so they could not say. Another version had it that the Emperor was among those crushed to death, when a panic-stricken crowd tried to squeeze through a gate ahead of the Turks into the inner city.

The Emperor had not intended that his body should be found, or if found, identified. But as the Sultan was passing from Hagia Sophia toward the palaces of the Acropolis, where later the Old Seraglio was to stand, a Serbian soldier appeared carrying a man's head. He lifted up the still-dripping thing, which began to bleed again with the sudden motion, and shouted loudly, "Glorious Lord, may happiness always be thine; this is the head of Tzar Constantinos."

And so it was: Constantine had forgotten to shed his slippers, which were purple and embroidered in gold with the double imperial eagle, and the corpse had been identified by these.

The cavalcade halted, and Kyr Lucas Notaras, who by this time had been found, was sent for, along with some other nobles, to identify the head. At the first glance, the Greeks burst into tears. Perhaps Notaras did too. It was indeed the right head. The Serbian, intent no doubt on a reward, took some officers of the Sultan's suite to show them the body from which the head had been taken. It was lying on the square now known as Sandjakdar Yokushar.

Mahomet ordered that Constantine's head should be exposed on a column of porphyry which stood on the open space in front of the imperial palace. It may well have been the pillar on which the Holy Ikon of the Virgin Mary as protectress of the city had until recently been placed. This exposure was made to prove to the Greeks that their Emperor was indeed dead.

Others say the head was placed between the feet of the equestrian statue of Justinian, a favorite way of wishing a Turkish conqueror well being to say, "May the heads of your enemy fall beneath the feet of your horses."

Though the body has never been found, its tomb was for long displayed in Constantinople, and the legend arose that Mahomet had given orders that a perpetual lamp should burn there. Actually the lamp seems to have burned over the sarcophagus the next over, which contained the bones of an Osmanli saint, and the unornamented coffin shown to visitors as being that of Constantine was the invention of the proprietor of a nineteenth-century coffeehouse who wished to add to his revenue in this way.

Constantinople is noted for its fireflies. In popular legend, fireflies are the sad and gentle ghosts of the dead. The weather was still sultry and portentous. That night they flitted and wavered as usual, through the abandoned gardens and open spaces of the city, around flowering shrubbery gone wild—for it was late spring—twinkling in and out of sight, no higher than your waist. For nothing ever changes. It is only we who go.

It must have been quiet in the gardens. In the narrow alleys of the city it was less so. There were shrieks from time to time, and the fires of bivouacs crackled on cracked marble, and there was some rapine and loud murder no doubt, particularly about dividing the spoils, and some restless clanking of slave chains.

In a day or two, after he had rested, Mahomet, with his customary thoroughness, proceeded with plans for the occupation of the city.

XIX

FIRST, he dealt with such of the prominent defenders as yet remained alive.

On the 30th of May he moved into the imperial palace, probably that of Blachernae. It had been stripped of everything portable. The halls were echoing, drafty, and bare. The courtyards were unweeded. And he was, even though he meant to stay, an intruder.

He was also a poetaster. Entering one of the larger halls, he looked down the dusty length of it and up at the decrepit windows, and recited two verses from the famous Persian poet, Saàdi (1184–1291):

"Now the spider is chamberlain in Caesar's palace
And the owl hoots the watch on the towers of Afrasiab."

The quotation, written about the downfall of a Persian dynasty, was just as apposite to the removal of the Byzantine. Mahomet was admired both for his learning and his taste.

He next asked what had become of the imperial ladies, and was told that Justiniani's ships had got them safely off several days before.

Then he began to tidy up. The bailo of the Venetians, together with his son and seven fellow countrymen, was beheaded. One of them was Contarino, who had already been ransomed. When this was pointed out—for Mahomet meant to have him—a second and impossible ransom of 7,000 gold pieces was imposed, and when it could not be raised, his head followed that of the others. The Spanish, or rather Catalan, consul and five or six of his companions were next. Those of the Latins escaped with their lives who could pay liberal ransoms, the sum for a noble being 70,000 sequins payable to Zagan Pasha; for a commoner, if he could raise the money, less.

Phrantzes did not get away so easily. He was made a slave for fifteen months before escaping to the Morea, and then from it, to write his history. His wife and children had been sold to the Master of the Sultan's Horse. His wife Phrantzes was able to redeem a year later, but his daughter Thamar disappeared into the seraglio. She was fourteen at the time, and died a few months later, in 1454. His son John, equally attractive in a similar way, killed himself in December, so we are told, rather than have the Sultan find him so, a piece of prudery for which he preferred to pay with his life.

The most unfortunately to suffer, however, was Notaras. He had hidden himself but was betrayed, in return for his own freedom, by one of his servants. At first Mahomet treated him favorably, found and restored to him his wife and daughters, condoled, gave gifts, and even condescended to visit his wife. His first thought was to make Notaras governor of the city.

With this in view, Notaras handed over a list of the principle dignitaries and officials of state, which made rounding them up much easier. We are told that the soldiers were offered 1,000 aspers for each one of their heads.

Mahomet then asked why Notaras had not put his wealth at the disposal of the defenders of the city.

"It was yours. God has reserved it for your hands," said Notaras.

"If that is so, why did you withhold it for so long, by a fruitless and fatal resistance?"

To this there seemed to be no immediate answer.

"What is it that has put these treasures into my hands?" persisted Mahomet.

"God," said Notaras.

"Then it is to Him I owe thanks, not you," said Mahomet. There were other incidents. In his cups, Mahomet demanded

Notaras' younger son for pleasure purposes. Notaras said the Christian religion forbade such practices, and in order to save his sons from apostasy, asked that their execution precede his own. "For this man," says Critobulus, "was pious and renowned for his knowledge of spiritual things, for the loftiness of his soul, and the nobility of his life." He was also renowned for his confirmed plotting, and one of these stratagems being detected, he, his two sons, and nine nobles from the list he had supplied to the authorities were beheaded. His wife was taken toward Adrianople, but died on the way.

In general, the Greek heads of households were executed; male children sent into the Janissary schools, or into the personal service of Mahomet as pages; and the women and girl children, unless extremely attractive, were left alone.

"All Greece felt itself struck by that disaster. In the Morea and in the islands men fled without knowing whither to go. The sea was covered with vessels and barques bearing away the families and the wealth of the Greeks. The mountains, the monasteries, the islands occupied by the Genoese and the Venetians, served for refuge.... It was a dispersion like that after the capture of Jerusalem," says a much later historian, Villemain.

A few weeks later Mahomet published an edict proclaiming that all former inhabitants who had paid ransom, or who were ready to enter into an agreement to pay it, should be considered free and be allowed to live in the city free from taxation. A similar order had been issued within three days of the city's capture. Mahomet wished the city repopulated as soon as possible. He ordered, as his conquests went successfully on, 5,000 families from Trebizond, Sinope, and Asprocastron to be sent to Constantinople. To these, in the next six years, he added 2,000 Serbian families, 2,000 Peloponnesian, two-thirds of the population of Amastris, Trapezus, Caffa, Euboea, and Samothrace. Turks, Greeks, Serbians, Bulgarians, Albanians, all were forced to contribute to the populousness of the capital, and in truth did not suffer by the change.

In this way was founded that peculiar institution, the Greek families of the Phanar, who living in the shadow of their conquerors, claimed a distinction and nobility predating the conquest, often, from their behavior, seeming to predate Adam; served the Osmanli in administrative capacities; and in the early nineteenth century contributed much to the liberation of Greece. Even to this day they constitute, or feel themselves to constitute, the aristocracy of those parts.

Mahomet set about planning to rebuild the city. On the third day after the capture, the tomb of Ayu or Job was revealed in a vision. He was an Arab fakir who had fallen in the first Arab siege of the city, in the seventh century. It was ordered embellished.

Mahomet decreed that a palace be built for him at Seraglio Point, and imported artisans from Karamania (once he had conquered it) and Iconium to do the work. Hagia Sophia, once plastered over, made an excellent mosque, and so could not be returned to Christian use. Of the forty chief churches in the city, many were too splendid to be left in Christian hands, and also became mosques. But some churches were tolerated.

On the site of the Church of the Holy Apostles, Mahomet had built the Mosque of the Conqueror, with an appropriate inscription from the Koran, 1st Sura, on the exterior. That is the Sura known as "That which opens and subdues hearts." The Prophet's traditionally accepted words, "They will take Constantinople, and happy the Prince, happy the army, which conquers it," were inscribed over the main door. This building he equipped with eight colleges, with poorhouses, and with kitchens.

In 1477 he repaired the entire circult of the walls, and in general instituted so much building that today Trebizond looks more like Byzantium as it looked then, than does Constantinople.

For political reasons, Mahomet had decided to protect the Christian Church. The old Patriarch had died during the siege, and as Gennadios seemed an excellent substitute, his anti-Latin feelings being all too well known by now, a search was made for him.

Gennadios was difficult to find. He was in Adrianople, the slave of a pasha, but treated with distinction. He was finally rooted out and sent to Mahomet, who gave him the ruined Church of the Apostles as official residence, until such time as it could be torn down to make way for his own Mosque of the Conqueror.

A local synod was called, Gennadios was elected, and so, though perhaps under slightly different circumstances than he had hoped for, achieved his ultimate ambition.

The ceremony attendant upon the elevation of a patriarch had been unchanged for centuries. The Patriarch rode a white horse of the royal stables from Hagia Sophia to Bucoleon, where he was received and his election confirmed by the Emperor, while the choir sang *The King of Heaven.* The Patriarch prostrated himself three times before the assembly of churchmen and once before the Emperor. The Emperor then touched his scepter on the Patriarch's head, saying, "The Holy Trinity, which has given me the Empire, invests you with the Patriarchate of New Rome." The Patriarch then gave the Emperor communion.

Except that Hagia Sophia was now a mosque, and the Holy Trinity was out of the question, Mahomet followed the same ceremony, saying, "Be Patriarch, and Heaven watch over you; use my friendship in all circumstances; enjoy all the rights and all the privileges which your predecessors have enjoyed."

Gennadios was then given the Church of the Holy Virgin (also in time to become a mosque) as his seat. He was authorized to continue the Christian Rite, to decide questions of civil and ecclesiastical law among the Greeks, and to keep open the gates of the Greek quarter where his palace was, and which was to become a virtual ghetto, for three nights during Easter.

Mahomet found Gennadios as impossible to get along with as everyone else had, and after eight years he was persuaded to retire from the Patriarchate into a clamorous and embittered old age, railing alike against the Turks, who did not understand the purity of his motives, and his fellow Greeks, who, alas, did.

Just the same, under Mahomet, and for the first sixty years

of the conquest, the Christian religion was fully tolerated, for Mahomet could ally himself with it without being put to the inconvenience of indulging in it. The Patriarch had the rank of vizier and carried a gold pastoral staff studded with diamonds, given him by Mahomet, as symbol of his rank. He also had, whether he wanted it or not, a guard of Janissaries, and religious tolerance was maintained at the price of a double capitation tax.

During the sack of the city, the miraculous ikon of the Virgin Chodegetria, on the Acropolis where formerly the altar of Minerva Embasia had stood, one of four portraits presumed to be by St. Luke, had been cut up into strips. Otherwise, though there was a shortage of vessels, services (and theological arguments) went on as before. The Latin Church suddenly found its prestige diminished by the loss of a Christian outpost, no matter how disaffected and rebellious; and the Orthodox Church, which had had for centuries a stronger, more extensive, and far richer empire than the Byzantine Empire with which it had once been territorially co-extensive, now became transnational. The Russian Orthodox Church became autocephalus, like those of Serbia and Bulgaria, and Byzantine culture migrated to Moscow and Novgorod, where it was to persist, first in revival, later in an ignominious repetitive degenerate condition, until the Russian Revolution swept the last remainders of all that away. Or perhaps not quite all away. The paranoia of an orientalized hierarchic bureaucracy probably still remains, as do many of its habits. Russia became known as "the Third Rome." The more hysterical aspects of Byzantine Orthodoxy are adequately figured forth so late as Dostoevski; the Tsar became in fact a Basileus, his emblem the Byzantine double eagle; and even in our own century the corrosive antics of Rasputin fully recapitulate Byzantine palace intrigue.

On the 2nd of June Mahomet dealt with Galata in the way best calculated to annoy its inhabitants, by taking inventory of the goods of all those who had fled and giving them three months to present an evaluation of their goods and pay tax;

otherwise, the goods were to be confiscated. He also had leveled most of the walls. On the 18th of June he returned to Adrianople, to plot further maneuvers and to remove his grand vizier, Chalil, whose traitorous correspondence with himself Notaras had obligingly turned over to Mahomet.

Mahomet was not surprised to read it. One day, seeing a fox tied up at a door, he cried, "Poor fool, why haven't you asked Chalil to buy your liberty?" On hearing this, Chalil decided to make the pilgrimage to Mecca, but was persuaded to stay on, be denounced and go to heaven direct, though without his head.

To the European view, the capture of the city, which Europe had done so little to prevent, was a salutary shock. The Podestà of Pera, writing in June of the same year, said that Mahomet intended to become lord of the whole earth, and that in two years he would go to Italy. "By God, unless the Christians take care, or there are miracles worked, the destruction of Constantinople will be repeated in Rome." Aeneas Sylvius, at the Diet of Frankfort, pointed out that now Constantinople was captured, the way to Hungary lay open to the Turks; and if Hungary went, Italy and Germany would be next. The fear was certainly great, and it continued. Nobody expected the Turks to be defeated at Lepanto, a hundred years later. When they were so defeated, the Venetians, whose shipping had perhaps been harried most, shouted at each other that the Devil was dead.

He was dead by sea only. He went on terrifying everybody by land, until Sobieski successfully drove the Turks back from the siege of Vienna in 1683.

XX

THIS, however, was in the future. At the moment Mahomet had other plans. It was said at the time, on the Turkish side, that "the conquest of the city had been the key which opened the lock of difficult things." The key was chiefly psychological, but all the same, for so long as Constantinople remained free, it had interposed something between Christian and Turk, even if that something was nothing more than intrigue, bribery, and a possible naval and military depot. But now there was nothing between Christian and Turk.

The habit of regarding the Turk as the Infidel somewhat disguised to the Europeans that they were confronted with a matter of political, rather than merely of theological, inevitability. As the Turkish Empire flowed smoothly around the last flotsam of the Empire like an oil slick burning at sea, Christian delight at the suppression of a heretic rival soon turned to dismay, as Europeans found themselves confronted by an onrushing and seemingly omnipresent militant state intent upon empery.

One curious fact of prudently conducted international war is that the enemy is usually careful not to take the capital of the other side, the object of war being not to destroy the foe, otherwise there would be nobody left to fight, but merely to reduce him.

Such, certainly, has been the strategy of wise European states on most occasions. But this means that everyone must play the same game according to the same rules, and utterly collapses as a successful strategy when buffer capitals are invaded by an ethnic horde with a different set of values. To take the capital of a foreign state confronts one at once with an obliterated buffer and a new, overextended and hostile border. And this is what, within ten years of the conquest of Byzantium, both the West and the Osmanli found themselves faced with—Hungary, the only European state whose borders marched with those of the Osmanli, being used and subsidized by both sides. And as Mahomet took successively the Morea, Wallachia, Serbia, Bosnia, Albania, the Crimea, and the Venetian, Genoese and Frankish islands in the Archipelago, the consequences of not having contained him earlier became clearer and clearer.

After Constantinople fell, there remained three Byzantine enclaves to deal with: the Morea; the independent city-state of Monemvasia, a seaport in one of the eastern folds of the Peloponnesus; and the completely independent and far distant Empire of Trebizond, under the rule of the Grand Comneni.

In Morea, Demetrius and Thomas, far from attempting to relieve the city, had employed themselves in the more congenial task of intriguing against each other. They were both appalled and surprised by the fall of the capital. Their first thought was to flee to Italy. But Mahomet accepted from them a tribute of 12,000 ducats a year, and for seven years left them in peace. Or rather, it would have been peace if Demetrius and Thomas had not continued their fratrical wars, to which purpose they devoted any money sent from Europe to relieve them. They were not popular with their subjects.

In October of 1454 Mahomet sent an army into the Morea, supposedly to defend his loyal vassals against Albanian incursions led by Scanderbeg. He called the Palaeologi together, and told them that their administration was vicious and that they should rule their people better. He also suggested that they try not to provoke their own ruin by their own actions. He then proclaimed Demetrius emperor.

Thomas, though younger, would not agree to this, and once safely out of sight, amused himself by removing the eyes and cutting off the nose, hands, and ears of the son-in-law of the Prince of Achaia. He then revolted against the Sultan, but instead of attacking Mahomet, first paused to destroy the possessions of Demetrius. Demetrius naturally appealed to the Sultan, who appeared with a large army, reconciled the two brothers, and took over their possessions for himself. He had already taken Athens in 1456. The 30th of May, 1460, Demetrius handed over Mistra, and was retired to Constantinople (he refused to go to any Latin nation, on religious grounds). His daughter was put into the seraglio; he was given an annual pension of 50,000 aspers and one eunuch to serve as an honor guard; and eventually he assumed monastic habit. He had no descendants, apart from his daughter, whose eventual end is not known. Presumably she merely died of natural causes in the harem.

Thomas resisted somewhat longer, and then escaped to Corfu and from there to Italy, taking with him the head of St. Andrew to sell as a bribe. The Pope and the Cardinals made him an annual pension of 6,000 ducats, and his sons, Andrew and Manuel, were educated in Italy. Andrew made an unfortunate marriage to a local prostitute, and sold his rights to the nonexistent Empire first to France, and then all over again to the House of Aragon. Manuel eventually returned to Constantinople, where he accepted the gift of two female slaves from Mahomet, and had a son who eventually became a slave in the Osmanli royal household. Nothing more than that is known about him.

By 1461 the Morea was a well-organized, if reluctant, Turkish province, with the sole exception of the autonomous republic, only a town really, of Monemvasia, under the rule of Manuel Palaeologus, a cousin. He placed the town under the protection of the Pope, and when a papal crusade failed to materialize, transferred the protectorate to Venice. The town, an important trading depot, was tolerated by the Osmanli because of both agreements and quarrels with Venice, and remained semi-independent until 1540, when Venice was at last forced to give it over.

These conquests left only Trebizond independent. That 250-year-old autonomous state at the far end of the Black Sea, which regarded itself as the true Byzantium, certainly behaved itself in a thoroughly Byzantine manner. In 1461 it consisted, for all practical purposes, of a long narrow valley with a capital, Amasia, built on either side of a rushing torrent, and of a narrow coastal strip with a port. On one side of it was Amastris, a Genoese trading depot, and between Amastris and Trebizond a small independent Turcoman state, Sinope.

This was the area where, 1,500 years before, Mithridates, who died old, maintained himself and the state of Pontus for so long against the Romans, chiefly because of his enormous financial skill. The Emperors of Trebizond had no financial skill. Their commerce, like that of Byzantium, had for long been in the hands of the all-consuming Genoese, except for those brief periods when the Venetians had been able to engross it. The inhabitants of Trebizond, no less than those of the mother city, were ruinously given to dynastic intrigue and theological dispute. In addition, there was much ill will between the native nobility, the Comnenan nobility and, now, the refugees from Constantinople.

Murad II had sent an army against Trebizond in 1430, without success. In 1454, Kalojoannes, its ruler, was forced to become a vassal of the Osmanli and to pay 3,000 gold pounds a year for the privilege. But such a center of future Byzantine intrigue could not be tolerated. Kalojoannes most unfortunately died in 1458, leaving, even more unfortunately, a boy of four, Alexius V, as his heir. Kalojoannes' brother David usurped the throne at once, and sent to the West for aid against the Turks.

David's niece, Theodora Comnena, who was married to Ouzoun Hassan, the neighboring Turcoman sultan of Sinope, and who was an ambitious woman, countered by forcing her husband into an overt act against Mahomet II and, like the Byzantines before her, demanded more tribute money—owed her state, so she claimed, since the days of Tamerlane, of whom Hassan was a descendant. It is extremely difficult to follow the logic of this maneuver, for it has none. It is also most unwise for mice to ask that the cat remove its claws. Mahomet replied by sending a fleet to reduce Hassan, which was done, and then advanced on Trebizond, to which his armies laid siege. After 28 days, David turned over the keys of the town, and while the Janissaries were occupying the Acropolis, set sail with his family for Constantinople.

There he could have lived in honorable retirement, had not his niece attempted another uprising. Mahomet intercepted the relevant correspondence; offered the royal family Islam or death; put the Princess Anne in the seraglio; convinced one son to circumcision and survival; and had the rest decapitated, sparing only the Empress Helena, who died shortly thereafter. That was the end of Trebizond. It is now an obscure, degenerate and extremely beautiful, if little visited, Turkish town.

Except that Thomas's daughter, Zoë-Sophia, had married Ivan III of Moscow, and that a cadet branch of the Palaeologi governed the Italian petty state of Montferrat until the line became extinct in the mid-sixteenth century, the royal houses of Byzantium had now finally been abolished, though various collateral branches of the Palaeologus family continue to the present day, the last notable man of that name in recent times having been an early twentieth-century French journalist, Maurice Palaeologue. They had been, however, the longest ruling of all the Byzantine houses.

But, as every military leader with some purpose other than mere conquest has discovered, from Alexander to Napoleon to Hitler, no matter how one may wish to consolidate one's holdings or even to stop at a certain point, one cannot stop, since the only way to control a large military establishment is to use it, otherwise the whole structure, and in particular its improvised economics, collapses. Robbing Peter to pay Paul unfortunately and inevitably means that all the other ten apostles must be levied in their turn, until one reaches the end. Despite complete economic ignorance, Mahomet and his predecessors had so well constructed the state, and so recent and ill-founded were the European states who alone could have halted him, that the end of prosperity for the Turks was not to come for another two hundred years. Nonetheless, armies had to be kept on the move.

Mahomet's progress was greatly assisted by the interior maladministration of the states he wished to attack. Writing to Pope Pius II (Aeneas Sylvius Piccolomini) in 1463, Stephan, last King of Bosnia, endeavored to explain. "The Turks promise to all who side with them freedom, and the rough mind of the peasants does not understand the artfulness of such a promise, and believes that such freedom will last forever; and so it may happen that the misguided common people may turn away from me, unless they see that I am supported by you."

Freedom may not have lasted forever, but at least it had the charm of novelty. When, in 1464, Mahomet II invaded Bosnia, the peasantry refused to fight in defense of their native rulers, saying, "It is not our business to defend the king; let the nobles do it." The nobles did not do it, having quarrels of their own, and so Bosnia fell.

The condition of Bosnian religious affairs greatly assisted the fall. In this case, refreshingly, it was not a matter of fanatical disagreement between Orthodox and Latin, but between Christian and Bogomil. One of the constant countercurrents within the Church had always been Manichaean or Catharist heresy. Though the Manichees themselves had been wiped out in the fourth century, their doctrine that the world was inherently evil, and had to be charred good, became a part of popular Christian belief and budded heresy from time to time. The Bogomils were such a group, and had had great success. Bosnia gave them shelter. When conquered by the Turks, those of them who had not previously been massacred by the Christians frequently became Muslims rather than fall into Christian hands. Their exact doctrine has never been fully elucidated, and neither has the symbolism of the extremely odd sepulchral sculpture they left behind them.

Christian warfare against the Turk was made anomalous by the vassalage system, since as often as not a Christian vassal was obligated to send troops to his Osmanli suzerain, who would use them against other Christians. Thus at the battle of

Rovine, in 1394, King Marko of Serbia, forced to fight on the Turkish side, said to his relative, Constantine Dragases (another Constantine Dragases, not the Emperor), "I pray God to give victory to the Christians, though I pay for it with my own life." Needless to say, the Turks won. And at the battle of Nicopolis in 1396, the French, Polish and Hungarian cavalry would have carried the fight, had not the Turks brought up a reserve of Serbian cavalry led by Prince Stephen Lazarevič. These wars were conducted before an emergent nationalism had made personal fealty a state offense.

Mahomet's principal foes remained Scanderbeg, Hunyadi, and the Wallachian tyrant, Vlad.

He began with Wallachia. That country had been ruled for the past thirty years by a man called Vlad or Bladus, usually called Drakul, or the Devil, by his subjects, Wlad the Executioner by the Hungarians, and Wlad the Empaler by the Turks. There have not been many real sadists in this world, most of them being harmless neurotics or else people with devious nervous systems who, since they restrict their activities to equally harmless masochists, on the whole do little damage. Wlad, however, was an authentic sadist. Beginning modestly, he made away with 400 Transylvanians because they were preaching a crusade, 600 merchants because they were too rich, and 500 nobles because they had said he was too cruel. He solved the problem of poverty by asking all the beggars of the country to dinner, and then setting fire to the hall in which they were eating. His chief pleasure was to dine with his court, surrounded by prisoners empaled on poles until they died. One way or another, he managed to dispose of some 30,000 people. With this man Mahomet first signed a treaty of amity, but since he shortly thereafter empaled two Turkish ambassadors, one higher than the other in deference to his rank, and somewhat later, when fresh ambassadors refused to remove their turbans in his presence, had their turbans nailed to their heads, a war was inevitable. At first Wlad won it. Mahomet, arriving at Praelatu shortly after this engagement, was treated to the spectacle of a forest of 20,000 poles, on each of which a Turkish or Bulgarian man, woman or child was empaled and writhing.

"How can I despoil of his states a man who does such things to save them?" demanded Mahomet. But he succeeded in driving Wlad out. The man took refuge in Hungary, and fifteen years later reappeared, but was assassinated.

It was now at last the turn of the Venetians and the Genoese to suffer from a conquest from which they had expected nothing but profit, and which they had done so little to prevent.

Wars are fought not over principles, but on pretexts. The Venetians refused to give up a slave who had taken refuge with them, because he had become a Christian. The Turks marched, and though the Venetians held their own by sea, by land they were repeatedly beaten.

The Pope released Scanderbeg from any obligation to the infidel incurred by the mere signing of a secular treaty, and Scanderbeg obligingly destroyed five more Osmanli armies. The only Janissary who ever rebelled, the son of John Castriot, hereditary Prince of Albania, he owed his power less to the loyalty of his Albanian and Epirot subjects, which remained as always minimal, than to his income, which was enormous, for he derived 200,000 ducats a year from the salt pits of Selina. He fought the Turks successfully, but he was another one-man dynasty, there were cabals against him, mostly Venetian, and he was forced to flee in 1462, and died discredited, which is to say poor, in 1467. He was honorably buried, though after Scanderbeg died of fever in 1467, his vertebrae and ribs were worn as amulets by the Janissaries, who made their own saints. His son was forced to abandon his capital of Croia to the Venetians, who rightly deduced it would make an important trading depot, and fled to Naples. The last descendent of Scanderbeg, the Count of St. Angelo, died at the battle of Pavia, in 1525. It is to the population movements of this period that the present large Albanian colonies in South Italy owe their existence.

Scanderbeg was the most difficult of Mahomet's foes to dispose of. John Corvinus Hunyadi, the Hungarian ex-regent and the only man who could really hold the Hungarian resistance effectively together, was wounded at the defense of Belgrade in 1456, and died a month later. His son John was made King of Hungary, but was first of all a minor, and second, despite himself, a weakling. "Alas, I no longer have hope of avenging myself on the only Christian who could boast of having beaten me," Mahomet is alleged to have said, when learning of Hunyadi's death.

Meanwhile, the Genoese found Turkish rule much less profitable to trade than Byzantine had been; and the Venetians tried to save what they could, for the Turks penetrated as deeply into Europe as Croatia, Carniola, Carinthia, and Syria (1470–1473), thus threatening the Venetian provinces as well as the Hungarian and Austrian.

The Genoese had been easy to dislodge. Since the invasion of Tamerlane, they had maintained trading posts in the Crimea and had established a flourishing mercantile city there, called Caffa. As Mithridates had discovered 1,500 years before, the Black Sea could be dominated just as well from the Crimea as from the west or south shores. Mahomet sent a fleet and an army, Caffa was betrayed by a traitor, and the Genoese in the rest of the peninsula surrendered and were driven out. It had all been soon done.

The Venetians had been at war with Mahomet for thirteen years. In 1476 he reached the Salzburg Alps, and in 1477 invaded Croatia and Dalmatia again, crossed the Julian Alps and entered Italy for the first time, sacking Friuli, advancing as far as the Piave, and by sea menacing Venice herself. At night, from the city, across the lagoons, the mainland could be seen burning.

The Turks were not always successful, but they were usually successful in the end. Venice offered to abandon Croia, where Scanderbeg's last followers were shut up. Mahomet accepted, and demanded Scutari (the European Scutari in Albania) as well. This Venice refused to yield up, so he was forced to take it. Peace was then concluded between the Porte and Venice, on January 26, 1479. A Turkish ambassador appeared at Venice, and was received so well that rumors of a secret entente between the two powers were everywhere. They were, in this particular case, unfounded.

Muslims—Osmanli, Turcoman, Arab, and Persian—now controlled the Balkans, Greece, Asia Minor, the Black Sea, Syria, Egypt, the North African coast, and large parts of Spain, though those were going back to the Spanish. The Christian world had little to congratulate itself upon—least, perhaps, upon their lack of assistance to Byzantium.

Since, as has been said, an army must be kept on the move if it is not to decay, Mahomet now moved it. His enterprises were sometimes capricious. Wishing some colored eunuchs, he forced the inhabitants of Zante and Cephalonia to intermarry with African Negroes, matching skins as another man would match fabrics, and wanting apparently a special shade of mulatto brown. A conquerer is much like a small child; he always wants more. He next set sail for Italy and took Otranto, his first incursion into what the Italians, at any rate, considered to be Europe proper (the Venetians were not regarded as Italians by Italians of that day, but as a refractory people set apart). The taking of Otranto caused another panic. It was said that he had promised himself not to rest until his horse had used the high altar at St. Peter's as a manger.

His galleys sailed from Constantinople, as galleys had not sailed from there for centuries. No longer would the Venetians or anybody else fight domestic engagements under a defenseless city, and Galata was at last reduced.

Mahomet had not, as usual, announced his itinerary, but laid siege to the Knights of St. John of Jerusalem, who held Rhodes. Unfortunately, during the siege he died, in 1481, suddenly, quite young (he was only about fifty-one, the wonder of the age) but, since he had been able to make himself feared in the right way, of natural causes: a heavy-set man, with a beak nose and a rather weary, melancholy, secretive expression.

XXI

SO accomplished had Mahomet II been that after his death Christendom believed itself to be delivered of its worst enemy. Christendom would have done better to wait upon events, for later, when there was time to make comparisons to his successors, he was as widely praised as previously he had been denounced.

As a matter of fact, he was a better legislator than he was a commander, owing his victories chiefly to the number of his soldiers and the weakness of his enemies. The Osmanli, like the Spartans of ancient Greece, had had virtually no art but that of making war. Mahomet II changed all that. His code of laws, the *Qanunname,* or Fundamental Law, was the means by which he did it, and is divided into three parts: that governing the hierarchy of the state; that governing ceremonies; and that which regulates finance, crime, and municipal government.

As modified by Suleiman the Magnificent some 70 years later, it remained the Turkish code of law until the end of the First World War. Incorporated into it was almost the entire legislation, forms, ceremonies, etiquette, and governmental system of Byzantium. To take over all this showed great political wisdom. There is nothing more likely to make a conquered people revolt than laws to which they are not accustomed, or to new divisions of property and an alien and heavier taxation. Osmanli taxation was lighter. Otherwise, they sensibly left things as they were.

Later, of course, modifications were introduced; confiscated land was distributed into fiefs, the holders of it distinguished, or anyhow competent, warriors who were expected not only to defend the land but also, on summons, those who had given it to them. This was the system whereby the Byzantines some centuries earlier had both rewarded the loyal and insured that they would remain so.

Under Mahomet, the greater number of conquered Christian farmers kept their holdings and were on the whole better off, chiefly because of the soundness of the administration, than they had been before, even though enormous latifundia grew up, the peasants at the bottom of the social ladder being virtual economic slaves, if not slaves in fact.

Unfortunately the Asiatic provinces were allowed to go to wrack and ruin, partly because, due to the taxgathering system, harvest had to wait for two months while taxes were gathered (payment was in kind, on the spot). But the decay of this system occurred long after Mahomet established it, for no matter how good the initial administrator, there is nothing he can do to control either the competence or the corruption of his heirs. That the system persisted and functioned for so long after him, despite corruption, is at least testimony to how well he succeeded in articulating the state.

It was a maxim of the Osmanli that sons of Christians should hold the highest offices of the Empire. First, because there were not enough Turks; second, because a military state prefers to have its civil work done by somebody else; and third, to prevent the Turkish overlords from becoming suicidally corrupt. For of course a Christian could be removed without much loss—there were always more Christians—but there were very few Osmanli Turks. The result of this policy was that under Mahomet II, four of five successive grand viziers were of Christian origin, and under Suleiman the Magnificent, 90 years later, eight out of nine were. Needless to say, they had been brought up as Janissaries.

It was under Suleiman that the Turks were able to threaten not merely Hungary but all Europe as well. He was ambitious and came upon a world entirely, if unconsciously, suited to his imperial plans.

Except that Germany and Italy were still divided up into small states, Europe had by now assumed its modern nationalistic shape; and the Emperor Charles V and Francis I of France were much too busy fighting each other to unite against a common foe. Both men were to be reckoned with, but the difference between them may perhaps be summed up by saying that Francis I was wily and Charles V powerful, the one apt to impose, the other by nature imposing. By a series of dynastic chances, Charles V ruled Spain, Austria, Flanders, Burgundy, and part of Italy, and was Holy Roman Emperor of the Germans as well. He thus surrounded France, and Francis himself, who had been captured at the battle of Pavia on February 25, 1525, was held prisoner at Madrid.

It is curious that the main impulse of Europe should have become secular and political at the time that the Osmanli began to fight their battles of self-aggrandizement under the guise of a holy crusade. Francis I, who was not a religious man though he held the title of Defender of the Faith, having no one else to succor him, called the Turks in. As a Most Catholic Majesty, he could not do so openly; he could not have done so openly anyway, being a captive in Madrid; but nonetheless he managed the matter. This pact was referred to as "the impious union of the Lilies with the Crescent," and caused a stir in the chancelleries. Francis is known to have said that he would have invoked the Devil to free himself from the hands of his enemies, and now he had. The days when the Duke of Burgundy could lament the approaching downfall of the Christian Byzantine Empire with a centerpiece to entertain guests at dinner, in which a lady mourned the tardiness of her defenders, were long gone. At the moment, Francis was only too glad to have Islam there, and Suleiman was only too delighted to come. Charles V's Austrian possessions and Hungarian pretensions marched with the borders of the Porte; and to make alliance with the worst enemy of his worst enemy, Suleiman was willing to do much. For the first time, the Porte actually sent complimentary presents, instead of receiving them.

"Moved with compassion," says a Turkish historian, Suleiman determined to make war. No treaty was established to this effect, however, for to undertake an alliance with a Christian infidel was as great an impiety to the Turks as to undertake such an understanding with a Muslim infidel was to the Christians. Instead, Francis was sent a reassuring letter.

"To thee, Francis," it began, "who art king of the country of France. You have sent a letter to my Porte, asylum of sovereigns, by your faithful agent Frankipan; you have also commanded him to make certain verbal communications. You have made known that the enemy has seized upon your country, and that you are actually in prison, and you have asked here asylum and succor for your deliverance. All that you have said having been laid open at the foot of my throne, refuge of the world, my imperial science has embraced it in detail, and I have taken complete cognizance of it.

"It is not astonishing that emperors are defeated and become prisoners. Take, therefore, courage, and let not yourself be cast down. Our glorious ancestors and our illustrious grandfathers (may God illumine their tombs) have never ceased to make war to repel the enemy and conquer countries. We also, we have marched in their footsteps. We have conquered at all times provinces and strong citadels difficult of access. Night and day our steed is saddled and our saber is girded on.

"May the very exalted God facilitate the good! To whatsoever object your wish may attach itself, may it be granted. For the rest, after interrogating your agent about affairs and news, you shall be informed thereon. Know it to be thus.

"Written at the commencement of the moon of Rebiulakhir 932 [15 February, 1526], at our residence in the capital of the Empire, Constantinople, the well guarded."

This has very much the high-handed tone the West had so objected to in the pronouncements of the Byzantine Emperors, but Francis was asking for help.

By early 1526, the Hungarians had learned that to help Francis, Suleiman was making elaborate preparations to invade their kingdom. Weakened by their wars with each other, the Hungarian magnates were in no position to resist and the population was in no mood to, for a good part of it had become Protestant, and Luther was most unwisely on record as having said: "To fight against the Turks is equivalent to struggling against God, who has prepared such rods for the chastisement of our sins."

In the spring Suleiman, praying first at his own holy places, entered Hungary by way of Serbia and Belgrade with an army of 100,000 commanded by himself and his three viziers, 300 cannon, and 800 vessels, or enough to pave the Danube. The war went well, and despite some show of resistance, the entire Hungarian ruling class and their king, Louis, were killed at the Battle of Mohacz, in a stampede into a marsh. After this, resistance was nominal and the Turks advanced on Buda, burning as they went. Suleiman supplied the Hungarians with a puppet king, John Zapoly, a man of neither cunning nor courage, admirably suited to his new role; took off the antique statues from the royal castle to decorate the Hippodrome; and in 1528 availed himself of Croatia, Slavonia, and Dalmatia as well. Louis of Hungary being dead, Ferdinand of Austria presented himself as rightful claimant to the Hungarian throne. The Osmanli backed Zapoly.

Suleiman, who had kept the ambassadors of Ferdinand of Austria in jail for nine months, in the Prison of the Seven Towers (the old Golden Gate to Constantinople), now sent for them. "Your master," he said, "has not felt sufficiently up to the present moment the effects of our friendship and our vicinity, but he will shortly. You may tell him that I shall go in search of him myself with all my forces, and that I earnestly hope to restore with my own hand that which he claims. Tell him also that he may prepare everything for our reception."

Then, on the 10th of May, 1529, he set out from Constantinople with an army of 150,000. The Byzantine Emperors had regarded themselves as delegates of Christ and representatives of His power on earth, owners of the world whether it happened to be in their possession at the moment or not. The Osmanli had a similar conceit; wherever the horse of the Grand Seignior had stepped that territory was for all time Osmanli. Suleiman had slept in the palace at Buda, and had left it standing only because he intended to sleep in it again. All Hungary, as far as he was concerned, now belonged to him.

Ferdinand had no forces with which to fight. Therefore, though to offer tribute would have been degrading, he offered Suleiman an annual pension instead. Unfortunately Suleiman took the contrariwise view—no one pensions off the supreme ruler of the world—and on he marched, reaching Vienna on the 27th of September, 1529.

Ferdinand had retreated prudently to Linz to await developments, turning the defense of his capital over to somebody else. It was in some ways a symbolic defense, no less than that of Byzantium though to far less effect; Vienna was in some measure a sacred city, insofar as it was the residence of the Holy Roman Emperor, a title by now virtually hereditary in the Habsburg line. That one of the heartland capitals of Europe should now be besieged by the same force which had taken Constantinople while everybody tactfully looked the other way, only 75 years before, struck terror into the hearts of many, and hardened the resolve of at least a few. Even the German Protestant states, in fact primarily the German Protestant states, sent reinforcements, the Elector of Saxony 2,000 men. Even so, Vienna had only 16,000 men to defend it, which is 7,000 to 9,000 more than Constantinople had had, and 72 guns, which could not be mounted on the walls, which had fallen into disrepair. Suleiman had 300,000 men, counting camp followers and domestics, 300 cannon, and a flotilla large enough to blanket the Danube, entirely too visible from the spire of St. Stephen's Cathedral. Also visible from there were the tents of the Osmanli encampment, which dotted the hills for miles.

To complete the parallel, the West was again divided by religious controversy, this time between Protestant (indeed the name had only just been given them, after the Protest at Spires in the spring of the year 1529), and Catholic. However, perhaps because its pretensions were so undisguisedly temporal, the Church had never so undermined and infiltrated the civil governments of the West as had the Orthodox Church that of the East, and rancor was not yet so strong between Protestant and

Catholic as it was to become later. The inhabitants of the city put up a stout defense. Unlike the Byzantines, the citizens consented to fight for their city side by side with the troops.

Suleiman sent in a message that if the garrison would surrender, he would not even enter the town but go in search of Ferdinand instead; if they did not surrender, he proposed to dine in Vienna on the third day of the siege, and not so much as spare children in the womb. To this message he received no reply.

Though good at battles and running tactics, the Osmanli were not good at sieges. Mahomet II had traveled light and moved quickly; but the pomp of success required that Suleiman move in clumsy caravans. His army was divided into 16 badly coordinated commands. Worst of all, the Osmanli were not accustomed to the damps and danks of European good weather. The Janissaries complained of the cold by Michaelmas, and since their supply lines were overextended, provisions were beginning to fail. Flour was supplied by trains of 22,000 camels, but the camels were even less used to a brisk subalpine autumn than were the men.

The Turks were forced to raise the siege, though in retaliation they laid waste the countryside as far as the gates of Linz. Harried on their retreat, which was as bad to them as the Russian campaign was to be to Napoleon some time later, the armies arrived back in Constantinople November 10th. This was the first real check the Osmanli had suffered in their campaigns against Europe, and though it did not diminish their power, it did diminish their ambitions.

Nonetheless, the siege of Vienna had given Europe a bad start in the sense that though it did not unite it against a common invader—after all, what could?—it did leave it with a permanent, from the Turkish point of view an effective, fear of the Turkish Empire. This fear was felt particularly strongly in the Germanies.

"We have not to combat an enemy of the same species as ourselves," said Busbeck, the Holy Roman Empire's ambassador to the Porte. "We have to do with the Turk, a vigilant, adroit, sober, disciplined enemy, one inured to military labors, expert in tactics and fit for all the hardships of the service. It is by these qualities that he has made for himself a way through desolated Empires, that he has subjugated all from the frontiers of Persia, and that he has threatened Vienna."

One way and another, this statement, consciously or unconsciously, tells much about the virtues and vices of the European nations and their armies at that time.

With the siege of Vienna, the military power of the Turks reached and then declined from its peak, but the European nations had no way of knowing that then, and neither of course did the Turks. Suleiman did not regard his failure at Vienna as a defeat, but as an affront. The following spring, with an even more cumbersome army even harder to maintain, he set out to avenge it, leaving Constantinople on the 26th of April, 1531, with 300,000 men, more than 120 cannon, 8,000 picked Janissaries, droves of camels to carry the baggage, 2,000 horsemen to escourt the Eagle of the Prophet, a banner encrusted with pearls and precious stones, and the Sultan's crown (made in Venice, to order, at a cost of 115,000 ducats), 1,000 giants, domestics of his household, armed with bows and arrows, leading paired hounds and bearing hawks. Suleiman rode in the midst of them, in a crimson robe trimmed with gold embroidery, a jeweled snow-white turban, a jeweled dagger and sword, and mounted on a chestnut horse. His four viziers came behind him, and the court nobles and their servants after that.

It was gorgeous. It was impressive. It was in all likelihood deliberately designed as propaganda; but as it wound over the hills and out of sight away from Constantinople and its music was swallowed by the landscape, there must have been a few in the city, Greeks most likely, to remember the tiny processions with which the later Palaeologi had set forth on their campaigns, together with the complete and easy informality with which they had as frequently come scampering back; and history would remember with what similar panoply the armies of a richer Byzantium had once gone to their defeat.

Hungary was again overrun, and the Turkish fleet went up

the Danube as far as Pressburg. Unfortunately the entire army was brought to a standstill by the insignificant village of Güns, which beat off eleven assaults. This, and a defeat in the mountains, saved Austria; and Suleiman, who had been attacked in the Morea by Charles V's admiral, Andrea Doria, retired.

However, he might be presumed to be lurking, and this threat was enough to make him an all-powerful and undisturbed force in European politics for the rest of his life, which ended in 1566.

Suleiman was the last of the nine successively competent sultans. His son was Selim the Sot, of whom there is little favorable to be said, and after his death the power of the Osmanli began to ebb until eventually, toward the end of the nineteenth century, the actual power of the sultans themselves was restricted, as had been the power of the later Palaeologi, more or less to the city itself and its suburbs, Asia Minor being often intractable. Just as Byzantium had done centuries before, the Osmanli lost Egypt, the Crimea, the Balkans, and Greece. The period of migrations having ceased, they kept Anatolia, and also Constantinople, which they have still.

Thomas Coryat, the eccentric English traveler who visited Constantinople in the early seventeenth century, shows, by implication, what the Osmanli so rapidly came to. In his time, all ambassadors but that of the Holy Roman Empire were forced to live outside the walls at Galata, known to the Turks as the Pig Quarter (by then all non-Muslims had become pigs, and as much turned upon the eating or noneating of pork as formerly had turned upon whether the Host were of leavened or unleavened bread).

The gentleman seen fishing under the wall of the Seraglio turned out to be Rama, the sultan's soothsayer, a most important personage. There were many fires, not all accidental, for "Janissaries do of purpose set Houses on fire, even to the great endangering of the Citie for prey and spoyle sake, especially the houses of Jews. For which cause the Jews within these few years, have both made their houses stronger than they were wont to be, and also have made Vaults under their houses, into which they may conveigh their Goods whensoever there chanceth any sodaine Fire." One night while Coryat was there, such a fire broke out, and was with difficulty extinguished by the chief gardener (who was also the Lord High Executioner), and the admiral, who felled a Janissary with his mace when the fellow was discovered looting a house.

When there is no order left to maintain, the show of it is usually kept up by sanguinary execution, and Constantinople was no exception to this rule. Brothers of the reigning sultan were strangled with a bowstring—that was their privilege, equivalent to the silk rope with which nobles in Europe were entitled to be hanged; military officers convicted of theft were shot from the mouth of a cannon; adulterous women sewn in sacks and flung in the sea; but the most popular punishment was gaunching. Felons were allowed to fall on a sort of meat hook. If it punctured their guts, they died rapidly. If it caught them in the thigh or somewhere else, they sometimes lived so long as a day or two, and were allowed to talk to each other.

The sultan at this time was Achmet I. His father, Mahomet III, had murdered nineteen of his brothers on coming to the throne, and then relapsed into safety and sloth. The Osmanli Empire was already weak, but fortunately saved by what had so often saved Byzantium, the internecine wars of its enemies.

None of this showed in the outward pomps of the capital, any more than it had shown in, say, the days just before the Crusaders sacked it, in 1204. Achmet entered the city with a retinue of 15,000. "The pompe of it was so gallant that I never saw the like in my life, neither doe I thinke that the like hath beene used amongst any Princes of the world saving these Musulmen, since the time of the Romane Emperours." But then, the Palaeologi had regarded themselves as Roman emperors.

Since the sultan had slipped into the city at dawn, surrounded by his women, and had headed directly for the Seraglio, it was an empty pomp.

Perhaps history has no lessons, only examples, and yet the weaker grows the power of great states, the greater grows the show. Of course, during the Renaissance the state procession was a recognized means of propaganda, as effective in showing one's power, and in the same way, as the military review is in our day.

And yet there is something a little eerie—even if Constantinople by now was an entirely Turkish city in fact and appearance, despite its cosmopolitan horde—about these diminishing processions, winding through streets still dominated by the enormous ruins of the last Empire but one, still protected by the walls of that last Empire, and still wending its way past that enormous cathedral, 1,100 years old now instead of merely 900, equipped with minarets and whitewash, but though different in name, no different in nature.

In our day it is almost 1,400 years old, and is neither church nor mosque, but a state museum. It still dominates the city; but there is perhaps something disturbing about our habit of turning things into museums. It is a very recent habit—it scarcely predates, in the modern sense, the conquests of Napoleon—and it is apt to make us forget that in past time the world was in private hands, and that almost certainly it will be in private hands again; that the two kinds of state, the declining, the aspiring, the conservative, the acquisitive, alternate over and over again, beyond any whim we may have toward stasis.

There seems no moral to be drawn from these events. History is its own parable and its own moral, and though certain virtually immutable principles of process may be derived from it, these have no ethical meaning. A system of ethics could perhaps be constructed empirically upon them, but this few individuals, and no states, have ever been so foolhardy as to do. For the strength of an ethical society comes neither from its professed nor from its actual conduct, but from the constant tension between the two; the tiny leeway between what people say they have done, and know they should do, and what they actually do do being the only freedom a stable society can ever grant to its individuals, a freedom which is usually adequate to their needs, and one which at least avoids total anarchy.

The last powerful aggressive act on a world scale of which the Osmanli proved capable was the siege of Vienna in 1683. By that time, the Osmanli had themselves changed. The sultan did not lead the armies himself. He sent a vizier. Two hundred years of corruption and of insufficient vigilance had greatly retarded both supplies and economies. The power of the navy had been broken at Lepanto, a century before. Religious tolerance was gone, and the provincials so restless that they could be oppressed into obedience, but not otherwise relied upon.

The Turks were successfully driven back, not by the Emperor Leopold of Austria but by Sobieski, elected king of Poland, with about 60,000 men. The vizier, attacked from the rear and driven back from this last attempt to storm Vienna, fled in the night of September 12th, leaving his entire and luxuriously furnished camp to the Christians. "The grand vizier," wrote Sobieski, "has left me his heir, and I inherit millions of ducats. When I return, I shall not be met with the reproach of the Tartar wives: 'You are not a man because you come back without booty.' "

When Sobieski entered the liberated city, he was acclaimed. He had saved not only the Viennese but Europe from the Turk. The Emperor Leopold, on his return, met with a less enthusiastic reception. This did not please him, he avoided his ally, and asked whether an elective monarch *could* be admitted to an interview with an hereditary sovereign, and if so, how he should be received. "With open arms," said the Duke of Lorraine, in disgust. The eventual meeting, on horseback, did not go well, and the five days spent settling the protocol of it gave the Turks time to make their retreat.

After the siege of Vienna, even though Sobieski withdrew to Poland in disgust and refused to pursue the war in Hungary, the Turks were continuously beaten back, defeated, or diplomatically outmaneuvered. In 1691 the new sultan, Mustapha, who commanded his army in person, was put to the mortification of watching his own defeat. He rallied, and it was not until the year 1697 that he had the privilege of seeing, from his station on the opposite bank, 29,000 of his men driven into the

River Treiss. He was forced to flee, and a peace was concluded with the Porte November 14, 1697. This, the Peace of Karlowitz, put a stop to that universal terror which the Turks had up until now inspired. By it the Turks lost almost half their European possessions.

As a major threat to Europe, the Osmanli Empire, dating from the fall of Constantinople, had lasted 244 years; as the impotent bulwark against them, the Palaeologi had lasted 192. From this period on, Turkey gradually sank until, by the nineteenth century, she was known as "the Sick Man of Europe." The pomp remained enormous and impressive, right up until the time of the First World War. But the power was gone. In short, history repeated itself. Historians inform us it does not, and yet it does. The details differ. The burden is the same.

One may ask whether the Oriental custom of abandoning a capital upon a change of dynasty, if not upon a change of rule, is not the better one. Egypt, Persia, Afghanistan, Turkestan, India and the Orient, and the high Indian cultures of the New World are strewn with the ruins of abandoned capitals, with the paved tombstones of forgotten dynasties. Only in Europe are we compelled to live with the combined futility of the past. From being their capital, Constantinople became the prison of the sultans. When not shut up by their own eunuchs and ambitious bureaucrats, they shut themselves up. Abdul Hamid, the terrible Turk of the nineteenth century, lived in a state of terrified paranoic seclusion. The last sultan, deposed at the end of the First World War, though not secluded, simply does not seem to have known what to do, and let the power dwindle away from him out of a mixture of apathy and congenital inability (though Abdul Hamid had been clever enough, his only fault being to make so many different plots that they all canceled each other out, and to make allies of the Germans, who, alas from the Turkish point of view, lost the war, a problem he left to his successor). The last sultans had almost Byzantine bad luck.

Somewhere, in one of his poems, Louis MacNeice says that the trouble with Africa is that its rivers "flow out of too little history into too much." The latter day Turks of Constantinople suffered from the opposite ill, of coming out of too much history into too little, and even a broken wall may sometimes mock. It was perhaps for this reason that Kemal Atatürk, the father of the new Turkish state of today, wisely moved the capital to the ancient site of Ankara (anciently Ancyra, Angora, taken by Orchan in 1354), in the interior of Asia Minor, where Osmanli power had first permanently settled and arisen.

It remains only to say a word about the eventual wanderings of the Palaeologi. The last of them with imperial pretensions is buried, oddly enough, in the West Indies. This we owe to the extensive, though seldom mentioned, territorial and political diplomacy of Oliver Cromwell. Don Ferdinando Palaeologus turned up in England during the Protectorate, petitioned for a pension, and was given one, though under a faith it is difficult to believe, considering his heredity, he could admire. Before the end of the Protectorate, he migrated to the island of Barbados, then the most aristocratic (in the English sense) of the West Indies, and was churchwarden of Old St. John's Church in the Scotland parish of the island from 1655 to 1666, and vestryman for twenty years, dying there on October 3, 1678, or about twenty years before the eventual turning back of his ancestral enemies.

His career at least forms a pleasant contrast to that of Misha Pasha, a member of the Byzantine royal house who, inspired chiefly by greed and ambition, made common cause with Mahomet after the fall of the city; participated in the siege of Rhodes in 1480–81; fell out of favor with his master but regained it under Bayazid II, whose chief vizier he caused to be denounced and strangled at Adrianople for his own ineptitudes. He was particularly noted for the vigor of his persecution of his once fellow Christians, had they any property worth adding to his own, was himself in time denounced, and vanishes from history, no one quite knowing how he met his end.

Don Ferdinando's tomb, in the Little England district of Barbados, is of unornamented white marble, overshadowed, through a window, by a large bougainvillea. The church itself is in the standard seventeenth-century English style, and has a pleasant, neglected atmosphere. One could not well think of a more agreeable place to be buried.

One other observance connected with the Palaeologi either survived, or more probably was invented, during the Greek wars of independence, in the early nineteenth century. A mass for the dead was said on the 29th of May, and a special kind of cake, decorated with almonds and cinnamon and iced with sugar, was displayed in the churches flanked by lamps swathed in black and bearing the inscription: KONSTANTINOS PALAIOLOGOS.

Such, at any rate, was the custom in Crete, according to Kazantzakis, the novelist. The parishioners then partook of this cake as of a sort of sacrament, and prayed for freedom from the Turks. It seems strange that the Church, which in his lifetime had done much to bring him down by cursing him for an apostate, should later take him for a patron saint and a guarantee of its own freedom from the same yoke from which he had tried to free it. But then it was not until the nineteenth century that Joan of Arc, his contemporary, was forgiven either, and not until the twentieth that she was canonized.

Life so often proceeds by parallels as to make us, in the end, a little sad. And yet it is agreeable that at least two of the three bravest people of their day should be admired in ours; and as for Mahomet II, he is not exactly dispraised by the contemporary Turks, either. All these people leave a memory.

DYNASTIC TABLE

(Corrected to Ostrogorsky's Hand List)

Constantinople, founded by Constantine the Great circa 330, became a separate state when Theodosius the Great (346–394) divided the Roman Empire between his two sons, Arcadius and Honorius. It reached its greatest territorial extent under the Emperor Justinian (died 565), and its greatest power and prosperity under the Macedonian Emperors (867–1057) who were succeeded by the House of Comnenus who, though often astute, had too much to contend with, and let the Empire slip. They in turn were succeeded by the House of Ducas (1059–1078) and by the utterly worthless

House of Angelus:

Isaac II	(1185–1195)	(By usurpation)
Alexis III	(1195–1203)	(By usurpation)
Isaac II	(1203–1204)	(Restored)
Alexis IV	(1203–1204)	(Co-Emperor)
Alexis V Muzurphlos	(1204)	(By usurpation and election)

Constantinople was then occupied by the Crusaders, resulting in a conflict between the two following houses, the simultaneous efforts of the Despot of Epirus and of the Emperors of Trebizond to capture the Empire proving ineffectual:

THE LATIN EMPIRE
(At Constantinople)

Baldin, Count of Flanders
1204–1205 (He disappeared in battle)

Henry, his brother
1206–1216 (He died young, probably of poison)

Peter of Courtenay
1217 (He had married their sister, Countess Yolande of Flanders)

Yolande of Flanders
1217–1219 (As regent and widow)
1219–1221 Interregnum

Robert of Courtenay (Her younger son)
1221–1228

Baldwin II (His son)
1228–1261 (During his minority the Latin Empire was ruled by a regent, John de Brienne (1231–1237). Baldwin's rule was terminated by the retaking of the city and the fall of the Latin Empire.)

EMPIRE OF NICAEA
(At Magnesia and Nicaea)

House of Lascaris

Theodore I. Lascaris
1204–1222

(Probably elected, but not a member of the previous dynasty)

John III Vatatzes
1222–1254
(He married Theodore's daughter)

Theodore II Lascaris
1254–1258
(Son of above, but took back his mother's name)

John IV Lascaris
1258–1261 (By succession, son of above) Deposed by his co-emperor, founder of the

House of Palaeologus
(At Constantinople)

Michael VIII
1261–1282
(By usurpation and election)

Andronicus II
1282–1328
(By succession)

Michael IX
1295–1320
Co-Emperor, predeceased his father)

Andronicus III
1328–1341
(By succession)

John V
1341–1391
(By succession) Who during his long reign put up with the following usurpations:

John VI Cantacuzenos
1347–1354

Matthew Cantacuzenos, his son, Co-Emperor, 1354–1357, and harder than his father to dislodge; after which John V held effective power, but was himself driven out by his son Andronicus IV, 1376–1379, and by his grandson, John VII, 1390, but was succeeded, all the same, by his son, Manuel II, 1391–1425, who associated with him John VII, 1400–1402, and was succeeded by his son John VIII, 1425–1448, who was succeeded by his brother, Constantine XI Dragases, last Byzantine Emperor, 1449–1453.

The pretenders to the empty
throne being Thomas, and
after him, his son Andrew,
who sold his rights to the
succession, first to Charles of
France, and second to the
King of Naples.

The Byzantine Empire was conquered by the Osmanli Turks who were ruled by

THE HOUSE OF OSMAN

Suleiman	died 1231	
Ertoghril	1231–1288	
Osman or Othman	1288–1326	(During the last four years of his father's life he had been regent)
Orchan	1326–1362	
Murad I	1362–1389	
Bayazid I	1389–1402	
Interregnum:	Civil War among the sons of Bayazid. 1402–1413	
Mahomet I	1413–1421	
Murad II	1421–1451	
Mahomet II	1451–1481	(The conquerer of Byzantium)
Bayazid II	1481–1512	
Selim I	1512–1520	
Suleiman the Magnificent	1520–1566	

After whom the dynasty swiftly declined, though it was not abolished until the end of the First World War.

BIBLIOGRAPHICAL NOTE

I would like to express my indebtedness to the staff of the University of New Mexico Library, and in particular to Miss Dorothy Arlene Wonsmas, for getting me all sorts of books from all sorts of places.

The literature on the siege and sack of Constantinople is not extensive. Chedomil Mijatovich, former Serbian minister to the Court of St. James, published a life of Constantine XI in 1892. Naturally enough, he shows a Serbian bias, but he also quotes extensively from Serbian chronicles not otherwise readily available. In 1903, Edwin Pears published his *The Destruction of the Greek Empire and the Story of the Capture of Constantinople by the Turks,* extensively quarried by Schlumberger, in his *La Siege, prise et le sac du Constantinople en 1453,* Paris, 1915. George Finlay, in his magisterial History of Greece, Vol. III, 1877, with his usual eye for significant detail, includes some picturesque ones. And that, as far as any extended treatment goes, is all.

It should perhaps be added that almost everything is conjectural or rests upon conflicting evidence, when it comes to the dates, statistics, and layout of the city at the time of the siege. I have chosen therefore what seemed to me most logical, relying on the whole upon Barbaro and Tedardi—whose own name, for that matter, is as frequently written Tedaldi. This confusion even applies to the reign dates of many of the Emperors and Osmanli Sultans. In the text I have used the conventional ones, but in the hand list at the end of the book, have listed Ostrogorsky's corrected ones. These are among the matters which can never be absolutely settled, of which there are a great many. For instance, the most important focal point of the siege was the St. Romanus Gate. Even at the time this was sometimes called the Pempton, and, by the defenders, the Civil Gate. All are close to each other if not identical. I have taken them to be identical.

It should also be added that I have deliberately allowed myself to be unfair, in the sense that there is a tendency in our century to shrug off responsibility for the holding of an opinion, in favor of a noncommittal impartiality. But the general opinion of past men is not made any the more invalid for the few good acts of a bad man, or the few bad ones of a good, and there is no reason to avoid the expression of prejudice, given that one suppresses no evidence. This is particularly evident in the treatment of Notaras and Gennadios. But in the entire literature both of and devoted to the period, there is not one single authority who has not, eventually, been unable to suppress a restive irritation at the eternal theological squabbles of the time. Like them, however, I would not, despite this, like to be thought to condemn the general in the particular. We must always respect the faith of another, given he respects ours, which is not often.

The original sources are as follows. Since I do not read Greek (or for that matter, Serbo Croat, Polish, or Russian), and my Latin is on a lapidary level, I have had to consult most of them either quoted in secondary sources or in translation, or with a crib.

EYEWITNESS REPORTS:

George Phrantzes, *Annals*. Printed in *Corpus Scriptorum Historiae Byzantinae*. Bonn, 1838.

The protégé and confidant of the Emperor Manuel II, who recommended him to his heirs, related through his grandfather to the royal house, and the constant companion and trusted confidant, as well as the head of the palace household, to the Emperor Constantine, he was also an excellent writer. He was a day-to-day spectator of everything that happened during the siege.

Leonardo of Scios, *Lettera de la presa di Constantinopli, di Leonardo da Scio, Arcivescovo di Metelino, scritta a Papa Nicolo*

V, intorno la presa di Constantinopli. Sansovino, Venice, 1573.
He accompanied Cardinal Isidore to Constantinople in November of 1452, and was there throughout the siege.

Cardinal Isidore, *Lettera d'Issidoro Ruteno, Cardinale e Vescovo Savino, della presa di Constantinopoli, nella quale egli si ritrovo Legate del Papa.* Sansovino, Venice, 1573.

Giornale dell' Assedio di Constantinopli, 1453, di Nicolo Barbaro, P. V. Enrico Cornet, Vienna, 1856.
Barbaro was a Venetian nobleman, who helped defend the city. He had a sharp eye, a dry manner, and he is probably the most levelheaded of all those who described the events.

Jehan Blanchin and Jacques Tedardi: *Informacion envoyée par Francesco de Tresves à J. R. père en Dieu, Monseigneur de Cardinal d'Avignon, etc., par Jehan Blanchin et Jacques Tedardi, Florentin, de l'entreprise de Constantinople, faicte par l'Empereur Turc le 29 jour de Mai l'an 1453, à laquelle le dict Jacques etstoit présent.* Printed in *Chroniques de Charles VII, roi de France,* by T. Chartier. Paris, 1858.
Tedardi fought on the walls.

Ubertini Pusculi Brixiensis, *Carmen de capta Constantinopolis libri quatuor.*
A poem, with a few details.

Θϱηνος δης Κωνοδαντῖνοποπολεως.
An elegiac poem, but so graphic in detail as to be useful. It is anonymous. This and the above printed in von A. Elisser, *Analekten der Mittel und Neu-Griechischen Literatur.* Leipzig, 1857.

Skazaniya o Vzyatii Tzar-grada bezbojnim turetzkim Saltanom (The reports of the capture of Constantinople by the godless Turkish Sultan). Usually called the *Slavonic Chronicle,* and undoubtedly the report of an eyewitness. I have used Mijatovich's citations of it. Printed in *Memoirs of the Second Division,* Imperial Academy of Science at St. Petersburg, 1854, in abstract.

Memoirs of the Janissary Michael Konstantinovich.
Published by Galezowsky, in his *Zbior pisarzow Polskieh,* Vol. XXXXV, Warsaw, 1828. I have used Mijatovich's abstracts.

Michael was a Serbian knight attached to the Sultan's camp, opposite the Adrianople Gate. Later he became a Janissary. He wrote his *Memoirs* as an old man, in 1490.

CONTEMPORARY WRITERS NOT EYEWITNESSES:

Michael Ducas, *Historia Byzantina*. Bonn, 1834.
A descendant of the imperial house of Ducas, not present during the siege. He supported the Union of the Churches.

Laonicas (Nicholas) Chalcochondylas, *Turcica historia*. Bonn, 1834.
The only Athenian Byzantine historian attached to the court of the Despot Demetrius.

Critobulus of Imbros, *De rebus gestis Mechemetis II inde ab anno 1451 usque ad annum 1467*.
A Greek in the Turkish service, who writes from the point of view that Mahomet was a great man. As indeed he was. But he is fair to the Greeks.

Tarich Muntechebati Evli Chelebi.
A Turkish historian, translated by Mordtmann in his *Belagerung und Eroberung Constantinopels durch die Turken im Jahre 1453, nach Original quellen bearbeitet,* Stuttgart, 1858 (used heavily by Broadribb and Besant).

Zorzi Dolphin, *Assedio e presa di Constantinopoli nell' anno 1453, estratto dalla Cronaca delle famiglie nobili di Venezia e della stessa citta dall sua origine sino l'anno 1478*.
Dolphin says he used eyewitness reports. Printed by George M. Thomas, *Sitzungs Berichte der Kgl. Bayerischen Akademie der Wissenschaften*. Munich, 1868.

Theodore Spandugin Cantacuzin, gentilhuomo Constantinopolitano, *Comentari, Del Origine e costumi Turchi, Fiorenza 1551*.
Available edited in O. N. Sathas, *Monumenta Historiae Hellenicae,* Vol. IX. Paris, 1888.
A Cantacuzenos who seems to have written down details accepted by his family as being traditionally true. Mijatovich follows him for the last days of the siege. His version does not tally with the standard ones, though.

Abraham the Armenian, *Mélodie élégiaque sur la prise de Stamboul.*

Trans. by M. Brosset. Printed in LeBeau's *Histoire du Bas-Empire,* Vol. XXI. Paris, 1835.

An absolutely miserable work, pedantic, archaicizing, self-conscious and treacly. But I have quoted from it in the introduction. The Byzantines were much given to "melodie." It was a literary genre. And not a good one, in most hands.

A few other bits and scraps have been uncovered mostly in the Vatican libraries, but they do not amount to much.

The following is a list of books principally consulted:

Baynes, N. H., *Byzantine Studies and Other Essays.* London, 1955.

Baynes, N. H., and Moss, H. St. L. B., *Byzantium: An Introduction to East Roman Civilization.* Oxford, 1948.

Brehier, L., Vie et mort de Byzance.

I. *Le Monde Byzantin.* Paris, 1947.

II. *Les institutions de l'Empire Byzantin,* Paris, 1948.

III. *La civilization byzantine.* Paris, 1950.

Broadribb, Rev. W. J., and Besant, Walter, *Constantinople: A Sketch of Its History from Its Foundations to Its Conquest by the Turks in 1453.* London, 1879.

Cambridge Medieval History, Vol. IV: *The Eastern Roman Empire.* Cambridge, 1923.

Chapman C., *Michael Paleologue, Restaurateur de L'Empire byzantin.* Paris, 1926.

Diehl, Charles, *Figures byzantines,* Vols. I, II. Paris, 1925, 1927.

———, *Histoire de l'Empire byzantin,* Paris, 1919.

Finlay, George, *A History of Greece,* edit. Rev. H. F. Tozer, Vol. III. Oxford, 1877.

Gardner, A., *The Lascarids of Nicaea, The Story of an Empire in Exile.* London, 1912.

Gibbon, E., *The History of the Decline and Fall of the Roman Empire.* Bury's edition, with notes. London, 1923.

Gibbons, H., *The Foundation of the Ottoman Empire.* Oxford, 1916.

Hammer-Purgstall, J. von, *Histoire de l'Empire Ottoman.* Paris, 1836. (Trans. of German original)

Mijatovich, Chedomil, *Constantine, the Last Emperor of the Greeks, or the Conquest of Constantinople by the Turks* (A.D. *1453*). London, 1892.

Miller, W., *The Latins in the Levant. A History of Frankish Greece (1204–1566).* London, 1908.

———, *Trebizond, the Last Greek Empire.* London, 1926.

Milligen, A. van, *Byzantine Constantinople, the Walls of the City and adjoining Historical Sites.* London, 1891.

Ostrogorsky, George, *History of the Byzantine State.* New Brunswick, New Jersey, 1957. (Trans. from the German.)

Pears, Edwin, *The Destruction of the Greek Empire and the Story of the Capture of Constantinople by the Turks.* London, 1903.

Runciman, Steven, *Byzantine Civilization.* London, 1933.

———, *History of the Crusades,* Vol. III. Cambridge, 1954.

Vasiliev, A. A., *History of the Byzantine Empire 324–1453.* Madison, Wisconsin, 1952. (Trans. from Russian, enlarged with new material.)

Wittek, P., *The Rise of the Ottoman Empire* (trans). London, 1938.

INDEX